The Power of Scientı

It is often said that knowledge is power, but more often than not relevant knowledge is not used when political decisions are made. This book examines how political decisions relate to scientific knowledge, and what factors determine the success of scientific research in influencing policy. The authors take a comparative and historical perspective and refer to well-known theoretical frameworks, but the focus of the book is on three case studies: the discourse of racism, Keynesianism, and climate change. These cases cover a number of countries, and different time periods. In all three the authors see a close link between "knowledge producers" and political decision-makers, but show that the effectiveness of the policies varies dramatically. This book will be of interest to scientists, decision-makers, and scholars alike.

PROFESSOR REINER GRUNDMANN is Chair of Science and Technology Studies at Nottingham University. He has published in journals such as *New Left Review*, *British Journal of Sociology*, *Current Sociology*, *Journal of Classical Sociology*, *Science, Technology & Human Values*, and *Environmental Politics*. His book publications include *Marxism and Ecology* (1991) and *Transnational Environmental Policy: Reconstructing Ozone* (2001).

PROFESSOR NICO STEHR is Karl Mannheim Professor of Cultural Studies at the Zeppelin University, Friedrichshafen, Germany, and director of the European Centre for Sustainability Research at his university. His recent publications include *Who Owns Knowledge: Knowledge and the Law* with Bernd Weiler (2008), *Knowledge and Democracy* (2008), *Society: Critical Concepts in Sociology* with Reiner Grundmann, (2008), *Climate and Society* with Hans von Storch (2010), and *Experts: The Knowledge and Power of Expertise* with Reiner Grundmann (2011).

The Power of Scientific Knowledge

From Research to Public Policy

Reiner Grundmann
and
Nico Stehr

CAMBRIDGE
UNIVERSITY PRESS

CAMBRIDGE UNIVERSITY PRESS
Cambridge, New York, Melbourne, Madrid, Cape Town,
Singapore, São Paulo, Delhi, Mexico City

Cambridge University Press
The Edinburgh Building, Cambridge CB2 8RU, UK

Published in the United States of America by Cambridge University Press,
New York

www.cambridge.org
Information on this title: www.cambridge.org/9781107606722

First published 2012

A catalogue record for this publication is available from the British Library

Library of Congress Cataloguing in Publication data
Grundmann, Reiner, author.
  The power of scientific knowledge : from research to public policy /
Reiner Grundmann, Nico Stehr.
    pages cm
  Includes bibliographical references and index.
  ISBN 978-1-107-02272-0 (hardback) – ISBN 978-1-107-60672-2
  (paperback)
  1. Science–Social aspects. 2. Science–Political aspects. 3. Research–
Political aspects. 4. Political planning. 5. Political science. I. Stehr,
Nico, author. II. Title.
  Q175.5.G78 2012
  338.9′26–dc23   2012016903

ISBN 978-1-107-02272-0 Hardback
ISBN 978-1-107-60672-2 Paperback

Contents

Figures

Tables

Preface

Intense discussions of the social function of science in society can be traced to its very origins. Interest in the practical virtues of scientific knowledge has arisen for obvious reasons. From the beginning of the scientific revolution, scholars, philosophers, and laypersons alike have been vigorously engaged in discussions about the nature of the practical impact of knowledge on social, political, technical, and economic matters. Likewise, the social role of the scientist became a topic for debate. After a period of growing resources for scientific endeavors, especially in publicly funded institutions such as universities, science today is faced with funding constraints. This leads to vigorous competition for scarce resources, and to attempts to find measures and rationales for public spending on science. In this context, claims about the practical efficacy and promise of scientific knowledge are not only turned into crucial symbolic capital – but can also be a matter of survival for some fields of inquiry. Where concerns are expressed about the usefulness of science, this can become a serious liability with regard to competition for economic support, attraction of new generations of students, and societal attention.

Dealing with the question of why knowledge sometimes becomes powerful, and sometimes remains unused or is regarded as useless, the traditional answer was to point to the very success of science and technology in transforming our living conditions. Longer, healthier, and better lives due to scientific discoveries and applications are prime examples. Scientific progress in medicine and other applied fields is paraded as incontrovertible evidence of the usefulness and power of knowledge.[1]

In our analysis of the conditions that enable knowledge to become powerful, we are not content with the simple but tautological answer

---

[1] In a recent study, Sarewitz and Nelson (2008) compare the differing success of vaccination and education programs. They argue that this difference can be explained by the availability of a functioning "technical core" in the first case, which is not available in the second.

that it is the practical success of science and technology. Of course, this has been, and in many quarters still is, the dominant answer. Listen to the British chemist and Nobel Prize laureate Harold Kroto, who says that there are innumerable theories, but only a few that are true. True theories, in his view, are facts that work in practice.

There are countless theories but they can be clearly classified into two groups: Scientific Theories which are considered "true" or "facts" because they have been found experimentally to work and we know why they work, and Un-scientific Theories which have been found wanting when similarly experimentally tested. (Kroto, no date)

Examples of such working and true theories are: Newton's theory of gravity, Maxwell's theory of electromagnetism, Einstein's theory of relativity, Mendeleev's periodic table, the theory of quantum mechanics, and Darwin's theory of evolution.[2] This statement could be taken as representative not only for the community of scientists, but for the dominant view about the relation between science, truth, and practical effectiveness.

While we do not doubt the practical success of knowledge, this answer allows at best for an *ex post facto* response to the question of what exactly gives rise to the power of knowledge. In so doing, Kroto and others combine old theories with new technical applications. Newton did not aspire to devise a journey to the moon, and Darwin did not tell us how to treat modern diseases. In a similar vein, one could say – and many indeed do say – that Marx was the mental originator of the Soviet Union, or that Nietzsche was responsible for the Holocaust. Such superficial, anachronistic, and functionalist allegations are ubiquitous. However, their frequent repetition does not make them more plausible.

Not all theories have practical applications or are aimed at them. Kroto's criterion that only proven theories ("facts") are scientific is mistaken. There are good theories which have no application whatsoever and theories where proof cannot be obtained for practical reasons, or because it is contested. As the history and sociology of science tells us, every research frontier shows uncertainty, experimenter's regress (Collins 1985), and trials of strength (Latour 1987) between proponents and opponents of such theories. Often these debates have no visible conclusion and a generational shift decides the fate of the theory. As

---

[2] Kroto lists the following successful practical applications of these theories: the landing on the moon (Newton); electricity, radio and TV (Maxwell); nuclear fission and satellite navigation (Einstein); silicon chips and synthetic pharmaceuticals (Mendeleev); laser and DVDs (quantum mechanics); the fight against life-threatening diseases (Darwin).

Max Planck famously put it, "a new scientific truth does not triumph by convincing its opponents and making them see the light, but rather because its opponents eventually die, and a new generation grows up that is familiar with it" (quoted in Kuhn [1962] 1970: 150).

In this book, we therefore aim at a much more precise account of the links between knowledge creation and practical political application.

Pointing to the ways in which knowledge has in fact altered our existential conditions, whether in anticipated or even in surprising ways, does not enable us to tell whether current knowledge may be powerful under future conditions unless we are prepared to assume what must, fortunately or unfortunately, be taken for granted: future conditions are rarely a carbon copy of past circumstances.

Knowledge can become powerful in two different ways, either through technical or through social applications. In the first case, we are looking at scientists and engineers, and the technical artifacts they produce. In the second, we are looking at social scientists and their links to the political, economic, or social world. In the first case the power of knowledge manifests itself in working machines or drugs, in the second in social action, especially effective political interventions into economy and society through laws, regulations, and policies. In this book, we focus mainly on the second aspect of practical knowledge.

Although views differ about the details of this link between knowledge and society, it seems to be common sense that the kind of knowledge that emanates from established science can indeed be quite powerful and beneficial in practice. The most recent thesis in this regard asserts, using the prominent Marxian categories of base and superstructure, that the superstructure becomes the motor of major historical transformations. It follows, of course, that knowledge increasingly displaces those factors and processes that were once held to be the "cause" of history, i.e. the economic base of society, including its property relations. Now the emphasis is much more on the "superstructural" elements which form part of the productive forces.

Despite there being no consensus on how the tight coupling between knowledge and social action works in detail, many would agree that knowledge produced by the sciences can in practice have a major impact. If science becomes so central for the production of societal wealth, the question arises of how we can tap into this productive force and use it optimally. The development of productive forces in the knowledge society means first of all – for us anyway – understanding the process in which knowledge becomes practical.

Running the danger of oversimplifying, we identify two approaches in the literature which analyze the relation between knowledge and power, using an established distinction between technology push and demand pull. On the one hand, there is the thesis that knowledge flows into society, originating at the source of basic research, continuing through applied research and ending in technical or other practical applications. This linear model makes use of the flow metaphor and implies that for knowledge to become practical, barriers have to be broken down so that knowledge can run freely ("science push"). On the other hand, there is the thesis that knowledge is commissioned from users, which implies that it can be produced on demand and deliver solutions as required ("social pull"). This approach has many variants; we mention only the function that science is said to fulfill as provider of legitimation (Habermas 1970; Salter et al. 1988). The first approach emphasizes the supply side of science producers, the second the demand side of science users. In both cases the unit of analysis is not clear. It is rarely made explicit whether we are dealing with single scientists, groups of scientists, scientific disciplines, or science as an institution. We shall therefore limit our analytical frame to the investigation of the *activities of scientists* who produce practical knowledge and introduce it into contexts of application. What exactly counts as *practical knowledge* is the topic of this book.

Reflections on the power and promise of scientific knowledge preceded systematic considerations about the influence of social conditions on knowledge. Once interest in the social basis of knowledge was firmly established, the concern with the impact of knowledge on society receded as a problematic issue. The matter of the function and the influence of knowledge on society appeared to be solved. Of course, it never disappeared. But the prevailing view was, and perhaps still is, that we should mainly fear a deficit of knowledge.

In exploring in this study both the nature of economic discourse, climate science, and race science, and the features of the practical context within which such bodies of knowledge aspire to gain influence, our study of knowledge production, and of the contribution of knowledge to major societal transformations and historical processes, represents an effort to specify some of the characteristics of knowledge that make knowledge powerful or that appear, for that matter, to substantially reduce the practical efficacy of science. We concentrate on the kinds of attributes that make knowledge powerful in practice, and therefore approach the process of policymaking in modern society from the angle of the role knowledge can play. Heretofore, the answer to the issue of the power of knowledge was found in the philosophy of science. We will try to show that the answers that epistemology offers are not entirely helpful.

But it is not only epistemology that has hampered the analysis of knowledge and power. A number of further, interrelated issues have weakened the power of the analysis of the relations between ideas and practical affairs, including politics. Among them is the often taken-for-granted term "knowledge," and in its wake the relation of knowing, action, and power. A careful genealogy of the concepts of power and knowledge may assist in dissolving the outward appearance of an essential unity of power and knowledge (cf. Foucault 1980). A careful specification and differentiation of these terms should be of help, as would a differentiation of different phases of policymaking in the case of political action. However, the relationship between knowledge and power, and therefore the question of the power of knowledge, remains the core issue of our inquiry.

However, our aim in this book is not primarily a conceptual clarification. At the heart of the book, we present three case studies containing knowledge claims generated within different disciplines, both established and emerging, from social and natural sciences, at different historical times. The actors are oriented to national as well as transnational policy communities. The "operational" or practical knowledge generated in the different scientific communities we are examining emerges in close proximity to social, economic, and political contexts. In each of the three cases, prominent members of the science communities and forceful circumstances contribute to efforts to disseminate knowledge claims widely and assure that they appeal to and resonate with the political agendas of the day. At the same time, agenda-setting efforts are also part of the interests that motivate the knowledge-generating communities.

We do not claim that the selected cases fit some kind of experimental design which would enable us with certainty to factor out processes and dimensions that are crucial for the practical success of knowledge. However, we are convinced that the range and the diversity of cases improve our ability to discern those attributes that allow one to speak about the possibility that knowledge becomes powerful. Our aim is not to produce a general theory of knowledge application but to provide some historical-analytical tools and data for such an endeavor.

Within the context of each of the three case studies, we stress different elements of the knowledge/power constellation. In the case of Keynes, it is perhaps only a slight exaggeration to say that he changed economic policy in Western democracies singlehandedly. While his recommendations were not accepted and implemented during his activity as a government advisor, he laid the theoretical foundation for a new economic policy during these years. It is remarkable that he based his policies on only a few variables. His theory did not reflect the complexity of economic reality – which in the view of many is the precondition of a theory to become practical.

In the case of climate science, we refer to the role of transnational epistemic communities in placing research topics on the global political agenda. In this case, it is remarkable that there is little practical success visible in climate policies, despite the size of the epistemic community and its scientific consensus.

In our case study of race science as a theoretical and applied science, we emphasize the extent to which scientists take up cultural and political resources of the day in order to generate knowledge claims that resonate closely with the politics of the time. As in the case of climate policy, we see a close relationship between scientific experts and political actors. In contrast to climate policy, race science in Nazi Germany led to practical applications of knowledge claims in the form of race policies, culminating in the Holocaust. This case raises the questions of whether knowledge as such can be "neutral," and whether the growth of knowledge is always accompanied by societal benefits, or whether it represents a moral value in itself.

We are grateful to Jay Weinstein for allowing us to make use of the case study on race science and the Holocaust in this monograph. The initial chapter entitled "The Power of Knowledge: Race Science, Race Policy and the Holocaust," authored by Jay Weinstein and Nico Stehr, was first published in *Social Epistemology* (1999). Although enlarged, our case study of the practical power of race science is significantly indebted to the earlier analysis. Permission to reprint the relevant parts has been granted by Taylor and Francis.

The case for and the examination of the socio-economic context in which the influence of Keynesian economic discourse may have considerable historical importance was first made in Nico Stehr's *Practical Knowledge* (1992). We have enlarged and extended the argument found there, embedding our case in more recent work on John Maynard Keynes, who was after all one of the most important social scientists in history, especially when judged by the practical influence he enjoyed in the immediate postwar era and more recently, in the wake of the financial crisis of the years 2008–10. Permission to reprint the relevant parts has been granted by Sage Publishing.

1 Introduction

The roads to human power and to human knowledge lie close together, and are nearly the same; nevertheless, on account of the pernicious and inveterate habit of dwelling on abstractions, it is safer to begin and raise the sciences from the foundations which have relation to practice and let the active part be as the seal which prints and determines the contemplative counterpart.

Francis Bacon, 1620 (Book II, 4)

The fact that science contributes to the social life-process as a productive power and a means of production in no way legitimates a pragmatist theory of knowledge.

Max Horkheimer ([1932] 1972: 3)

The prevailing view

In order better to understand the task we have set for ourselves in this study, it is useful first to refer to the prevailing view in response to the question of the conditions that make for the *Power of Knowledge*. The two mottos above, Horkheimer's taken from an essay written in 1932 for the inaugural issue of the *Zeitschrift für Sozialforschung,* and Francis Bacon's from *Novum Organum* of 1620, both endorse a clear separation between questions pertaining to the *truth* and *utility* of knowledge. The distinction between truth and utility is one of the traditional philosophical distinctions in reflections about attributes of knowledge that may make ideas powerful in practice. The year 1932 is symbolic and significant, of course, and Horkheimer's insistence that it is not for societal interests to decide what is true echoes emerging, profound political struggles about the role of science in society. Science and the ideas that materialize from the scientific community are not the handmaidens of power, nor should they be deprived of their proper autonomy. In defending the autonomy of science, Horkheimer ([1932] 1972: 4) also insists that the philosophical perspective that favors a clear separation between the utility and the truth of knowledge does not lead to a separation or alienation between theory and action (practice).

Horkheimer's position, though using different terms, refers to a primary and a secondary code of knowledge production. The primary code of knowledge production represents truth; the secondary or derivative code refers to the utility of knowledge claims. The implication of the thesis of a primary and secondary code governing knowledge production suggests that the most useful theory is a good theory or truthful knowledge claim. Theory and practice are alienated from each other, but the ruling code in science is truth and not usefulness. Truth controls use. And this is why it is useful for society to allow the autonomy of science.

In a simplified way, one could state that the prevailing view of the relation between power and knowledge can be described as the *instrumental model*.[1] It is characterized by the following principles:

First, the structure and culture of human groups, as producers of knowledge, have no influence on the production of knowledge or on the context of justification. The development of knowledge is driven and determined by the "logic" of science in conjunction with the nature of the world of objects. Second, the use of knowledge is largely independent of the context of application (hence the frequent statement that knowledge as such is value neutral, and can be applied for good or bad purposes). And third, the utilization of scientific knowledge is not impeded by the special circumstances of time, place, and social conditions (sometimes called the *objectivity and rationality assumption*). A scientific body of knowledge is said to be true everywhere.

The model of instrumentality conceives of scientific theory and research as a kind of intellectual tool to be employed in practical situations. Theoretical knowledge, as long as it is true or adequate, is also reliable and useful. Theoretical knowledge alone does not guarantee a successful execution of desired social action, nor does it ensure the value of the means chosen to reach a specific goal. But theoretical knowledge, if utilized, secures a kind of technical relief (*Entlastung*) for

---

[1] We are aware that the terminology needs clarification. In the philosophy of science before Popper, the *instrumental view* meant Bishop Berkeley's view that scientific theories might work in practice, i.e. they are instrumental, but they are not necessarily true. This was in the early days of modernism, as for many it was sacrilegious to use the concept of truth outside of church scholasticism. However, this view was dominant among practicing scientists, who left the philosophy to the philosophers. Popper (1956), of course, did not sympathize with this attitude, which he described as "science as plumbing." According to Popper, science must never give up the concept of truth. In this book we use the term *instrumentalism* to denote a connection between theory and (successful) application – as expressed, for example, in Kroto's quote above.

actors. Actors are not themselves required to manufacture the knowledge to be utilized, nor is it necessary for them to comprehend the
scientific context in which the theoretical knowledge was generated in
the first instance. What is sufficient is an adequate understanding of
the conditions of application; the desired effect is then guaranteed by
virtue of the truth of the theoretical knowledge.

In an essay entitled "Causality in the Social Sciences," Lewis S. Feuer
(1954) notes that the loyalty of social scientists to particular theoretical
traditions is driven by their adherence to one of a pair of meta-sociological
convictions. Feuer calls these meta-convictions *necessitarian* and *interventionist*. Social scientists who adhere to the necessitarian model are
persuaded that a predicted state of affairs cannot be prevented from
being realized. The interventionist perspective assumes that one can
intervene to alter a given state of affairs, but also to block the predicted
states from coming into existence. There is an elective affinity between
Horkheimer's distinction between the truth and utility of knowledge
claims and Feuer's necessitarian and interventionist models. As Feuer
(1954: 683) observes, social science theories win allegiance from social
scientists not so much because they are able to muster more empirical
evidence than competitors, but rather because of the ways they open up
possibilities of human action and of human intervention.

In this book we want to revisit and critically consider what appears to
many other observers to be the set of self-evident reasons that account
for the power of knowledge. The taken-for-granted answer among the
public, many policymakers and members of the scientific community is
to be found, in the first place, in the conflation of knowledge and truth.
What counts as objectivity and truth is subject to historical change, as
several studies have shown (Shapin 1994; Daston and Galison 2007).

In modern society, what warrants the conflation of knowledge, truth,
and power is mainly linked to dominant norms in the scientific community. These norms postulate that knowledge claims are at their best
if they are trans-historical and trans-situational. The decline or loss of
context-specificity of a knowledge claim is widely seen as adding to the
validity, if not the truthfulness, of the claim. For the citizens of modern
society, the solution to the problem of the conditions that give rise to
power of knowledge is delegated or relegated to sanctioned procedures
of knowledge acquisition as practiced in science, particularly natural
science.

We do not question the assertion that knowledge can be powerful. But this assertion does not answer the question of *why* knowledge
can be powerful, or for whom knowledge may be powerful. Nor do
we doubt that the source of many contemporary powerful knowledge

claims originates within the scientific community. We certainly concur with a growing number of observers that we are living in a knowledge society, and that the command of knowledge is constitutive for authority, inequality formation, participation in civil society, or generally for the identity of individuals.

But it is equally evident that science advances and continues to issue numerous claims that prove to be completely ineffective in practice. What turns such an observation about the "impotence" of science – with respect to many practical social and personal problems – into a most intriguing and puzzling observation is that such ineffective claims are often warranted by the scientific community as in strict conformity with the procedures that otherwise constitute eminent, reputable, and reliable scientific claims. As a result, it is misleading to ascribe to science a kind of boundless power.

One should therefore examine exactly why knowledge is effective in one case but has no effect in another, although in both cases the authenticity of knowledge is guaranteed. Today's standard and rarely doubted response refers to an identification of knowledge with power. This comforting response assumes knowledge to be something so compelling that its power stems from its own genesis (within science!). But in so doing we cannot distinguish between different forms of knowledge on the one hand, and we have no explanation for the successful or unsuccessful application of knowledge on the other. In the first case one assumes that traditional knowledge was too weak to stand up to scientific knowledge. In the second case one seems to rely on the different degrees of veracity of knowledge. Accordingly, knowledge assets would therefore be ineffective because they are theoretically inadequate. We deliberately exaggerate in order to explore the implications of these arguments. We are well aware that there exist approaches that challenge the traditional concept of knowledge and power. This often happens only implicitly; for example, when implementation research asks why a "good" theory was not effective in practice; or when researchers show that technologies quite often work even in the absence of full theoretical explanations (Perrow 1984). What these approaches lack is a systematic analysis of the characteristics of knowledge and power.

Unlike the traditional models of the effect and power of knowledge, we point out that the source of the effectiveness of knowledge does not lie in the process of knowledge production, or in certain norms of the scientific community when it tries to clarify controversial knowledge. Rather, it is crucial that if knowledge is going to be practically relevant, it must include the policy options that should be manipulated in a certain way so that reality can be brought into line with the relevant knowledge. This means, first, that a lot of knowledge is never put in a position directly to transform reality (and is therefore not in a position to reshape the reality). It means, second, that in order to become effective in practice, a theory need not contain all aspects or variables of the current reality to which it refers. The proposition that only a complex theory is capable of effecting change in a complex reality should be discarded.

Taking a comparative and historical perspective, this book poses the broad question of how political decisions relate to scientific knowledge, and in what sense we can actually speak of the power of knowledge. We will do this through some theoretical considerations and the study of empirical data. We shall examine two cases from the early, and one case from the late twentieth century. Race science was a policy-relevant theory and body of research before World War I, and Keynesian economics from the 1920s on. Race science could look back at the heritage of evolutionary theory, with many prominent scholars espousing it, including Darwin himself (Sewell 2010). In Germany it came to be used as a political tool, and provided a legitimating basis for the Holocaust. In the 1920s and 1930s, John Maynard Keynes proposed economic policies to help solve problems of the crisis-ridden British economy. These initially fell on deaf ears, but became dominant after World War II. Keynesian policies were implemented in all developed capitalist economies. At one point, a US president famously pronounced that "we are all Keynesians now."

Late in the twentieth century, concern about the Earth's atmosphere arose, initially instigated by atmospheric scientists. A small group of advocate scientists in the 1970s alerted the world public about an imminent global ecological catastrophe, the depletion of the ozone layer. With the establishment of a largely successful international regime, basic institutional features for a science/policy interaction were established. Several influential actors tried to repeat a similar approach in the case of climate change (after 1988), though so far with little success. While the political success in ozone politics is widely celebrated, climate policy and politics seem to be in a mess. In this book we will particularly examine the institutional framework that was set up to ensure an effective transmission of scientific research into political action through the Intergovernmental Panel on Climate Change (IPCC). Again, as in the case of race science, one could say that the science base was the same, at least at first glance, but the policies implemented by various nations were different.

Within the context of each of the three cases, we introduce a comparative dimension which is useful to address questions of policy variation across national jurisdictions. In the case of Keynesian economics and its impact on the evolution of modern economies, we discuss, among other things, the role of the notion of "complexity" of social phenomena and the extent to which the complexity of the social world has to be mirrored in social science knowledge as a precondition for its practical effectiveness. We also ask what the reasons were for a difference in the appeal of Keynesian policies in different times and places. In the case of climate science, we refer to the role of an internationally unified scientific assessment and the question of why national climate change policies have varied hugely. Similarly to the discourse of climate change, we see how race science was embedded in cultural and political resources of the day and generated knowledge claims that resonated closely with the politics of the time. We will highlight that knowledge production in itself need not be a virtue in modern societies. The national variations will be addressed again as the question arises as to why race science led to the Holocaust in Germany, but not in other countries.

The linear-rational model and its critics

Scholars of public policy, especially in the United States, have been using the instrumental model described above. In a well-known contribution, Harold Lasswell and Abraham Kaplan (1950) depict a linear-rational model of policymaking.[2] It follows an enlightenment model of politics, in which scientific knowledge helps to solve societal problems. If science produces true and valid knowledge, this can be used in the political process, where it produces the "right" political decisions and effectively resolves politically motivated debates. This view has been shared by many authors before and after Lasswell and Kaplan's book was published. The hope was that a science-based solution will be agreeable to warring parties, since it transcends the ideological (metaphysical) differences.[3]

It might be useful to distinguish between two strands in the public policy literature: a rationalist and a pragmatic strand. The rationalist

---

[2] This model covers technological applications of scientific research as well. Godin (2006) has argued that the "linear model" is a stylized artifact that emerged out of various institutional practices (US government accounting schemes and OECD statistical definitions). It cannot be attributed to single individuals alone, as has been the case with regard to Vannevar Bush (1945), although this is common practice.

[3] Otto Neurath, founding member of the Vienna Circle, put it like this: "Metaphysical terms divide; scientific terms unite" (quoted in Cartwright et al. 1996: 179).

approach tries to base political decisions on the best available knowledge, whereas the pragmatist approach aims at incremental, negotiated solutions that work.

Charles Lindblom's classic description of public policy as the "science of muddling through" can be read as a pamphlet in favor of a pragmatist approach. Lindblom contrasts the rational approach (which involves a huge information collection exercise plus a systematic comparison of available alternatives of action) with a more modest approach, where the policymaker considers only a few policy alternatives (most of which will be familiar to him from past controversies), relying on a record of "past experience with small policy steps to predict the consequences of similar steps extended into the future" (Lindblom 1959:79). Echoing James March and Herbert Simon's (1958) bounded rationality thesis, Lindblom argues that the first of these approaches is impossible with complex problems, since limitations of time and resources (monetary, intellectual, and informational) are overwhelming. He even suggests that in practice, administrators are advised not to practice the first model, but rather to restrict their consideration of policy alternatives to just a few. It is therefore curious that "the literatures of decision making ... and public administration formalize the first approach and not the second" (Lindblom 1959: 80). In other words, practitioners know that they cannot cope with the demands of the rationalist model, but academics are oblivious of this and theorize exactly such a model.

In a later article Lindblom returned to the topic, defending the second approach which he now calls "disjointed incrementalism." His argument rests on the case that we will never achieve a "full picture" or a *synoptic view* of all relevant elements (values, information, factors, causes ...) that are prior to a decision. Instead, we have to proceed from a grossly incomplete analysis, but do this in a conscious way. It is of no help to appeal to the ideal of synoptic analysis, as this will lead to worse outcomes compared to decision-makers who are conscious of the limitations and muddle through open-eyed, so to speak. As he put it, "a conventional synoptic (in aspiration) attempt to choose and justify the location of a new public housing unit by an analysis of the entirety of a city's land needs and potential development patterns always degenerates at least into superficiality if not fraud. A disjointed incremental analysis can do better" (Lindblom 1979: 519).

Another line of inquiry has developed the view that politics and science are at odds with each other, mainly due to epistemological reasons and language barriers. The "two communities" model (developed, *inter alia*, by Caplan 1979) casts doubt on the concept of a linear rational model and sees the relation between science and politics as difficult.

The two are characterized by different logics and cultures.[4] While the scientist wants to arrive at the truth, the politician is concerned about power. Asserting the theory of functional differentiation, Luhmann (1984) makes a more basic point about the problematic nature of communication between social systems. Communication between politics and science is problematic, or "highly improbable."

Whenever ideas have become institutionalized in policies and have therefore become real, it seems only natural to think that what has happened had to happen. In other words, the link between knowledge and politics seems unproblematic, even inevitable. It is the task of the historian and critical social scientist to unravel this apparent inevitability. Michel Foucault used the term *discourse* to describe the reality of thoughts and practices enshrined in a specific historical period. He used the term *archaeology* to describe the efforts needed to analyze and deconstruct these discourses. Of course, social scientists know that the roles of academics and policymakers are different, and that actors from these two fields inhabit different epistemic universes. One can therefore assume that it is unlikely that these roles will intertwine easily. Unlikely does not mean impossible, but the possibility of such "meetings" needs to be investigated carefully.

It has been observed by people who were active in both roles that it is nearly impossible to step out of the role one currently embodies – all prior knowledge and empathy with the "other" role notwithstanding. Consider this everyday example: A car driver wants to get to his destination quickly, and therefore endangers a pedestrian crossing the road. The pedestrian could do the same a few moments later after she gets into her car and drives off. Likewise, the car driver whom we saw in a rather reckless manner will eventually revert to his role of pedestrian. Imagine he has just stopped by the roadside and wants to get to the shop on the other side of the road. He will now find himself complaining about irresponsible drivers trying to "knock him over." We are all familiar with such everyday examples which teach us how difficult, perhaps even improbable, it is that "lessons learnt" from one role will swiftly improve one's performance in the other roles. One might say that only accidents or near misses will produce the necessary shocks for a re-examination of routines.

---

[4] The two communities model has been superseded by policy network approaches (Heclo 1978; Marsh and Rhodes 1992) and discourse coalitions (Hajer 1995; Gottweis 1998). Here, a close exchange of information between actors of different social subsystems is postulated (including representatives from industry, science, administration, and the public). They participate in a public discourse and at times also cooperate within less visible networks in order to influence political decisions. They confront another set of actors who support different interests, values, and political goals.

Hernes has given an account of his personal experience commuting between the worlds of (social) science and politics. He notes that politicians and social scientists show a mutual benign neglect for each other, "politicians funding research but taking little interest in the results; researchers describing the world, but not really expecting much in terms of changing it" (2008: 258). Hernes goes on to construct a typology of the two roles.[5] He suggests that the first step in the work of a social scientist is always an observation in need of explanation, whereas the politician starts with the definition of a political issue that needs to be addressed (and remedied). It is therefore "the aim of the scientist ... to explain reality, the aim of the politician to turn something into reality" (Hernes 2008: 262). The politician needs "levers of action" in order to change reality – moreover, a skilled politician should be able to foresee side effects and unintended consequences. Hernes concludes with the remark that the task of the scientist is to "invent explanations and validate them," whereas the task of the politician is to "invent interventions and implement them" (Hernes 2008: 263). It would be interesting to carry the argument one step further and see what happens when scientists (or other non-politicians) try to affect political changes, and are savvy enough to understand the nature of the political process. Following Marx's dictum ("The philosophers have only interpreted the world in various ways. The point, however, is to change it"), many have tried to do so, and not only Marxists. Scientists working in nearly all disciplines, from anthropology to zoology, have made attempts to influence political outcomes through their open or hidden advocacy. So have non-governmental organizations (NGOs) and business organizations, at times working closely with scientists, at times providing knowledge claims themselves.

We can identify a potential overlap between the roles of scientist and politician, revising the role Hernes assigned to the scientist as an exclusively cognitive being. Suppose a scientist knows that politicians want to act and be seen as proactive on an issue. If his or her scientific research indicates "levers for action," and if he or she manages to present the complexity of the issue as manageable, then the chances are much higher that such research will be considered relevant for the policymaker. It would seem that the more scientists understand the nature

---

[5] Without going into too much detail regarding his typology and some problems associated with it, suffice it to say that he seems to adhere to a rather naïve, Popperian view that scientists would reject a theoretical model if empirical evidence did not conform to it (Hernes 2008: 262).

of the political process, the more they are likely to smuggle research results into political practice, thereby making them effective.

Data and consensus

Knowledge, it should be noted, rarely comes in a form that is unambiguous or simple. To be sure, policymakers may prefer simplicity, and experts sometimes comply with such requests. But even if knowledge is presented at the outset as a simple set of facts, predictions, and recommendations, more often than not it turns out to be complex at a deeper level. This point is apparent in the diversity of policies based on similar, or the same, scientific advice.

We will show how this plays out in our three case studies. With regard to race science, it is obvious that there were vast policy differences across nations despite a common science base. After all, the Holocaust was carried out by one government, not by others. Equally, the case of Keynesianism shows varieties of implementation. To be sure, one could say that there was no overall agreement on the term "Keynesianism." However, the theory entailed policy recommendations drawn up by one idiosyncratic scholar who made specific recommendations to policymakers. Climate change, our third case study, shows how a transnational effort at orchestrating science and policy could not eliminate variations in domestic policies.

Gormley (2007) suggests that economists (in contrast to other social scientists) have been particularly influential in shaping public policy. Writing on the deregulation atmosphere of the United States in the 1980s, he argues that much of the deregulatory push had been advocated by distinguished economists from elite universities, and gained wide acceptance within policy circles. Environmental policy is one telling example where we witness a move away from command-and-control approaches to cost–benefit analysis and market-based approaches. The US Clean Air Act amendments of 1990 introduced emissions trading, an instrument applied to sulphur dioxide (SO_2) reduction. It soon became a favorite in international negotiations regarding climate change. Before that, market-based approaches had been seen with great skepticism, not least by European governments (Damro and Luaces-Méndez 2003; Gilbertson and Reyes 2009). Gormley cites other examples of successful application of policy proposals developed by academics, including those coming from political scientists. However, he notes that there are also many examples where their proposals have fallen on deaf ears. He goes on to offer an explanation for the differing results. In this account, expert consensus is especially important. Proponents of policies armed with "good, unambiguous empirical research in support of policy proposals" have a major advantage in controversies of this kind. This "enables interest group advocates to make both instrumental and normative arguments in favor of the policy proposal, whereas opponents must content themselves with normative arguments alone" (Gormley 2007: 310).

Gormley attributes the defeat of some of these ideas to a lack of empirical evidence, which prevented expert consensus; or, as he put it, "each paper produced by one of these experts is sure to be skewered by someone from the opposing side. Under such circumstances, experts are much more likely to provide 'ammunition' to opposing sides in the debate than to change anyone's thinking on how to proceed" (Gormley 2007: 310).

This is a lesson that has been drawn by many. As we shall examine in Chapter 4 on climate change, the IPCC has proceeded along exactly these lines of thought. However, no matter how strong the IPCC consensus was, it failed to lead governments to agree on climate policy. Climate change seems to be the prime example where experts have been providing "ammunition" to opposing sides in a debate *despite* a far-reaching expert consensus.[6] Dan Sarewitz (2004) describes this situation as an "excess of objectivity," and Roger Pielke Jr. (2007) contrasts the (ideal typical) cases of "abortion politics" and "tornado politics" to illustrate the intertwinement of science, morals, and politics in decision-making. Climate change resembles abortion politics, despite all attempts to make it look like a case where it is all about facts and risk assessment (i.e. tornado politics).

The power of ideas

Coming back to the relation between ideas and interests in the policy-making process, we shall now consider the intriguing idea that ideas by themselves could exert a special power. Variations of this argument are present in various contributions from the political science and international relations literature, for example in Thomas Schelling's "focal points" (where points of convergence are "obvious"), or in Judith Goldstein's notion that the "power of the [economic] idea itself explains its acceptance" (Goldstein 1994: 2). It has been objected that the strong version of the argument would require a demonstration that in order

[6] Gormley himself recognizes the limits of the knowledge consensus model when discussing the example of gun control. Here, interest groups matter because "they are well-organized, well-financed, and persistent."

"to have causal weight, ideas must have an independent effect on policy, apart from the interests of actors who defend them" (Jacobsen 1995: 295). However, Goldstein eventually retreats from this rather bold statement into an assertion that it is salient ideas, i.e. those embraced by elites, that count most.

But there is another way in which ideas become powerful and shape reality. This is familiar to sociologists and media studies scholars who speak of *issue framing* (Goffman 1974; Hajer 1995). As we know, frames not only select segments of reality for further attention, but also provide schemata of interpretation that people use to locate, perceive, identify, and label (Entman 1993). Frames define problems and determine what a causal agent is doing; they identify the forces creating the problem. Frames are instrumental in diagnosing causes and they solicit moral judgments. Frames also suggest remedies, offer and justify treatments for the problem and predict their likely effects. In this sense ideas can be said to have an independent power. That is to say, if in any policy issue the problem was framed in a different way, we would see a different sequence of events unfolding, leading (in all likelihood) to a different outcome. In a somewhat slimmed-down version, political scientists have acknowledged that the way a problem is defined determines the nature of the solution (Schattschneider 1960).

Still, frames need to be constructed and introduced into the policy process. This is where policy entrepreneurs, journalists, and political and academic elites can play an important role. There needs to be some affinity, however, in order for frames to become aligned with specific political projects and political orientations (parties). As Hernes (2008: 263) noted, "you can choose your opponents, not your allies – and you can eliminate some unwanted allies by the option you decide on."

Peter Haas has put forward a much-acclaimed model to explain international policy coordination. He notes that "speaking truth to power" is a fraught exercise: "Even when scientists think they have developed truths for power, power appears disinterested at best, and possibly even uninterested" (Haas 2004: 570). So under which conditions does power listen to truth? It is a rare phenomenon, Haas reminds us (but not so rare as to be entirely dismissed, as is practice among many policy analysts). One precondition is that scientific knowledge is transformed into "usable knowledge," which is "accurate information that is of use to politicians and policy makers." Echoing the linear model, Haas postulates "that science must be developed authoritatively, and then delivered by responsible carriers to politicians." This is done via a transmission belt "of like-minded scientists ... called an epistemic community" (Haas 2004: 576).

He defines an epistemic community as a "knowledge-based network of specialists who share beliefs in cause-and-effect relations, validity tests, and underlying principled values and pursue common policy goals. Their orientation is perhaps best expressed in the words of one member, who voiced his willingness to accept the 'plausibility of a causal link without certainty' (Haas 1992: 187f.). In another place he writes: "Because of their environmental values, the members of the group advocated anticipatory action despite the range of uncertainties" (Haas 1993: 176).

Haas assumes that "the more autonomous and independent science is from policy the greater its potential influence." First, science needs to be developed behind a politically insulated wall, and then transmitted by epistemic communities to decision-makers. He further assumes that decision-makers recognize "the limits of their abilities to master new issues and the need to defer or delegate to authoritative actors with a reputation for expertise" (Haas 2004: 576). It has been commented that "Haas is encouraged by the increasing number of scientific staff in government" and the "increasing deference paid to technical expertise and in particular that of scientists." However, at the same time it has to be noted that "data are usually ambiguous and scientists are usually divided over public issues, concerning, for example, the environment and energy" (Jacobsen 1995: 302–03).

When are epistemic communities influential? Adler and Haas (1992: 380–81) seem to argue that "where policymakers have no strong preconceived views, and the issue is a first foray, then these bands of experts will exercise a lot of influence." However, as Jacobsen rightly points out, "if the issue does not matter very much, then experts do – not an appealing analytical agenda" (1995: 303). To the rescue of Haas and Adler, it could be said that experts in such situations play an agenda-setting role. Their ideas are instrumental in getting an issue onto the political agenda. This point is conceded by Jacobsen when he states that "[b]y persuading players to accept a 'definition of the situation,' one gains some control over the outcomes because how a problem is defined determines the nature of the solution" (Jacobsen 1995: 292).

There are two basic assumptions in Haas's framework: that policymakers turn to specialists to ameliorate uncertainties, and that policymakers act on the basis of expert consensus. There are other possibilities that might be more effective in the process of governance under conditions of uncertainty. First, epistemic communities react to challenges posed by other actors in society, such as NGOs (see Toke 1999). Second, the need for shared knowledge is more limited than

Haas perceives. What we frequently observe is that the specialists are divided. By definition, uncertainty means that there are at least two competing theories (Elster 1979: 384). This suggests that the decision-makers' problem is aggravated instead of ameliorated. Yet at the same time, this opens the way for other than cognitive mechanisms to play a role in the contending struggle over the right policy answers. Whereas the first point suggests that Haas underestimates the potential initiative role of NGOs, the second suggests that he overestimates the cognitive capabilities of epistemic communities and their influence on public policy (we shall return to his analysis of the IPCC in the Conclusion).

Politics of knowledge

In this section we start to explore the relations between knowledge and policy. We argue that policies are never based on a comprehensive knowledge base. Rather, they rest on selective bodies of knowledge that are available to policymakers, either by accident or by design (i.e. strategically). Some think that a comprehensive knowledge base for policy, while desirable, is not feasible. Others think that it is not even desirable. Recall Lindblom's statement that a "synoptic view" is not only unavailable, but even harmful if endorsed by practitioners.

Pielke (2007) and Sarewitz (1998, 2004) have convincingly argued that politicians are cherry-picking results from research that suit their political agenda, drawing attention to findings favorable to their views or policies. As Sarewitz put it, there is an excess of objectivity: there are too many research findings which open up too many policy alternatives. More research will lead to more options. Any hopes to solve the problem of uncertainty through more scientific research are dashed. Scientific results are essentially used to legitimize political options that existed prior to the new research. Steven Krasner (1993: 238, 257) has labeled this view as "ideas as hooks": "Ideas have not made possible alternatives that did not previously exist; they legitimated political practices that were already facts on the ground. Ideas have been one among several instruments that actors have invoked to promote their own mundane interests ... Only after ideas became embedded in institutional structures were they consequential for political behavior."

Max Weber was one of the first to emphasize the importance of technical experts in policymaking. In *Economy and Society*, he delineates "legal authority with a bureaucratic apparatus" or the superiority of technical knowledge. Bureaucracies not only accumulate knowledge, but also attempt to protect this knowledge from access by "outsiders" (cf. Weber [1922] 1978c: 990–93) and strive almost completely to avoid public discussion of their techniques, while political leaders are increasingly "dilettantes." "The ruler ... seeks to fend off the threatening dominance of the experts. He keeps one expert in check by others" (p. 995). Who controls the administrative apparatus? Weber asks. His answer is that such control is possible for the non-specialist only to a certain degree; in general, the "trained permanent official is more likely to get his way in the long run than his nominal superior, the Cabinet minister, who is not a specialist" (p. 338). We will see whether our case studies support the reading that expertise reduces the politician to a "dilettante," or whether he is in charge of decisions. In order to do so, we will have to consider specific political and historical contexts.

Collingridge and Reeve (1986) point out that there are situations where a policy consensus exists before research is undertaken. The research output merely legitimizes predefined policy options.[7] Policy decisions are made through negotiation and compromise: "Compromise of this sort requires next to nothing by way of technical information." But why do so many scientific experts participate in policy advisory functions, and why are governments eager to mobilize so much expertise for decision-making processes? The answer is that interest groups try to block each other by way of knowledge claims:

The role of scientific research and analysis is therefore not the heroic one of providing truths by which policy may be guided, but the ironic one of preventing policy being formulated around some technical conclusions. Research on one hypothesis ought to cancel out research on others, enabling policy to be made which is insensitive to all scientific conjectures. (Collingridge and Reeve 1986: 32)

In fact, Collingridge and Reeve argue that "no choices of policy are ever made which are sensitive to any scientific conjecture, and that no such choice ought to be sensitive to any scientific hypothesis" (Collingridge and Reeve 1986: 28). This very much ties in with the arguments developed by Lindblom. Good policy decisions are flexible and open to revision; and reduce the "error cost," to use Collingridge and Reeve's term (e.g. burden on human health, the environment, or the economy).

Barry Barnes highlights a potential weakness in this argument. In Collingridge and Reeve's view, political controversies are assumed to be independent and/or to predate the scientific research. The interests of the participants in the controversy are seen as independent of

---

[7] They depicted two scenarios for scientific advisory panels: (1) an over-critical policy environment where scientists and policymakers are divided. As a result, there is endless dispute and technical debate. (2) An under-critical policy environment where research is used to justify existing policy options.

knowledge. But this assumption is questionable. According to Barnes (1988: 561), "objectives and interests are formulated in the light of knowledge." This is an insight which has come from various authors who write on the relation between ideal and material aspects of social action. Well-known, of course, is Max Weber's analysis of the role of religious ideas for economic interests (Parsons 1938). Likewise, Foucault has pointed to the role of discursive formations, which include material interests and systems of thought. Interests cannot be determined independently of ideas. And Peter Hall (1989b) emphasizes how ideas are crucial in defining one's interest. When new knowledge comes into a policy field, it can destabilize existing social relations. Interests have to be redefined; they are no longer given. There is an additional reason for the special role of ideas. In public discourse, not all arguments are legitimate. An appeal to self-interest will not do, unless one can point to legitimate principles, such as the principle of fairness or justice. If a scientific finding supports one's interests, this would legitimately be an argument to be used in support, too. For this reason knowledge claims, especially scientific claims, are important resources indeed.

Another point is worth emphasizing: while it may be true that research rarely, if ever, prescribes policy, it may play a significant role in agenda-setting. What people think *about* is important for the policy process. And *how* people think about issues is likewise crucial, too. Again, the framing of a problem at the beginning of a controversy is significant, and can have a lasting impact on the development of a debate.

We may gain a better understanding of the issue if we distinguish between scientific research and expertise. The two are often used interchangeably (and we follow the same practice on occasions). Collingridge and Reeve have a point when using the term "research": this has been carried out and published in scientific publications, but mostly sits somewhere in a database. It is unlikely to influence policy in any way; and how could it? The argument becomes less convincing when one substitutes the term *research* with the term *expertise*. Experts translate research findings into contexts of application. They are the brokers who provide knowledge for their clients and audiences (see Stehr and Grundmann 2011). In contemporary societies, it would be hard to imagine that political decisions (or important private decisions, for that matter) are being taken without the input of some kind of expertise.

We propose to define knowledge as the *capacity to act* (or capability of taking action),[8] as the possibility of "setting something in motion."

---

[8] We do not claim that this is exclusive to knowledge. In the social context, cognitive findings do not have a monopoly on human capacity to act. A similar function can be

Knowledge is a *model for reality*. Thus, for example, social statistics are not necessarily (only) a reflection of social reality, but rather an explication of its problems; they refer to that which could be, and in this sense they confer the capability of taking action.

Research results and findings are not mere passive knowledge. Knowledge should be understood as the first step toward action; knowledge is in a position to change reality. Our choice of concepts is based upon Francis Bacon's famous thesis that "*scientia est potentia*," or as this formulation is frequently, but misleadingly, translated: *knowledge is power*. Bacon claims that the particular utility of knowledge derives from its ability to set something in motion. The concept of *potentia*, this ability, here describes the "power" of knowledge. Knowledge is creation. Human knowledge is the knowledge of the rules of action, and thus the capability of setting in motion the process in question, or producing something. The successes or results of human action can accordingly be seen in the alteration of reality. The result of this, at least for the modern world, is that its reality is increasingly based upon knowledge and consists of knowledge. Knowledge is not power (in the usual sense of the word *power*), but rather *potential* power.[9] Accordingly, we must differentiate between the capabilities of taking action and making use of the capabilities of taking action. This should be evident through the following considerations.

Knowledge fulfils an "active" function only where action is not carried out within essentially stereotypical parameters (Max Weber), or otherwise extensively regulated.[10] Knowledge plays an active role only where, for whatever reasons, there is latitude or necessity for decision-making.[11] For Karl Mannheim ([1929] 1965: 74), therefore, social

---

performed by the social norms internalized by actors, for example, or even needs and tendencies (Loyal and Barnes 2001).

[9] In its etymology, however, power is related to ability; and one of the most fundamental definitions of ability would be: to make a difference. In this sense, and not in the sense in which power is usually discussed in the context of social relationships, namely as power exercised to gain something, or over a person, the definition of power as ability is reminiscent of the idea of knowledge as *enabling* (cf. Dryberg 1997: 88–99).

[10] Building on the premise that knowledge constitutes an ability to act, one can differentiate between forms of knowledge, i.e. according to which capacity to act is embodied by knowledge. Lyotard's ([1979] 1984: 6) attempt to differentiate between "investment knowledge" and "payment knowledge," in analogy to the difference between expenditures for investment and consumption, can be considered an example of such a functional separation of forms of knowledge.

[11] Niklas Luhmann's (1992: 136) observations on the conditions for the ability to make a decision may permit an even broader application of knowledge. "One can only" decide, as he very plausibly emphasizes, "if and insofar as it is not determined what will happen." On condition that the future is highly uncertain, the deployment of knowledge in the decision-making process can extend to many more social contexts, even to those that are normally marked only by routine and habitual behavior.

action begins only "where the not yet rationalized latitude begins, where unregulated situations force decisions to be made."[12] Formulated more concretely:

It is not an action …, when a bureaucrat deals with a bundle of files according to existing regulations. There is also no action when a judge subsumes a case under a section of law, nor when a factory worker produces a screw using prescribed movements, nor actually even when a technician combines general laws of natural processes to some end or other. All of these modes of behaviour should be described as *reproductive*, because these actions are performed in a rationalized arrangement without benefit of *personal* decision.[13]

Consequently, for Mannheim the problem of the relationship between theory and practice is restricted to situations of just this kind. To be sure, even extensively regulated and thoroughly rationalized situations that are constantly repeated are not free of "irrational" (i.e. "open") moments. At the same time, this perspective points to the conditions of knowledge, and indeed of knowledge as the result of human activity. Knowledge can lead to social action, and is at the same time the result of social action. This indicates that it is by no means necessary to consider the capacity to act to be identical with actual action, i.e. knowledge is not itself already action.[14]

The social significance of scientific discoveries, then, lies primarily in the capacity to make use of knowledge as the ability to act. Or in other

[12] From an interactionist perspective, organizations and social structures of any kind are "negotiated orders" (Strauss 1978). However, this does not mean that any aspect of the social reality of an organization is permanently at the disposal of its members. Only certain very limited contexts of social structure are at their disposal, and with respect to these contingent action contexts, knowledge in the form of planning collective goals can be mobilized.

[13] Similar concepts can be found in Friedrich Hayek's essay "The Use of Knowledge in Society" from 1945, which is actually a paean to decentralization, the importance of local knowledge for taking action, and the price system as a mediator that conveys information and solves the problem of coordinating situative knowledge. Hayek ([1945] 1969: 82) refers to the fact that economic problems always "arise only as a result of changes. As long as things stay as they are, or at least do not develop differently from what is expected, no new problems occur that require a decision, and no necessity arises to make a new plan."

[14] A more recent study by an economist, which above all deals with various conceptual problems in the attempt to quantify knowledge and integrate it into economic theory, is reminiscent in several passages of the definition of knowledge as the capacity to act: "I define knowledge in terms of potentially observable behaviour, as the ability of an individual or group of individuals to undertake, or to instruct or otherwise induce others to undertake, procedures resulting in predictable transformations of material objects" (Howitt 1996 : 99). Aside from the somewhat ponderous form of the definition, the restriction of the concept to the manipulation of *material objects* is a step backward, into the *black box* of "procedures" and "observable behaviour." Ultimately, Howitt tends to equate knowledge with action.

words: knowledge gains in *distinction* on the basis of its ability to change reality.

Human action is indeed, as Mannheim also stresses, in manifold ways the result of a relatively set repertoire of fixed complexes of actions or modes of behavior, which play out in given triggering situations. This by no means applies to all the situations with which we are confronted in daily life, or in less routine contexts for action. As Friedrich Tenbruck (1986: 95) emphasizes, for example, due to internal or external circumstances human beings continually find themselves in new situations, for which highly automated and self-contained modes of behavior and habits are not appropriate. In these cases it makes a great difference *"which elements of the situation are given and which are open"* (our emphasis). Even the fixed nature of social relationships, or as this is also described by many observers, the existence of *"structural"* attributes of action, which work on social action as an external "force," can be conceived of as a set of *imaginable* or possible *options for taking action*, which are open for certain individuals or groups.

The qualities that research findings *should* have – which stimulate a demand for further knowledge, influence the assessment of the knowledge on offer, and co-determine the practicability of the findings – are thus to a crucial degree a function of the supposed openness of the life situation. The probability of implementing knowledge as the capacity to act into a particular social action is an essential consequence of the correspondence – in the broadest sense – between the type and content of knowledge and those elements of the situation that can be conceived of as *open*, i.e. controllable or manipulable by actors, and that can actually be influenced (see the detailed account in Stehr 1992).

It is thus logical to differentiate between "knowledge for practice" and "practical knowledge," particularly since the pragmatic relevance of knowledge is by no means certain a priori, so that knowledge can be turned into knowledge for action. To avoid misunderstanding, we should point out that this distinction is not congruent with the familiar distinctions between "explicit" vs. "tacit knowledge," "theoretical" vs. "applied knowledge," or "technology" vs. "craft knowledge." Our distinction aims to capture the difference between science's potential to be put into practice vs. the actual practical use made of science.

We should also make clear that knowledge can have different functions in politics and policymaking. Knowledge can be used for problem-solving and for legitimizing decisions (or both). Knowledge can also operate at the level of influencing the construction and framing of policy problems (see Weiss 1977, 1978, 1980) without leading to specific policies. Knowledge may thus have a big impact on shifting the parameters of the debate, but is *not* taken up in policy adjustments – so it may contain little guidance on practice, but nonetheless leads to a reconceptualization of the question.

Building on an insight of Karl Mannheim ([1929] 1965: 143), who in his study *Ideology and Utopia* made an attempt to formulate the problems of a "science of politics," it becomes clear that the successful "deployment" of findings in concrete situations for action demands that for such contexts, the possibilities for action, as well as an understanding of the actors' latitude for action and their chances of shaping events, must be linked together, in order that knowledge may become practical knowledge.

The qualities necessary for an understanding of practical knowledge, which make possible the *realization* of knowledge, are on the one hand particular findings, and on the other, i.e. on the side of those taking action, the control of situationally specific conditions. These abilities, which make implementing findings possible, can be called *capacity to shape*, in contrast to knowledge as the capacity to act.

We should emphasize that the main determinant of the influence of research does not only lie in features of the research. This would neglect a host of conditions influencing the take-up of knowledge that have little to do with any characteristics of research. The public policy literature has shown that in many instances the take-up and implementation of policies depends on many contingencies (see, for example, Kingdon's (1984) policy streams and Cohen et al.'s (1972) "garbage can" model). But we do wish to put forward the hypothesis that knowledge has to be practical in the sense outlined above in order to become effective; this is a necessary but not sufficient condition.

In modern society, at the intersection of possibilities to take action and to shape events, the rapidly growing group of *experts*, *advisors*, and *consultants* as mediators of knowledge find their employment and exert their influence (Stehr 1992; Stehr and Grundmann 2011). These functions are necessary in order to mediate between the complexity of changing and rapidly expanding (scientific) fields of knowledge and those who intend to enlist these findings as aids to taking action; for ideas do not "wander" from person to person, like an item of "luggage"; rather, knowledge is tied to individuals and to "networks" of persons. Varying interpretations must come to one single "conclusion"; only then do they become effective as capacity to take action (Wittgenstein) and, ultimately, as practical knowledge as well.

And it is exactly this function – the closing off of reflection, or the "rectification" of the frequent lack of immediate practicability of scientific findings, so that they can serve as the basis for action – which is performed by experts or knowledge-based professions in the modern knowledge society. The social prestige and influence of consultants, experts, and advisors is ultimately especially significant whenever their expertise extends to the access and control of *actionable* findings, findings that can be used for decisions that will make a difference.[15]

Conclusion

Our literature review shows that social scientists are divided on the question of what influence knowledge has on politics. On one side are the supporters of a rational policy concept, under which more and better knowledge leads to improved policy outcomes. This is often accompanied by the assumption that a epistemic consensus would make political action easier. We interpreted and critically evaluated contributions from Lasswell, Kaplan, Gormley, and Haas in this regard. On the other side, we see representatives of the thesis that policymaking is largely divorced from scientific evidence; and that this need not be a disadvantage, but rather can be an advantage. Lindblom, Collingridge and Reeve, and Pielke and Sarewitz argue in this way.

We tend to agree with the second group of authors; albeit we must point out that the introduction of the concepts of *frames* and *experts* leads to a modification of the previously discussed literature. First, when knowledge comes in the form of ideas which provide interpretations of the situation (frames), they offer solutions by way of defining the problem. Claims makers are thus essential in the political process, and this role can be played by experts, or policy entrepreneurs. Second, experts, in contrast to scientific researchers, are fit to make a difference at the interface between science and politics if they point out practical "levers for action." As the contributions of Weber, Mannheim, and Hernes make clear, knowledge can only lead to action if there exists latitude for action and practical levers that can set something in motion. It is still an open question how much "cognitive authority" is attributed to these claims makers, and how important such authority is. Here our empirical studies will provide some interesting results. Our literature review has primarily scrutinized some general and abstract conceptual tools. We will need to take a closer look at the specific political context in order to understand the role of knowledge in concrete historical situations.

---

[15] A note on terminology: we will use the terms *experts*, *knowledge brokers*, and *policy entrepreneurs* to indicate the role identified above. These terms are not synonymous, but rather allude to different aspects of the advisory role, from being a more passive expert to a more proactive, visionary, or activist broker or entrepreneur.

2 The savior of capitalism: the power of economic discourse

> Economics is a science of thinking in terms of models joined to the art of choosing models which are relevant to the real world.
>
> John M. Keynes (1938: 296)

The aim of this chapter is to trace the impact of Keynesian ideas on economic policies. We are not interested merely in making the case that knowledge – or even more generally, ideas – plays an important role in the political economy of the day. Although the role of ideas in politics and policy is at times considered less important than so-called structural factors, we will pay attention to the linkage between knowledge and structure. Knowledge is an enabling feature of action, and structure a constraining attribute of enacting knowledge as a capacity of action.

It will be our contention that economic ideas that constitute enabling knowledge for policy purposes have to focus on those features of political, social, and economic realities that are subject to the control of relevant bodies of governance, and not subject to "external" influences beyond their control. At times, influence over external actions that are not subject to the control of a particular state may have been relinquished voluntarily, as in the case of supranational organizations such as the European Union; or such actions may result from developments that limit the sovereignty of national institutions from the beginning, because these influential transformations are beyond their control (cf. Dahl 1994). Whenever internal economic policies are affected by developments outside the control of a country, it should be evident that knowledge that fails to take such features on board will not be enabling policy.

Whether "practical men," as Keynes called them – governments, politicians, and civil servants – actually adopt knowledge that deserves to be labeled *enabling knowledge* and take it on board for policy purposes is not solely determined by the ideas in question. A multitude of additional factors will play a role, including their assessment of whether these doctrines will in fact solve, perhaps with tools already in place, the problems faced by practical men.

That the economic ideas of John Maynard Keynes had such an impact in various countries, especially in the decades immediately after the end of World War II, is hardly a contentious matter. Our interest centers on the question of what essential attributes Keynesian theory commands that made it useful as basis for policy, at least at a certain juncture in the development of those nations that subscribed to a capitalist worldview. It is equally evident that the "heroic" influence of Keynesian ideas has passed; whether the decline in the political weight of Keynes's ideas is merely a matter of being out of "fashion" (cf. Hall 1989b: 4) is part of the knowledge-guiding interest of our inquiry into the reasons for the power of his economic theory.

It is not desirable merely to hint at the outlines of John Maynard Keynes's economic theory and the intellectual and socio-economic context in which his ideas originated. However, while we will sketch many of the details of Keynesian theory, a description of "Keynesianism,"[1] that is, an account of the many economic *policies* in different countries attributed to and justified with reference to Keynes need not be presented in this context in any detail (but see Bombach et al. 1963). Nor will it be required to take account of what has come to be known as "Keynesian economics," a largely formalistic and highly technical *economic* literature, divided into a variety of groups of economists over the past thirty years (cf. Davidson 1978; Diesing 1982: 114–19), all claiming to have explicated and developed assumptions and ideas that may be attributed to Keynes in one way or the other.

A more intensive and detailed critical discussion of Keynesian ideas, the thick and possibly opaque crust of interpretations it has generated or the changes his ideas have undergone in the meantime as a result of such vigorous interpretive work, are proper, for example, within a discussion of the history of economic ideas, but not necessarily within the context of a study of the *practical efficiency* of Keynes's economic doctrines. We will instead refer directly to the writings of Keynes and his role as economic advisor, and not engage in a discussion of the complex debates they engendered among fellow economists, and the developments or dilutions his program may have subsequently experienced at the hand of the same fraternity – however urgent and justified these amendments and deviations might have been.

---

[1] Donald Winch (1989) and other observers have repeatedly emphasized that it is important in this context to differentiate between the ideas Keynes himself developed and advocated and those of his followers.

The economist Keynes

It is widely recognized that John Maynard Keynes's self-conception as an economist was shaped, in the first instance, by his interest in economic policy. Eric J. Hobsbawn (Wattel 1985: 3) has summarized this view in the following terms: "From his dramatic entry on the public scene as a critic of the 1919 Versailles peace to his death, Keynes spent his time trying to save capitalism from itself" (also Schumpeter 1946a: 355–56; Robinson 1956: 11).[2] The thrust of this evaluation of Keynes by others corresponds quite well to his own, not necessarily humble, self-judgment of the practical importance of his theoretical ideas. In 1936, for example, he indicates that his doctrine offers, as a theoretical alternative to the neoclassical model, the only "practical means of avoiding destruction of existing economic forms ... in its entirety" (Keynes 1936: 380). But his economic ideas also found many followers among social democrats and active labor union leaders,[3] while some of his conservative critics have condemned Keynes's ideas as advancing a socialist agenda (e.g. Coddington 1974). This, of course, initially illustrates the fact that the ways and means of the possible practical power of Keynes's theories are quite complicated.

The dissemination process and the possible practical effect of Keynesian ideas will hardly conform to a structure that follows the main lines of political divisions and cleavages in modern society. Yet patterns of influence across political cleavages perhaps signal that his ideas were by no means without their theoretical looseness, and were therefore open to a range of interpretive possibilities.

The most important works of John Maynard Keynes are his *Treatise on Money* (1930) and *The General Theory of Employment, Interest and Money* (1936). These studies should not be seen, however, following the

---

[2] Joseph Schumpeter (1946a: 356) observes that it was what he calls the "ideological element" in Keynes's economic thought that gave impetus to his ideas (because "new departures" in science are impossible without it), and that accounts for its appeal at the time. He describes the ideological component in Keynes as "the vision of decaying capitalism that located (saw) the cause for the decay in one out of a number of large features of latter-day society."

[3] The labor union movement continues to be primarily impressed by economic theories that stress underconsumption, because such ideas appear to have greater strategic significance in struggles to raise wages. At the same time, such views also function as evidence for a kind of disinterested – that is, objective – legitimation of the goals of the union. However, it is not justified, it seems to me, to draw the dubious conclusion from an elective affinity between Keynesian ideas and the labor union movement, as for example O'Connor (1984: 202) has done, that Keynes's theory is "the unintentional result of working-class struggle" and therefore only "a doctrine to legitimate working-class demands."

great Marxian example and ambition, to constitute a universal history of capitalist development. *The General Theory* was published during or immediately following the global economic crisis of the 1930s. Keynes began to write his main work in 1932.[4] At the time Keynes commenced work on *The General Theory*, Great Britain had suffered for more than a decade from annual unemployment figures of more than 10 percent. Keynes's *General Theory* was published after he already had participated actively and publicly in debates concerning economic policies and purposes (cf. Chick 1987).

James Tobin (1986: 15), for example, indicates that "one evident purpose of *The General Theory* was to provide a professional analytical foundation for the policy positions he had been advocating in those debates." That Tobin's interpretation of one of the main purposes is correct can also be gleaned from Keynes's own introduction to *The General Theory*. In the introduction, Keynes suggests that the book is primarily intended for his colleagues in economics. And he adds (Keynes 1936: v) that the main purpose of *The General Theory* is intended to deal "with difficult questions of theory, and only in the second place with applications of this theory to practice."

But despite Keynes's own testimony to the contrary, one can concur with Adolph Lowe's (1977: 218) observation that *The General Theory* represents the beginning of the end of pure economic theory[5] and the start of politically minded economic theory, and forms the culmination of intensive reflection by Keynes about economic policy matters of the day (cf. Schumpeter 1954: 1157; Steindl 1985: 105–09). Though the treatise itself contains but few explicit suggestions for economic policies, it nonetheless may be seen as the end product of Keynes's (1938: 107) long-standing conviction that the orthodox laissez-faire doctrine was "wholly inapplicable to such problems as those of unemployment and the trade cycle, or indeed, to any of the day-to-day problems of ordinary life." In any event, as far as the retrospective and the contemporary interpretations of the nature of *The General Theory* are concerned, it is widely hailed as an eminent example of economic theory

---

[4] See the letter from Keynes and the editorial comments by Donald Moggridge in Keynes's collected works ([1973] 1987: 172, 243, 337) for further information. Moggridge refers to two "external" reasons why Keynes may have started work on the *General Theory*: first, the reception of the *Treatise* among fellow economists; and second, a discussion, also connected with the same work, among younger students of economics in the so-called Cambridge Circus at the University of Cambridge (cf. Keynes [1973] 1987: 338–43).

[5] Economic theory no longer merely refers to "situations where there is no practical need for theoretical guidance, since the automatism of the system ensures that all goes well" (Lowe 1965: 98).

with a practical intent. The circumstances which led to *The General Theory* appear to confirm the observation that important theoretical innovations in social science often form a response to, and develop as the result of, intensive reflections on pressing contemporary events, to which some kind of "intuitive" solutions are proposed.

The economic theory

Keynes's *General Theory* amounts to a new paradigm for modern economic theory.[6] Keynes was convinced that his theory would have a revolutionary impact. In a letter to George Bernard Shaw, written before the completion of the *General Theory*, Keynes ([1973] 1987: 492–93) expresses his belief that he is writing a book "on economic theory which will largely revolutionize – not, I suppose, at once but in the course of the next ten years – the way the world thinks about economic problems." And very much in the sense of the meaning of the term *paradigm*, as proposed by Thomas Kuhn ([1962] 1970) for the purpose of grasping the nature of intellectual revolutions in the history of the sciences, Keynes's radical innovation primarily consists of a "displacement"[7] of central economic concepts and a novel classification of economic phenomena (cf. Harrod 1951: 462–63; but disagreeing with this assessment, for example, Lowe 1977: 217).

The fact that Keynes's main work originated in the face of the socio-economic and socio-political consequences of the Great Depression, and was furthermore based on his personal involvement in policy discussions and his experience as a speculator, should be seen as pertinent for a number of reasons.[8] That Keynes's economic diagnosis concerns

[6] The view that Keynes's theory constitutes a radical break in economic theorizing is, of course, not shared throughout the community of professional economists; some suggest that he failed to be radical enough (e.g. Brothwell 1988), while others do not detect an intellectual break of any significance which would warrant the label of revolutionary.

[7] Compare the important notion of the "displacement of concepts" proposed by Donald Schon (1963) as a central category for a general understanding of the conditions for and the process of theoretical innovation and imagination. As Peter Hall (1989c: 365) notes with respect to Keynes, in the same sense as Schon, "new ideas are most powerful when they change the basic categories through which we see reality, and, after Keynes, the economic world never looked quite the same as it did before."

[8] Keynes's gains and losses from his stock market speculations were huge. In 1927 his net assets were £44,000 (around £1million in 1992 prices). At the end of 1929 they had shrunk to £7,815 – just under 180k in 1992 prices (Skidelsky 1992: 342). However, in the mid 1930s his fortunes had multiplied again, outperforming Wall Street by far. Skidelsky (1992: 524) comments: "By 1936 his net worth had come to over £500,000, or about £13m in today's values. His capital had appreciated by twenty-three times, in a period when Wall Street's stock prices had only trebled and London's had hardly moved at all."

the phase of the depression in the cycle of economic development, for example, is quite relevant to the kind of therapy which might emerge from his analysis.

Later discussions and controversies about the "universality" or generalizability of Keynesian ideas refer to the immediate intellectual impetus and aims of his inquiry, and express doubt that Keynes's reflections can in fact be of greater relevance and pertinent to other economic circumstances. At the same time, and for the purposes of asking about the conditions for and features of the practical power of knowledge, it is noteworthy that ideas in social science that are developed primarily in conjunction with pressing external problems, rather than, for example, fashionable disciplinary theoretical controversies, may have a better chance from the beginning to evolve into recipes with workable solutions, though the range of situations in which such knowledge is perceived as relevant may turn out to be limited.

Keynes's economic theories represent the beginning of macroeconomics, as well as of the interest among economists – which continues until this day – in certain aggregate data of the economy of a society. Adolph Lowe (1977: 220) observes that this kind of *displacement in foci*, in comparison to neoclassical economic theory alone, assures Keynesian theory a greater instrumentality; that is, "by substituting for the innumerable micro-relations of the Walrasian model a few basic macro-relations, the General Theory arrives at propositions which easily lend themselves to statistical testing and, no less important, are handy tools for policy making."

The intelligibility of the economy no longer depends on an understanding of the rational decisions made by autonomous individual subjects. The object of reflection instead becomes the aggregate economy, with its own independent dynamic; the subject in Keynes's analysis, namely the government, or even more precisely the treasury, remains outside the boundaries of inquiry (cf. Diesing 1982: 82–85). The shift in the theoretical interest from individual to collective features represents of course a transition, which had its intellectual precursors in sociology and anthropology.[9]

A critique of the basic, harmonious assumption of neoclassical economics – that advanced economic systems, organized according to capitalist principles, tend to achieve an equilibrium at full employment levels – is usually seen as the characteristic starting point of Keynesian

---

[9] These attributes of Keynes's theory, and the stress on non-rational elements in economic decision-making, also led to criticisms that his work is too "sociological" (e.g. Brunner and Meltzer 1977).

economic theory. Many interpretations of Keynes that stress this point fail to recognize, however, that Keynes is concerned not only about the lack of full employment but also about the unjust distribution of income and wealth. Keynes is therefore convinced that his theory calls into question a number of economic views typically employed to justify a skewed distribution of wealth. He believes that less economic inequality is quite consistent with his own theory.

Keynes objects to the orthodox conceptions that the price mechanism alone assures the "normal state" of full employment of an economy; that the distribution of income corresponds to the marginal utility of the means of production (that is, capital, labor, and land); and that economic growth is a fairly assured prospect. The classical employment theory is primarily based on two assumptions:

(a) As a function of the interest rate at full employment, the savings rate and investment decisions are in equilibrium.
(b) The equilibrium between demand and supply of labor is determined by the real cost of labor, although its nominal downward flexibility is restricted.

The Keynesian conception of the process of economic action in its most important attributes, especially of the psychological determinants and dynamics, is also quite different from the views of its neoclassical predecessors, particularly in the emphasis of the latter on much more rationalistic factors (*homo oeconomicus*) as a determinant of the microeconomic behavior of individual and corporate actors. In a few words, Keynes chooses to stress the plasticity of economic action, its uncertainty, and the influence of a larger number of imponderables or "irrational" motives (cf. Schmölders et al. 1956). That is to say, Keynes's theory of economic action does not set aside the contingency of expectations, the importance of social conventions, and the influence of speculative behavior on economic decisions. In addition, the macroeconomic theory Keynes advances in his *General Theory* differs from its neoclassical forerunner in the following details:[10]

(1) Keynes's theory stresses the significance of investment decisions by businessmen for the rate of employment and growth. Investment decisions are primarily affected by uncertain or even speculative expectations about future economic data. The multiplier of investments, in addition, stimulates demand; but instability is endogenous to capitalist economies. The rate of investment and the savings

[10] Compare the first, classic description of these differences by Hicks (1937).

rate follow the economic decisions of different actors,[11] and a savings rate which is too high may impede potential investments.

(2) The decisive economic dimension for Keynes is not the supply side but the *demand* side. He thus inverts the emphasis compared to orthodox theorizing. In the context of Keynes's theory, consumption is no longer a function of supply; that is, supply does not generate its own demand, as it does in the case of Say's famous law, but rather supply is driven by demand. Commodities and services that are offered for sale are a function of the demand for such goods (Keynes 1936: 21–22; cf. Drucker 1981b; Stehr 2008); and the demand for goods and services could therefore be insufficient. Against the views of Austrian neoclassical economic theory as espoused by Friedrich Hayek, for example, Keynes supported government action during an economic slump, so as to nurture and increase demand.

(3) According to Keynes, *money* is more than merely a neutral medium of exchange. Keynes attempts to join value theory and a theory of money. The interest rate in an economy is determined, for example, by the demand/supply relation for money used for speculative purposes.

(4) One of the key observations of Keynes's macroeconomic theory concerns *employment*. He considers full employment to be a special case, and is therefore prepared to accept the possibility that an economy may be in a state of equilibrium accompanied by unemployment. Unemployment is no longer the result of a voluntary withdrawal from the labor market, as still postulated by neoclassical theory (that is, a segment of the proletariat refuses work because they consider the rate of real wages as too low), but is rather the outcome of the unique economic status of workers who are not in a position to determine the rate of real wages.

(5) Finally, Keynes rejects the view of neoclassical theory that the *income* distribution in society occurs in accordance with the marginal utility of the various means of production.

The differences between Keynes's *General Theory* and neoclassical economic theory also can be seen to reflect a decisive change in the capitalist economy itself: Until the early part of this century, the constitutive element of the economy was the interrelation between demand and supply for commodities and services, that is, the economy of goods.

---

[11] Keynes's (1930: 1975) initial observations on this matter, for example in his *Treatise of Money*, resonate at least partly with more conventional views: "An act of saving by an individual may result either in increased investment or in increased consumption by the individuals who make up the rest of the community."

Demand and supply of goods and services represented the "independent" variables of the economy. Later, and even more so in our age, the capitalist economy becomes one driven by monetary factors instead. Keynes (1936: vii) himself recognized this radical change and indicates that his theory, in contrast to neoclassical theory, revolves around the monetary economy or the "symbolic" economy, that is, it is especially concerned with the supply of money, with credits, budget surpluses and deficits, and interest rates. The Keynesian interpretation of economic facts is therefore a novel and unusual perspective: "Instead of goods, services, and work – realities of the physical world and 'things' – Keynes's economic realities are symbols: money and credit" (Drucker 1981b: 8).

A theoretical perspective of this kind is possible only after the monetary economy has reached a certain measure of importance and independence, and therefore becomes one of the significant determinants of economic activity generally. More recently, monetarists such as Milton Friedman have argued that these developments have accelerated, and the real economy today is the monetary or symbolic economy. Keynesian economic theory in fact reflects these structural changes of the capitalist economy. The movement of capital and investment decisions become a market, as the financial crisis at the beginning of the century underlines once again. Financial capital becomes detached from the flow of goods and services (e.g. Drucker 1971: 56–59).

Politics and the economy

Some of our most gifted economists would be useless in the tent of the Prince either in war or peace – even though as a result of the researches and theories, political economy is in a better position to render needed advice. (Paul A. Samuelson (1959: 188))

In examining the practical efficacy of Keynes's economic theory, it will first be necessary to indicate the features of the theory (and the policy measures) that might be used as standards. This task requires a general theory of the application of social science knowledge that transcends the orthodox model of instrumentality. As a matter of fact, the degree of "helplessness" engendered by the model can be illustrated quite well if one asks what procedures and what answers the standard theory of the application of social science knowledge might offer to the question of the possible utility of Keynes's economic ideas. The most sensible answer would be to indicate that any observable practical success of Keynes's economic theory amounts to an accident, or simply fortuitous circumstances, since his theory appears to be very far removed from the ideal social scientific theoretical model that the conventional view of application demands.

Although Keynes does signal – for example, already in the title of his major work – that he aspires to formulate a *general* theory of employment, interest, and money, his approach does not constitute such a *general* theoretical model as one might therefore imagine, especially when judged against widely supported and rather demanding methodological ideals about object-adequate social science knowledge. That is, Keynes fails to enumerate and examine as explanatory factors the intricate interrelation among innumerable attributes and processes of economic variables to other variables, any and all of which may affect the rate of employment, the value of money, and the interest rate. And one could surmise that the progress in knowledge represented by Keynes's ideas, when compared to the neoclassical economic understanding of the dynamics of the modern economy, would surely have to be linked to a significant degree to a much more faithful – that is, more elaborate and comprehensive – analysis of economic processes than that actually found in *The General Theory*.

Given such standards of adequate knowledge and advances in knowledge over time, the disappointment could not be greater. Keynes's general theory of employment, money, and interest is above all rather parsimonious when it comes to identifying relevant theoretical dimensions for reflection and inquiry. His theory refers to but a few attributes of economic action. As a matter of fact, for our purposes, Keynes's theory can even be summarized merely by indicating that, for the most part, his theory represents the discovery of the importance of investment decisions for the level of employment in the national economy. His theory is therefore about as far removed as possible from attending or capturing, as Seymour M. Lipset put it, the "total system behavior" of a major social phenomenon. On the contrary, Keynes's theory appears to be an intellectual "throwback" to the fallacies of classical social science theorizing, with its abundance of limited-factor theories.

It is useful to refer here to Collingridge and Reeve's observation that there is, in fact, the distinct possibility that access to impressive amounts of information and knowledge claims can be quite "dysfunctional" in practical decision-making processes. Their observation is also intended to combat the prevailing view of certain qualities of rationality; in particular, the thesis that the rationality of political decisions somehow improves, and in an almost linear manner, with the quantity of information available to the actors. Collingridge and Reeve (1986: 5) state that "it is simply not the case that a good decision can only be made once the uncertainties surrounding it have been reduced by gathering as much relevant information as possible. On the contrary, policy decisions may be made quite happily with the very scantiest information."

Despite the fact that only a few pertinent attributes of economic action appear to have been examined and taken into consideration by Keynes in his *General Theory*, voices could be heard almost immediately after its publication – and certainly a chorus of voices in later years – vigorously praising Keynes's theory and insisting that it may well have very important practical implications and benefits for the economic affairs of a nation.

Economic knowledge

Our final task might be to select those variables which can be deliberately controlled or managed by central authority in the kind of system in which we actually live. (John Maynard Keynes (1936: 247))

The practical economic lessons drawn from Keynesian economic theory are that his ideas constitute a "system of political control over economic life" (Skidelsky 1979: 55). More specifically, a careful reading of the *General Theory* shows clearly that Keynes explicitly tried to devise practically sound answers for economic problems, constructed with a certain corporate actor in mind: the British Treasury.

Keynes's theory is above all characterized by the fact that it consciously stresses the importance of but a few *aggregate* quantities of the national economy. But on the basis of these dimensions, it is possible to point to the decisive determinants of the employment level, or the conditions which *set* (un-)employment *in motion*. More precisely, Keynes is concerned with the annual total or aggregate production of goods and services of the economy, the aggregate demand for these goods and services and the aggregate income that can be distributed, which forms the basis for aggregate investments and demand.

The determinants of the employment level can then be ascertained on the basis of these aggregate quantities. In other words, Keynes stipulates a relation between the national income level and employment; five endogenous variables and one exogenous economic variable mediate this relation. In addition, the analysis is based on a number of mostly static assumptions – which, taken together, clearly indicate that Keynes's theory surely cannot claim anything approaching "completeness" or "comprehensiveness" in reflecting the intricate, complex, empirical nature of national economic relations (for example, Schumpeter 1954: 1175, 1183–84).

If the propensity for consumption (or the ability to consume) and the readiness of entrepreneurs to invest are insufficient to use national economic resources to the fullest extent, and if neither can be expected to rise in light of the prevailing economic data, the *state* should step in and stimulate the economy with additional expenditures. As a rule, additional state expenditures have to be financed by the central bank, or by way of money raised in the capital market; because a tax increase, the other potential source for additional revenue, would result in a decline in demand, and therefore achieve the opposite effect. But an economic policy which is committed to these means implies, in the anticyclical case, that the goal of the balanced budget has to be sacrificed; and since a continuation of compensatory state spending incurs a continually rising indebtedness, it is not surprising that proponents of "solid" and carefully drafted budgets have always resisted those policies supported by Keynes (cf. Spahn 1976: 216).

In contrast to the occasionally vigorous opposition of economists and politicians to state intervention, especially in the United States, it is precisely an *activist* conception of economic policies of the state that is a characteristic feature of Keynesian economic policies. Keynes (1936: 379) even refers to the necessity to greatly expand the traditional functions of the state in order to secure full employment. In a significant passage from his *General Theory*, Keynes (1936: 320) discusses the propensity to invest in broad terms, and suggests that "in conditions of laissez-faire the avoidance of wide fluctuations in employment may ... prove impossible without a far-reaching change in the psychology of investment markets such as there is no reason to expect. I conclude that the duty of ordering the current volume of investment cannot safely be left in private hands." In other words, in direct contrast to neoclassical theory as well as the recently favored monetarism, the fundamental presupposition that the state is capable of constructively intervening in the economy becomes a taken-for-granted feature of his theory and of Keynesian economic policies. However, such compensatory state activity today is not readily accepted, because many economists and politicians again emphasize the so-called self-healing abilities of markets. As a result, the primary economic function of the state is seen to concern policies that protect competition and a free market.

In the following section we will show when, where, and how Keynes's theoretical conceptions met ideological and socio-structural conditions and resonated with, or failed to converge with, such circumstances of action.

The aim is therefore not to demonstrate that Keynes has an intellectual monopoly and priority in regard to state interventionist economic policies. Indeed, a variety of politicians and economists before and after Keynes, without referring to him, advocated such action by the state in favor of specific social classes and economic goals.[12] But quite independently of the question of the intellectual genesis of certain ideas and any priority disputes, the problematic at issue here requires us to discover indications that a particular theoretical perspective incorporates, or has a strong affinity to, socio-economic conditions that are actionable. Such resonance between theory and practice should not be mistaken to signal that a particular theoretical conception is logically implicated, or that it has been established empirically and without doubt that certain processes and subsequent developments can only be the result of such a linkage or parentage. As a rule, societal conditions rarely, if ever, allow for the establishment of such definitive links. This is a mixed blessing. On the one hand, it restricts the reach of public policy when trying to fight social ills (poverty, public health problems, crime). On the other hand, this puts limits on what governments can impose on society. In this sense, one can draw consolation from the fact that society is rather resistant in this regard.

The state as entrepreneur

In 1929, unemployment in England had stood almost without interruption for a decade at approximately 1,500,000, and was about to reach the 10 percent level (see Figure 1).

The rate of unemployment became an important political issue in England, not surprisingly, and figured prominently in the parliamentary campaigns of both the Liberal and Conservative political parties of that same year. The Liberals, under the leadership of Lloyd George, promised in a political manifesto of March 1929 that should they assume the role of government, they would reduce unemployment to a "normal level." They proposed to reach this goal with the help of a government-financed program to create employment, especially in the field of transportation and housing. Lloyd George had already supported such a platform for economic initiatives of the state in 1924.

This program was opposed by the governing Conservative Party. The official government position at the time was equally clear. As Winston Churchill expressed it forcefully in his budget speech in 1929, "it is

---

[12] Peter Wagner (1990: 301), for example, underlines that the theoretical perspective which prompted and legitimized continental European elites to intervene more strongly in economic affairs after the crisis of 1929 was linked less to any Keynesian conception than to the old intellectual opponents of liberal theory from the era of the urgency of the so-called "social question," and to the role of the state in socio-economic issues, especially at the turn of the century in Europe. After the war, however, the linkage of economic policies to Keynes was quite explicit even on the continent.

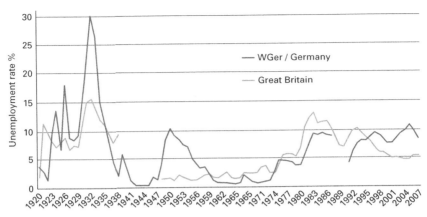

Figure 1: Unemployment rates for Germany/West Germany and Great Britain, 1920–2007.
Sources: Liesner (1985) and IMF International Financial Statistics.

orthodox Treasury dogma, steadfastly held, that whatever might be the political or social advantages, very little additional employment can, in fact, and as a general rule, be created by State borrowing and expenditure" (see Winch 1972: 111).

Keynes participated in the public debate that followed the election promises of the Liberals. In a campaign flyer written in a polemical style in collaboration with Hubert Henderson, Keynes ([1929] 1984b)[13] directly intervened in the campaign on behalf of the Liberals. He tried to justify Lloyd George's election promises and attempted to refute the arguments of his political opponents. The outcome of the election must have been quite disappointing for Keynes, because the Liberals only managed to finish third. The Liberal Party, however, was able to assume the role of power broker, since neither the Conservatives nor Labour won a majority of the seats. Ultimately, the Labour Party formed a minority government.

Here and in other essays written in the 1920s and early 1930s (Keynes [1926] 1984c, [1930] 1984d), Keynes voices his commitment to specific

---

[13] In Keynes's own collection of his most important essays and statements about contemporary economic policies, first published in 1931 under the title *Essays in Persuasion*, the statement still carries the programmatic title "A Programme for Expansion"; while the same essay is reprinted in Keynes's *Collected Writings* re-titled as "Can Lloyd George Do It?" (cf. Keynes [1929] 1984b). The latter version has been expanded by a few passages compared to the essay authorized by Keynes for his *Essays in Persuasion*.

economic policies in a much more insistent and explicit fashion than might be found in his more academic or scientific writings, including *The General Theory*. He argues for certain fiscal and monetary measures – in particular, for an increase in government spending on the basis of either a reduction in the interest rate or an intensification of public expenditures for investment purposes.[14]

Don Patinkin (1982: 200–20) has examined in detail the development of Keynes's conceptions of economic policy measures and the apparent contradictions in his economic policy recommendations. One of the foci of Patinkin's analysis is the question of when and why Keynes favors *monetary* over *fiscal* policies.

In his *Treatise of Money*, or in statements published in newspapers at the same time, Keynes recommends that in response to the prevailing economic conditions, the state take both monetary and fiscal measures. Patinkin does not believe that the emphasis on different policy instruments involves a contradiction. The stress on a reduction in the interest rate on the one hand, and an expansion in state expenditures on the other hand, reflects the different roles Keynes assumed at this time.

In the *Treatise of Money*, Keynes took on the role of a "pure" scientist and attempted to formulate "universally" valid claims. In his interventions in the public debates of the day, however, Keynes, as his country's best-known economist, tried to contribute ideas for the economic policy of Great Britain in response to her unique economic conditions (cf. Patinkin 1982: 208–09). Keynes suggests economic measures that could be enacted under these conditions, and which appeared to be in the interest of the country (see Lekachman 1968: 65–66).

The more polemical essays of the 1920s and early 1930s, and the academic writings of the same time, in other words, were written for very different kinds of audience. Nonetheless, the explicit advice in these essays for economic policies designed to reduce unemployment was compatible with the more reserved and usually implicit formulations and policy recommendations of the more academic work. In both cases, the general idea was to expand aggregate demand.

Keynes offered a straightforward, pragmatic calculation, intended to demonstrate that the promised increase in state expenditures, and therefore the expansion in demand, was in the interest of all citizens

---

[14] In an essay written in 1926, "The End of Laissez-Faire" (Keynes ([1926] 1984c: 292), as well as in his *Treatise of Money*, Keynes favors certain monetary policies to combat unemployment in England: specifically, a flexible interest rate policy for the Bank of England. He also recommends a reduction in the interest rate to the United States at the end of the 1920s.

and was less costly to the economy in the final analysis than was a continuation of high unemployment. The Liberal Party had promised in its
election platform to create an additional 400,000 to 500,000 jobs, and
calculated that the state would have to spend 1 million pounds for each
additional five thousand positions. Keynes actually considered these
figures to be on the conservative side, since the indirect effects had not
yet been taken into consideration. These indirect, cumulative effects
of additional state expenditures, later known as the multiplier effect,
should have a much greater effect on the national level of employment
(Keynes [1929] 1984b: 106). Additional expenditures were supposed
to be financed with the help of a public borrowing program. It was
assumed that the interest to be paid would affect the budget only to a
negligible extent.

In the context of this kind of economic advice, of course, such questions as why the state should become economically active at all; why the
state should become an entrepreneur; why inactivity, or the self-healing
power of the market, is insufficient to resolve the economic crisis (cf.
Keynes [1929] 1984b: 117–19); and whether "collective" policy measures in fact undermine the nature of the economy as a capitalist economy, become politically charged issues. Keynes rejected both sets of
arguments and expectations. The capitalist economy will not be undermined by the policy measures, nor are the self-healing powers of the
market sufficient to cope with the recession. In the past, a war had often
been required to lift an economy out of a deep depression. As Keynes
(1932a) observes with a measure of resignation,

formerly, there was no expenditure out of the proceeds of borrowing, which
was thought proper for the State to incur, except war. In the past, therefore, we
have not infrequently had to wait for a war to terminate a major depression. I
hope that in the future we shall not adhere to this purist financial attitude, and
that we shall be ready to spend on the enterprises of peace what the financial
maxims of the past would only allow us to spend on the devastations of war.

But beyond these fundamental factors, most of the infrastructure of
society (roads, housing, and communication system) was owned by the
state, and the quality of these structures constituted a decisive resource
for private business. Keynes pointed out at the same time that credit
funds raised by the state did not compete with private investment activities; on the contrary, since the profit expectations of business were
lacking, the propensity to invest among entrepreneurs must be stimulated with the help of a growing national income. A high level of savings is not automatically translated into significant investment activity
by business. For as Keynes ([1929] 1984b: 123) stresses, "the object of

urging people to save is in order to be able to build houses and roads and the like. Therefore a policy of trying to lower the rate of interest by suspending new capital improvements and so stopping up outlets and purposes of our savings is simply suicidal." Moreover, an expansion in the credit volume and the investment of these funds nationally during a recession does not go hand-in-hand with an increase in inflation. The sum total of the state investments and the general consequences of state economic activity, Keynes ([1926] 1984c: 292–93) predicts, by no means change the essential features of a capitalist economic system. Moreover, Keynes ([1926] 1984c: 294) adds, "I think that capitalism, wisely managed, can probably be made more efficient for attaining economic ends than any alternative system yet in sight, but that in itself it is in many ways extremely objectionable."

When the minority Labour government in 1931 embarked upon the opposite course of action to reduce unemployment, Keynes reacted with irony and disappointment. State expenditures were reduced; for example, the pay of teachers was cut and taxes increased. According to Keynes, such policies were destined tragically to worsen the economic situation of the country. His appeal that "something must take the form of activity, of doing things, of spending, of setting great enterprises afoot" (Keynes [1931] 1984e: 139) did not register, and his advice was not heeded. The unemployment rate continued to increase.

Keynes changed the substance of his policy advice once more, as it became evident in the early 1930s that the rate of unemployment was not declining despite a fall in the interest rate (cf. Figure 1). In light of the new situation, Keynes advised the government that both a drop in the interest rate and additional state expenditures were required to reduce unemployment (e.g. Keynes [1933] 1972: 353–55). A change in England's foreign exchange policy, moreover, would assure that such a concerted policy would not lead to a flight of capital from the country. Keynes also ultimately favored such a combination of policies in his *General Theory* (e.g. 1936: 164, 378).

These episodes in the development of and the reaction to Keynes's policy advice to realize certain economic goals in England at the end of the 1920s and the early 1930s show quite clearly that the manufacture and publication of social science knowledge do not automatically assure that such a capacity for action is translated into action. The opposite seems to be true, at least in this case. One might therefore ask whether it is possible to discern certain more general factors – factors transcending the specifics of the English political situation – that might account for the disappointment and failure that Keynes personally experienced. One could ask, for example, whether the advice Keynes offered to the government, both in private and in public, to combat mass unemployment already constituted a concrete enough capacity for action, or whether they still had to be translated into "instruments," as Smith (1987) indicates, which would have allowed the advice to be translated into action. Perhaps it is also possible to detect other general preconditions, for example, in the form of national economic statistics, which show that Keynes's advice in fact failed to point to economic factors that could be influenced with the type of means available to the government; or to determine whether it was possible to gain any insights in the likely effects of the measures. In any event, it is not surprising to see that there is little agreement on the reasons, aside from the politically motivated opposition, as to why Keynes's advice found such little acceptance in England at the time.

Keynes the advisor

Not only did Keynes develop a new economic theory which had practical implications, but he was also directly engaging in the political affairs of the day. He wrote articles for academic journals, newspapers, and magazines. Being a member of the cultural and political elite of the country meant that he was occupying the role of an opinion leader, mixing his worldviews, academic outlook, and political ideals in a way that sought to influence politics and policies. He was part of the Bloomsbury circle, had a keen interest in art (he had a collection of modern paintings), music, and theatre, and married a dancer. He bought a grand piano (and a Rolls Royce) from his friend Samuel Courtauld. Among his academic and political contacts were names such as Ludwig Wittgenstein, Piero Sraffa, Bertrand Russell, Virginia Woolf, Lloyd George, and Macmillan.[15] Kirshner (2009) argues that Keynes's theories and practical political interventions have to be understood as a consequence of his philosophical and normative orientations. His moral compass, so to speak, shows a disdain for the money motive, or economism, the view that we all are basically motivated by the drive towards ever greater wealth. In his essay "Economic Possibilities of Our Grandchildren," he famously wrote:

When the accumulation of wealth is no longer of high social importance, there will be great changes in the code of morals. We shall be able to rid ourselves of

---

[15] It is interesting to note that the Jews were stereotyped negatively in Keynes's circle. Skidelsky (1992: 239) comments that Keynes's stereotyping took place on the philosophical, not the vulgar, plane. Much like Sombart, he thought of Jews as embodying the "spirit" of capitalism, which to him was an abstract "love of money."

many of the pseudo-moral principles which have hag-ridden us for two hundred years, by which we have exalted some of the most distasteful of human qualities into the position of the highest virtues. We shall be able to afford to dare to assess the money-motive at its true value. The love of money as a possession – as distinguished from the love of money as a means to the enjoyments and realities of life – will be recognised for what it is, a somewhat disgusting morbidity, one of those semicriminal, semi-pathological propensities which one hands over with a shudder to the specialists in mental disease. (Keynes [1930] 1984a)

This near-Freudian comment formed the basis of his general views about the nature of economic activity and his normative orientation. He saw economists as dentists, whose job it is to solve people's pedestrian problems, such as economic security, so that they can focus on the good things in life (Kirshner 2009: 537).

His theories were developed in close contact with, and partly as a reaction to, positions taken by other significant commentators and decision-makers he knew. Keynes was part of an elite network in Great Britain that spanned government officials, intellectuals, artists, business people, financiers, and academics. He was appointed to government advisory bodies after the Great Slump in 1929. He became a member of the Macmillan Committee on Finance and Industry, which was charged with an inquiry into how the banking system affected the economy. He also became a member of the Economic Advisory Council (EAC) "after attending three luncheon parties hosted by [Prime Minister Ramsay] Macdonald. Previous attempts at setting up such a committee, on the initiative of Beveridge and Baldwin, were short-lived. But now, with the economic crisis unfolding, Macmillan was to establish the Council on 22 January 1930 to 'advise His Majesty's Government in Economic matters.'" Membership consisted of senior ministers and fifteen outside experts, including John M. Keynes (Skidelsky 1992: 343–44).

Through this involvement in politics, Keynes was drawn into political battles for which he was not well prepared. As Skidelsky (1992: 344) notes, "Keynes was not a political animal, but he was a political economist. He invented theory to justify what he wanted to do. He understood that his theory had to be usable for politicians and administrators: easily applied, offering political dividends. But he also understood that, before he could win the political argument, he had to win the intellectual argument."

Keynes was the central figure in the debates of the Macmillan Committee, dominating the proceedings both in examining the witnesses and in shaping the report (Skidelsky 1992: 345). It was in these discussions that Keynes rehearsed and honed his argument regarding controllable tools for government intervention. A crucial issue in the debate was the question of why wages had not fallen despite unemployment. Keynes was careful not to blame union power on this. Instead, he made a sweeping historical case about the "stickiness" of wages. He stated: "My reading of history is that for centuries there has existed an intense social resistance to any matters of reduction in the level of money incomes. I believe that, apart from the adjustments due to cyclical fluctuations, there has never been in modern or ancient history a community that has been prepared to accept without immense struggle a reduction in the general level of money income" (Keynes 1981: 318).

It was no surprise that his argument was supported by Ernest Bevin, the general secretary of the Transport and General Workers' Union, who also sat on the Macmillan Committee. Lord Macmillan, however, replied that social security benefits had prevented "economic laws" from working. Keynes disagreed profoundly, pointing out that these are "not sins against economic law. I do not think it is any more economic law that wages should go down easily than that they should not. It is a question of facts. Economic law does not lay down the facts, it tells you what the consequences are" (Keynes 1981: 83–84). For Keynes, unemployment benefits were not the cause of unemployment.

During the deliberations of the committee, Keynes made various suggestions to overcome the economic crisis. First of all, he rejected the Bank of England's policy of returning to the gold standard with the concomitant policy of restricting credit. Instead, he proposed to stimulate domestic investment through lowering interest rates, increasing the amount of credit, controlling foreign investment and public expenditure in infrastructure. When confronted with sceptical arguments about the central role of credit, Keynes admitted that the supply of credit may only be a "balancing factor," but that it was the "most controllable" (quoted in Skidelsky 1992: 358).

The following exchange between Keynes and Bank of England economist Walter Stewart exemplifies Keynes's approach:

STEWART : As an economist I cannot believe that all the ills of business can be cured simply by an increase or decrease in the volume of Central Bank credit.

J.M.K. It may be that the weather has much more influence on business than the matter of the bank rate; but nevertheless, when one is discussing what should be done, it would not be useful to keep on saying it is the weather which really matters. In a sense it is true it may be the biggest factor?

STEWART : It may be the only thing that the Central Bank can do; but it does not strike me as the only thing that business men can do ... I regard wage adjustments as ever more important in industry than ... anything bankers can do. (Quoted in Skidelsky 1992: 358)

As Keynes sharply observed, what matters for government are levers of action that can be controlled. Besides monetary policy, the volume of investment was an element which could be controlled, and if private business did not invest, the government always could. And it should, Keynes insisted.

Skidelsky (1992: 362) argues that Keynes's appearance before the Macmillan Committee "marks the start of the Keynesian Revolution in policymaking." While his role on the Macmillan Committee was to get bankers, policymakers, and economists to rethink their principles, he had an opportunity to influence government policy more directly as a member of the EAC, which was chaired by Prime Minister MacDonald. A broad-ranging consultation of experts and business people was suggested, to which Keynes was opposed, as this only could add to confusion. He persuaded the Prime Minister to install a small, select committee of economists who should come up with agreed solutions to the problems identified by his small group. Macdonald set this group up, and Keynes chaired it. The other members were Henderson, Pigou, Stamp, and Lionel Robbins.

Keynes's hope of arriving at a shared diagnosis rested on the assumption of a common language – he probably thought that the framework laid out in his *Treatise on Money* would be adopted by his fellow economists on the committee (Howson and Winch, as quoted in Skidelsky 1992: 364).

However, his former ally Henderson, who had shared his views expressed in the article "Can Lloyd George Do It?" shifted away towards more conservative proposals.[16] Nothing should be done that would lead businessmen to expect higher taxation. In the midst of depression, any kind of large-scale public expenditure would result in higher taxes. The anticipation of this would ring alarm bells among business leaders. Henderson wrote:

[T]he alarm might quite easily serve to counteract fully the employment benefits of the programme, and you would then be in the vicious circle of requiring a still bigger programme, still more unremunerative in character, with an increasing hole in the Budget, and increasing apprehension, until you were faced with either abandoning the whole policy or facing a real panic – flight from the pound and all the rest. (Quoted in Skidelsky 1992: 366)

And he added that such consequences would be anticipated by business: "where there are solid grounds for expecting that a certain event

[16] In this pamphlet written in 1929, Keynes suggested what was later known as the "multiplier effect": that an initial public expenditure would lead to an increase in effective purchasing power and thus create a cumulative effect.

will happen, and the grounds are of a kind which the business community can understand, then the results of that event begin to take effect in advance" (quoted in Skidelsky 1992: 671).

Keynes admitted that psychological factors were important, but insisted that interest rates were 50 percent higher compared to what they were before the war, and that reasonable means must be found to allow substantive investment to occur.

Apart from interest rates and the gold standard, which hampered private investment, there was the issue of wages. Virtually all economists were agreed that if money wages were completely flexible, there would be no unemployment problem. However, Keynes argued, wages were fixed, at least in the short term. While Pigou drew similar conclusions in terms of economic policy to those drawn by Keynes, another influential member of the committee did not. Lionel Robbins of the London School of Economics (LSE) argued that the slump was not the disease which needed a cure, but that it was itself the cure for the previous disease of Britain's living over and above its circumstances. The standard of living had to be adjusted to the new realities.

Keynes sarcastically praised him for having – almost alone – a consistent scheme of thought, with his political recommendations being in line with his economic theory. Both Keynes and Pigou, while agreeing with the diagnosis of the inflexibility of money wages, did not conclude that wage flexibility therefore had to be restored. On the contrary, solutions were sought which did not focus on wage levels.

Even on the analytical level, Keynes did not attribute the economic situation to high wages, as some of his opponents did. High unemployment and wages were both caused by a fall in prices and loss of export markets, due to the overvaluation of the pound. Only because there was a drop in output could wages get an increased share of profits. Keynes's analysis included the international dimension of economic activity from the outset, whereas it came only as an afterthought to other economists, such as Pigou (cf. Skidelsky 1992: 370).

The committee could not come to an agreement on economic policy. Robbins wanted the right to publish a minority report; Henderson and Pigou objected to Keynes's public investment plans. What remained as an emergency stopgap, likely to gain consensus, was a tariff on imported goods. Protectionism seemed to be politically acceptable, also by figures such as Oswald Moseley who were close to Keynes at the time. However, the redrafted document, which allowed Robbins to express his own views in a separate section, was a hodgepodge of different positions. The committee could not agree on wage policy, taxation, public spending, or import taxes. A Cabinet committee set up to consider the recommendations of the EAC stated that it was a disappointing document. Only the import tariff policy was to survive and become adopted as practical policy in the Import Duties Act of 1931. Skidelsky (1992: 377) comments on Keynes's political shrewdness: "In deciding to drop public works and go all out for a tariff Keynes once more showed his uncanny ability to anticipate what would soon be politically acceptable."

In what follows we will look at Keynes's involvement in economic policy debates in Weimar Germany. This will illustrate that the economic doctrine shared by a dominant circle of economists, which included ideological reservations, contributed to a protracted and successful resistance to Keynsian economic policies.[17]

Keynes in Germany

During the course of the Great Depression, Keynes did not only engage in efforts to persuade English politicians of the merits of his diagnosis and therapy. In the memoirs of Heinrich Brüning, the so-called "Hunger Chancellor," one finds a brief account of a one-hour meeting between Keynes and the then German Chancellor Brüning on January 11, 1932 in Berlin.[18] Brüning (1970: 506), who was head of the government in the Weimar Republic from March 30, 1930 to May 30, 1932, recalls that Keynes tried to convince him that the Chancellor's "propagation of an inflationary technique stifles any reasonable fiscal policy in Germany." Brüning adds the observation that the audience of a lecture to the International Economic Society in Hamburg on January 8, 1932, which carried the title "The Economic Prospects 1932" (cf. Keynes 1982a: 39–48), erroneously assumed that the British government shared Keynes's economic policy prescriptions. Keynes's visit to Hamburg and Berlin coincided with the announcement of the German government that it would henceforth cease any further reparation payments.[19]

---

17 A discussion of the much broader history and problems of the implementation of economic policies indebted to Keynes's theory in the postwar era in West Germany, in the United States, and in the United Kingdom may be found in a study carried out by Spahn (1976).
18 The meeting between Chancellor Brüning and Keynes was most likely arranged by Keynes's friend Carl Melchior, who also served as an advisor to Brüning (cf. Johnson and Johnson 1978: 59). Keynes's recollections ([1949] 1972b) about his friend Melchior may be found in his *Collected Writings*.
19 Keynes analyses the problem of the reparations payments, based on his recent experience and observations in Germany, in a newspaper article published in mid January 1932 in the *New Statesman and Nation*. In the article, Keynes favors a moratorium and therefore supports the position taken by Brüning in this instance (cf. Keynes 1978: 366–69).

The position toward the economy favored and implemented by Chancellor Brüning[20] – in particular his government's fiscal and economic policy efforts designed to operate in a pro-cyclical and deflationary manner – corresponded closely to the interests of business, but also found support among the Social Democratic Party (Landfried 1976). These policies were also supported with vigor, however, among the majority of economic experts and advisors during this economic crisis in the Weimar Republic (e.g. von Mises 1931; Röpke 1932; A. Weber 1932: 169; Kroll 1958: 131–93: Krohn 1981: 142–49; Landmann 1981).[21]

Most economists and practitioners in Germany, just as in Britain, were confident that the "natural healing" powers of the market (and the competition of workers for jobs) would be sufficient to ease the burden of chronic high or structural unemployment. As a matter of fact, prior to the depression of the 1930s, most professional economists were convinced that unemployment would be limited to frictional or casual unemployment. High unemployment rates for them represented the result of excessive wages, which impeded the formation of necessary investment funds. Imbalance in the demand and supply of labor should ultimately depress wages and interest rates, and contribute to a self-healing of the economy. By the same token, overproduction would be temporary and not general, the result of frictions and passing disequilibria, including the lack of knowledge of market participants, soon to be fixed by smoothly working market forces.

Thus, the economist Alfred Weber (1931: 29),[22] in a lecture addressing the annual meeting of the *Verein für Sozialpolitik* in September 1930 in Königsberg and devoted in part to praising the virtues of the capitalist economic order, suggests that there is a consensus among fellow economists. Weber observes that the precondition for substantial increases in investment funds can never be consumption, but rather an injection of new capital. Unleashing consumption can never, according to Weber and his colleagues, result in anything beneficial economically.

---

[20] Harold James (1989: 238) notes that the deflationary policies of the Brüning administration were also supported "by a number of high-ranking professional civil servants, the most influential of whom was Hans Schäfer, the state secretary (the highest-ranking civil servant) in the finance ministry."

[21] Historians of this area in Germany tend to conclude, in light of the convergence of the views of politicians and economists, that the economic and fiscal measures adopted by the government of Chancellor Brüning constituted, on the whole, a meaningful, even adequate response to the conditions the government had to face; however, economists, judging on the basis of current knowledge, are more likely to conclude that the same policies were an erroneous response to the same set of contingencies (cf. Sanmann 1965: 110).

[22] The economist Alfred Weber should not be confused with Max Weber's brother, the sociologist of culture Alfred Weber (1868–1958).

On the contrary, supporters of a "primitive theory of demand," for example certain labor union leaders in Germany or Henry Ford, are victims of an almost tragic error which can only lead to a collapse of the economy (cf. Weber 1931: 32).

No economist who investigates these issues without prejudice and in a disinterested manner, Alfred Weber (1931: 58) proclaims, thereby only serving the search for clarity and truth, can possibly reach the conclusion, after an objective assessment of the present crisis-like situation, that a solution would be possible without a temporary reduction in the level of wages (cf. Weber 1931: 40). Such a conclusion implies, of course, that policies which would involve borrowing of capital by the state for the purpose of relief works are at best meaningless and at worst dangerous. German economists are in virtual agreement, despite differences in worldviews and different methodological preferences, as Weber reports with pride in his lecture, that their theoretical diagnosis of the crisis and their prescriptions for policy measures are correct. Only marginal or eccentric members of the discipline violate this broad professional consensus. These deviant members do so out of self-evident psychological motives. But they are dangerous nonetheless. They are a danger for the profession and the public at large, with their support of superficial and non-scientific views (Weber 1931: 56).

Alfred Weber's judgment is representative of the kind of expert advice from economists that the German government received toward the end of the Weimar Republic.[23] This advice strengthened Chancellor Brüning's resolve to follow deflationary policies and reduce public spending as the answer to the economic crisis in general and the fear of inflation in particular. With these goals in mind, the German government increased various taxes, fees, and duties; for example, the income tax and the value added tax. Since these fiscal policies did not result in increased public income, expenditures were slashed broadly in order to achieve a balanced budget. The result of these measures was a kind of cumulative and self-sustained recessionary process.

When Keynes ([1932] 1982c: 61) complains at about the same period in time that the responsibility for widely ineffective economic policies of

[23] The economic doctrines that Alfred Weber and his colleagues represented did not monopolize economic discourse at the time. However, a group of younger economists around Adolph Lowe, Gerhard Colms, Eduard Heimann, and Emil Lederer did not have much intellectual influence and institutional support; their analysis of the crisis, which reflected upon and incorporated English contemporary economic theories, and their policy advice did not gain much credence during the days of the Weimar Republic. As a matter of fact, most of these social scientists were soon forced to leave Germany. Claus-Dieter Krohn (1981, 1987) has presented a detailed account of the views of these economists and their personal fates.

the state designed to combat the economic crisis must be linked to the *lack of knowledge* of economists and politicians, he undoubtedly displays a far more accurate sense of the reasons for the practical impotence of economic policies of the day than his many skeptical critics. Keynes ([1932] 1982c) stresses that he, at least, continues to believe that

we still could be, if we would, the masters of our fate. The obstacles to recovery are not material. They reside in the state of knowledge, judgment, and opinion of those who stir in the seats of authority. Unluckily the traditional and ingrained beliefs of those who hold responsible positions throughout the world grew out of experiences which contained no parallel to the present, and are often the opposite of what one would wish them to believe today.

The effects of the opposite strategy, namely an active economic policy, were widely unknown. But such an active policy as favored by Keynes in the early 1930s was by no means impossible in the Weimar Republic. Even foreign policy, often invoked as a constraint, would not really have constituted a serious obstacle to an active economic policy (e.g. Sanmann 1965: 125; Landmann 1981: 217).[24]

The great influence over economic policy that Keynesian ideas acquired in the United States in the wake of the 1938 recession (cf. Salant 1989; Weir 1989; Parker 2005) affirms his Weimar diagnosis. The influence in the United States was further strengthened during World War II. After the war, Keynesian ideas were exported successfully to other Western countries by the emergent American superpower. These developments led Hirschman (1989: 4) to conclude that the dissemination of economic ideas and their implementation as policy is fostered considerably if the theories come to be embraced, first of all, by the elite in a country. If that country happens to achieve global political influence and the elite finds occasion to disseminate these ideas, then such ideas will achieve considerable practical importance.

The policy conception that Keynes advocated was characterized by its simplicity and flexibility, though different concrete policy measures were consistent with its overall thrust.[25] But Keynes's economic views

[24] This conclusion is reflected in particular by Landmann (1981: 217, our translation): "Only the absence of any insight into the circular connections of the shrinking German economy could make the fulfillment-willing Brüning and the creditors of reparations fight against everything that was contrary to the unconditional price deflation" (see also Sanmann 1965: 134).

[25] The great appeal that Keynes's *General Theory* generated among economists is, in all likelihood, also linked to its relatively uncomplicated but persuasive explanatory scheme. Keynes gives a straightforward account of the imbalances generated by the capitalist economy *and* unambivalent economic advice to the state as an economic actor. Bleaney (1985: 37) observes that Keynes's theory "was a theoretically sophisticated exposure of the weaknesses of neoclassical pure theory, which by introducing

and his policy conception must be distinguished from the kinds of macroeconomic instruments and goals that emerged especially in the postwar era in the United States, but which nonetheless were widely perceived to be Keynesian ideas and policies. Keynes (1936: ix) himself describes and offers his *General Theory* as a perspective that is much less "based on narrow pre-conceptions than is the case for orthodox theory and can therefore be applied with greater ease to a wider range of circumstances."[26]

Keynes's theory and policy measures advocate the intervention of the state in an effort to balance the disequilibria of the capitalist economy. Specifically, (1) these interventions should create institutional conditions that lead to lower interest rates and contribute to expectations about economic growth that in turn should stimulate investments; and (2) the state should support demand by increasing public expenditures.[27]

A crucial, perhaps decisive premise of Keynes's advocacy of such economic policies is the *ability of the state to be able to act* in the desired manner (cf. Feuer 1954: 683–84; Lindblom 1972: 3–4). Such a premise is, as one might observe, an almost taken-for-granted assumption in economics since the days of Johann Heinrich von Thünen (1783–1850), who was the first economist to emphasize spatial economics, and who developed the notion of the "isolated state." The regularities of a national economy are most easily discerned if one discards any non-economic power over the economy (Marx), or assumes that such interference merely constitutes a phenomenon that is negligible.

the principle of effective demand yielded *a very simple* explanation of the problems of the Great Depression" (emphasis added).

[26] These observations may be found in Keynes's introduction to the 1936 German edition of his *General Theory*, written especially for the translation. In his introduction, Keynes stresses the relative flexibility and relevance of his theory to a wide range of circumstances. He thus suggests that his ideas, though formulated in the first instance for the case of laissez-faire economic orders, may in fact be applied to economic conditions in which the extent of "state intervention is much more significant."

[27] At times the suggestion is advanced that Keynes is a savior of the capitalist system. This observation is based on the idea that the non-productive programs of public expenditures that Keynes advocated help to solve the capitalist problem of underconsumption or overproduction. During the 1920s, output increased despite a decline in the amount of capital and labor used in production. Keynesian policy measures deal with these developments on two levels: On the one hand, the use of even more efficient means of production is slowed as a consequence of higher state expenditures, because the economy is drained of investment funds. On the other hand, these expenditures produce additional demand that balances the supply of goods and services. However, the survival of the capitalist economy Keynes is credited with is only temporary, according to some neo-Marxists (cf. Block and Hirschhorn 1979: 370–71).

But it took some time before Keynes's ideas would find acceptance and be carefully implemented in some countries. Initially, his economic policies were greeted with considerable skepticism among politicians, civil servants, and business leaders. The war years and the economic consequences of World War II affected the outlook of politicians and economists, and eventually led to a full-fledged acceptance and practice of Keynesian ideas in England, the United States (*Full Employment Act*), West Germany (the so-called law concerning economic stability and growth, 1967), and most other Western nations; it even found entry into the Charta of the United Nations. Keynes's economic theories and the policies they inspired became the new orthodoxy (e.g. Kaldor 1983: 29–30). But only twenty-five years later, in the seventies, it appears that economic policy measures inspired by Keynes to secure full employment fail; and economists are confronted, first, with the largely novel phenomenon of stagflation, and later, with its opposite. In the face of new realities, Keynesian policies are increasingly assumed to be impotent. The economic goals of a pre-Keynesian era – for example, inflation as the basic ill of an economy and efforts to direct and control the supply of money – acquire central importance. Even if one is able to distinguish between a level of full employment which might be achieved with the aid of genuine Keynesian policies, a notion advanced by John Hicks (1985: 23), and the residual portion of the unemployed, it remains a puzzle why the Keynesian rate of employment has constantly declined in the last two decades.

As the export ratio for a number of selected countries indicates (see Table 1), one of the more dramatic consequences of the worldwide recession in the early 1930s was an enormous reduction in exports and imports. The proportion of the Gross National Product (GNP) exported has rebounded, however, and continues to increase with each passing year in the postwar era. In the late 1980s, the ratio for some countries begins to approach the level reached in the late 1920s.

The trends reflected in the growing export ratios provide a first, approximate indication of the changing ability of the state to affect the development of its economy on the basis of economic policies directed toward national developments. In other words, the effectiveness of Keynesian economic policies varies with, or is dependent on, the ability of the state to influence and realize economic goals identified as desirable for the state and its citizenry (cf. Feuer 1954). For a country with a high export ratio, economic policies are much less effective than they would be in a country that generates a lower proportion of its economic wealth abroad, assuming that many of the other economic ties and effects which issue from outside the state can be largely

Table 1. *Exports as a proportion of Gross National Product, expressed in market prices for selected countries, 1928–2007*

	D/BRD	GB	USA	JAPAN
1928	33.24	22.75	5.29	
1936	12.00	16.36	3.79	
1950	9.33	17.55	4.41	
1954	13.83	16.69	4.51	
1960	16.02	17.33	5.21	10.71
1964	15.71	17.27	5.74	9.50
1970	19.91	21.55	6.49	10.82
1974	23.32	24.89	8.70	13.62
1980	23.47	27.50	10.79	13.49
1984	25.19	28.29	9.09	14.69
1988	29.29	23.04	7.60	9.75
1992	23.98	23.72	10.14	9.76
1996	25.03	29.49	11.16	9.72
2000	33.69	27.68	10.98	10.84
2004	38.07	24.91	10.06	13.04
2007	46.43	25.87	11.88	17.07

Sources: The reported ratios for Germany/West Germany, Great Britain, and the USA were computed on the basis of information found in Liesner (1985).

discarded. Of course, such an assumption is unrealistic, and increasingly so.[28] The most significant transformations of modern society – and that means also in the contemporary economy – are embedded, as Daniel Bell (1987: 2) observes, in a "world economy," while the "political orders are still *national*." In other words, political work on the

[28] Highly relevant, for example, though it advances much beyond issues of immediate importance in our examination, is the comprehensive analysis provided by Peter Drucker (1986: 768), who stresses that the global economy generates most of the decisive economic effects in the contemporary world, and not "the macroeconomics of the nation state on which most economic theory still exclusively focuses" (also Lipsey 1991). Some social theorists are not convinced that we are in the midst of a decisive globalization of national economies. They argue that the portion of the GNP generated abroad at the beginning of this century, as well as the subsequent decline documented in Table 2, shows that measured in these terms, globalization was far more significant in the early decades of the twentieth century than today (cf. Hirst and Thompson 1992). The growth of trade in recent decades may have been slowed by the appearance of multinational corporations with production sites in many countries (see Stichweh 1999). Economic globalization is not restricted to the flow of goods and services, but rather is embedded in the rapidly swelling stream of symbolic commodities across national boundaries.

changes induced by global processes, for the most part, continues to be bound and affected by national institutions and responses.[29] In the case of multinational organizations, especially the European Community, political efforts are designed to respond to globally induced economic changes in a coordinated manner. Yet these developments mean that the range and the instruments of national, sovereign economic policy are reduced. Economic discourse also reflects this contradiction; less so at the present time, perhaps, but just a few years ago, the nation-state was almost always defended as *the* most meaningful unit of economic analysis (e.g. Kuznets 1971). There are a few interpreters of the work of Keynes who maintain that his *General Theory* is by no means premised on the existence of a more or less closed, and therefore largely autonomous, nation-state, but rather has as its general reference a global economy (e.g. Hicks 1985: 22). In fact, in *The General Theory*, Keynes does not deal with international trade. However, whether such a deliberate void can be interpreted to mean that Keynesian theorizing had as one of its primary empirical points of reference the global economy must be a dubious conclusion.

The growing interdependence of national economic developments in the industrialized states, or the question of whether such change represents a historically new configuration, can perhaps best be gleaned summarily from a comparative analysis of economic trends for different countries in different periods of time. If one compares the developments of certain macroeconomic indicators – for example, economic growth as reflected in changes in GNP, unemployment rates, or long-term interest rates – the data should reflect the following structured pattern: After nationally specific movements in such trends, especially after the depression in the thirties and in the aftermath of World War II until about the early sixties, national macroeconomic indicators ought to converge more and more, almost to form a common pattern, if the thesis of a growing lack of differentiation of present economic developments is in fact accurate. The convergence should be reflected in closer and closer correlation coefficients between national economic indicators. Tables 2–4 summarize such a comparative analysis for the United States, Canada, Great Britain and Germany (West Germany). The

---

[29] It is currently a broad field for daily political speculation as to what consequences an increasing "integration" of national economies might have with regard to such issues as governability and the preservation of social and cultural characteristics of these nations. Is it true, for example, as Hotz-Hart (1983: 313) predicts, that increased international competition reduces the mode and possibility of national social security systems, because there is a conflict between the logic of the market and the logic of the welfare state?

Table 2. *Correlation coefficients between (de-trended) growth of Gross National Product for selected countries 1920–1938, 1948–1962, and 1963–1987*

Countries	1920–1938	1948–1962	1963–1987
USA/CAN	−.63	.82	−.05
USA/UK	.56	−.04	.68
USA/GER	−.11	−.52	.59
UK/GER	.70	.33	.83
UK/CAN	.20	−.24	−.29
GER/CAN	.82	−.81	−.60

Table 3. *Correlation coefficients between (de-trended) rates of unemployment for selected countries 1920–1938, 1948–1962, and 1963–1987*

Countries	1920–1938	1948–1962	1963–1987
USA/CAN	−.97	.81	.84
USA/UK	.56	−.54	.77
USA/GER	.92	.38	.55
UK/GER	.73	−.33	.74
UK/CAN	.68	−.75	.79
GER/CAN	.94	.63	.83

de-trended (by quadratic time trend) data for each of the four countries are used as the basis for the computation of simple correlation coefficients among pairs of countries. In addition, the reported correlations refer to three periods of time: 1920–38, 1948–62, and 1963–87.

The three periods of time chosen correspond to the most frequently noted broad eras in international economic development. If one compares the resulting correlation coefficients, first for the two most recent periods, which coincide with the division in the adoption and then rejection of Keynesian economic policies in most of these countries, one is able to conclude that the majority of the possible comparisons indeed appear to confirm the expected results. Aside from a smaller number of exceptions, the vast plurality of pairwise comparisons between the United States, Canada, Great Britain, and Germany for the periods 1948–62 and 1963–87 indicate that the correlation among these major economic indicators increases in the present period. The data indicate,

Table 4. *Correlation coefficients between (de-trended)*
long-term interest rates for selected countries 1920–
1938, 1948–1962, and 1963–1987

	1920–1938	1948–1962	1963–1987
USA/CAN	.87	.88	.83
USA/UK	.32	.32	.03
USA/GER	Na	−.56	.38
UK/GER	Na	−.14	.29
UK/CAN	.08	.08	.22
GER/CAN	Na	−.48	.26

Sources: The data for the USA, Great Britain, and Germany
(Federal Republic of Germany) for the years 1920–1983 are
taken from Liesner (1985). The data for Canada for the years
1920–1983 can be found in Parkin and Bade (1986), while the
most recent figures are extracted from the *International Financial
Statistics Yearbook, 1988* published by the International Monetary
Fund.

at the same time, that the relatively greater "sovereignty" – and therefore the conditions for the possible success of Keynesian economic
policies – in the postwar years may have been to a large extent the
outcome of the major dislocations brought about by the war. Such an
interpretation gains plausibility as one observes the rather close correlation between certain economic developments in the USA, Canada,
Great Britain, and Germany during the years 1920–38. The correlation
coefficient for the level of unemployment in these countries during this
period is in part rather substantial, and is as close as it is in the most
recent observational period.

On the surface, the data summarized in Tables 2–4 reflect no more
than the fact that the rather significant "interdependence" among
nations reached during the first part of this century – which was particularly high prior to World War I – took a considerable number of
years to reestablish after World War II, as well as the Great Depression.
As a matter of fact, one could almost reach the conclusion that the
degree of economic autonomy of different nation-states at the present
time is even more substantial than may have been the case at the beginning of the century. However, such a conclusion would constitute a
misinterpretation of the data. The reciprocal dependence of the major
trading nations today is much closer than fifty years ago. Even though
the export ratio still has not reached previous record levels in the case

of some countries, the structure and the extent of the economic interdependence among nations has grown as the underlying structural factors changed. While the sheer "physical" dependence of one nation on
other nations may in fact have declined over the past few decades, the
autonomy of nations has at the same time been undermined in other
significant respects (cf. Rich 1983). But in order to demonstrate these
differences in mutual dependency relations among the economies of the
industrialized nations, one has to examine the different nature of the
flow of commodities and services; the kinds of imported and exported
goods and services; the flow of capital and investments; the convert-
ibility of currencies; the exchange of knowledge, patents, education,
skills, inventions; and, generally, the growing importance of the "symbolic" economy, for example, of exchange and interest rate differentials.
Political developments both enable and inhibit the flow of all of these
tangible and not so tangible commodities. The growth of multinational
corporations is both a motor and an expression of these developments.
The production in different countries by the same firm reduces the need
to export, and reduces the risks associated with exports. Direct investments have the result, as Rosecrance (1987: 163) stresses, that "the
linkages among investments in industrial societies generate a common
interest in succeeding, a condition that was absent in the nineteenth
century up until World War I."

Both the economic and the political consequences of the present
interdependence of national economies are different from any earlier
interdependence; for example, the dependence of nations as expressed
in high export ratios in the decade of the twenties in the last century.
This mutual dependence forces nation-states to cooperate. Any attempt
to uncouple a nation from the global economy can only have serious
repercussions. Compartmentalized economic policies are past strategy.
National economic goals can paradoxically only be achieved on the
basis of international coordination and integration, which are of course
associated with the "cost" of a loss of sovereignty.

Global economy, or the conditions for the
crisis of Keynesian economic policy

We do not wish to argue that the limits to effective economic policy
measures that may be derived from *The General Theory* are identical
to the limits of such measures found in *The General Theory*. No doubt
there are such limits. But there also are limits to effective economic policies that derive from existing economic conditions, and that of course
change with these conditions. The "scientific" and logical limits of

Keynes's *General Theory* have been examined frequently, and by much more competent critics (e.g. Hansen 1952; Kaldor 1983). Our interest focuses, in contrast, on the practical opportunities offered by, and the limits associated with, social science knowledge, as such knowledge intersects or confronts specific socio-historical circumstances. This implies that attention centers not on the logical or the scientific *internal limits* to *The General Theory* but rather on the "historical," *actual practical limits* of Keynes's economic accounts.

For the most part, economists and others now appear to accept the view that economic policies inspired by Keynesian economics are, under present-day economic conditions (in particular since the mid or late 1960s), largely ineffective, or at least no longer as effective as they once clearly were. But the consensus about the evident practical limits of Keynesian economic policies under current economic conditions remains vague and ambivalent. One encounters a wide range of at times contradictory accounts designed to explain the diminished force of such economic policies. These accounts include, for example, the suggestion that in many Western countries economists and politicians have always responded to Keynes with considerable skepticism, and that his economic advice was at best translated into practice half-heartedly and with limited conviction (e.g. Steindl 1985: 116–18); or that Keynesian policies were "misused" in the 1970s because their effectiveness was limited to a specific "Keynesian situation" (cf. Schiller 1987). Still other critics, for example Alfred Weber, were never convinced that Keynes had produced economic ideas which could be translated into practice. That is, even after the war, Alfred Weber ([1935]1956: 42) was unrepentant in his opposition to Keynes. He writes: "[T]hough Keynes's epigones have been busy trying to assert that the ideas of the master really represent a *general* theory of macro-economics, they also carry a heavy burden of the guilt for the serious difficulties from which much of the free world suffers, at the present time."

The ability of the state, or for that matter any other economic actor, to act effectively must be seen in relation to the dynamic bundle of factors which determine the evolution of the economy, especially economic expansion, under changing socio-political and socio-economic conditions. As a result, the need for an alternative to classical economic theory arises, according to Keynes (1936: 1), first and foremost because classical theory is impotent in the face of changed economic conditions. Classical economic theory covers the special case of a full employment economy. It would therefore be misleading and dangerous to apply it to the case of involuntary unemployment. To apply classical theory to contemporary economic conditions in fact amounts to employing Euclidean geometry in a non-Euclidean world. The requirement can only be to develop a non-Euclidean mathematics. Keynes describes and assesses his own theory in these terms. He therefore expects that it will contribute to a much closer meshing between theory and practice. But Keynes can only cope to a limited degree with criticism that a particular economic theory is restricted to specific socio-economic conditions, because his own account responds to a unique situation.

Conditions or factors which are significant for present-day economies but do not figure in either neoclassical theories or in Keynes's theoretical program are, for example, scientific and technical developments and inventions (Freeman 1977). While Schumpeter ([1912] 1951) stresses the significance of innovations[30] for the expansion of the economy, there is no discussion of the importance of innovations in Keynes's *General Theory*. More precisely, perhaps, a discussion of the role of innovations is no longer contained in the *General Theory*. Keynes (1930: 85–86) does discuss innovations in his *Treatise on Money*. He explicitly follows Schumpeter's lead in an essay published in the same year, and refers to the significance for economic growth of technological change and inventions, fluctuating investment decisions by industry, changing interest rates, and the immense capital accumulation in the modern age (cf. Keynes 1930).

From the perspective of a nation-state, technological inventions and change can generally hardly be planned, controlled or limited. In any event, Schumpeter (1952: 283) is convinced that Keynes's analysis only applies to a restricted and temporary set of conditions, since the elimination of the dimension of technological change as a dynamic variable means the limited

applicability of this analysis to a few years at most – perhaps the duration of the "40 months cycle" – and in terms of phenomena, to the factors that *would* govern the greater or the smaller utilization of an industrial apparatus *if* the latter remains unchanged. All the phenomena incidental to the creation and change in this apparatus, that is to say, the phenomena that dominate the capitalist process, are thus excluded from consideration.

There can be little doubt that the limited practical relevance of Keynes's theoretical perspective, if indeed such a restricted usefulness can be demonstrated for present-day conditions, is linked to the kinds of policy

---

[30] Joseph Schumpeter's conception of innovations is not restricted to scientific and technical innovations. He uses the word in a much broader sense, in order to stress the occurrence of (progressive) discontinuities of various sorts in the course of economic development.

goals, especially the possibility of full employment,[31] and economic "variables" chosen by him for analysis. By the same token, limits to its effectiveness should be associated with the neglect of other variables or means of action. In economic discourse, the selection of specific conceptions of economic goals, dimensions of economic conduct, and concrete economic indicators is governed both by intellectual concerns internal to the economic profession, its theoretical and methodological standards and preoccupations, and by prevailing economic conditions within a primary socio-political and socio-economic context of reference – for example, the nation-state.

The Keynesian analysis, for example, does not contain an explicit discussion of the question of *productivity*. On the one hand, one expects such an analysis in Keynes because productivity is widely seen an important indicator and reference point for the supply side of economic conduct. On the other hand, the neglect of the dimension of "productivity" reflects existing economic conditions. That is, particularly the years between 1900 and 1920 saw one of the most significant improvements in productivity in the modern era. These facts supported the optimistic expectation that the scarcity of economic resources, always emphasized in the writings of classical economic theorists, represents a much less serious limiting issue for economic conduct in modern societies. Drucker (1981b: 10) therefore stresses that the reversal of the "theory of productivity from one that postulated a built-in tendency towards diminishing returns to one that postulated a steady increase, was a major factor in the Keynesian 'scientific revolution,'" because it made the switch from "supply-focus to demand-focus – that is, to the belief that production tends inherently to surplus rather than to scarcity."[32]

Among the factors that currently influence economic development in advanced societies are attributes of economic conduct and contextual constraints that, though already identified by Keynes as relevant, have since been transformed to a considerable degree. An important

---

[31] It should be noted, however, that Keynes (1936: 38) considers unemployment a kind of permanent affliction of the capitalist economic system. That is to say, the aim of permanent full employment is not merely unattainable as the result of present-day technical developments, but is also a structural feature of the overall economic system. Nonetheless, the consensus on the desirability of full employment as a goal of state-sponsored economic policies, irrespective of political ideology, has been considerable for decades in the West and East. Later the political and economic premises facilitating the consensus about full employment, or the "right to work," began to fall into disrepute (cf. Gorz [1980] 1982; Keane and Owens 1986; Keane 1988: 69–100).

[32] It is beyond the scope of our study to examine the issue of military Keynesianism; see Melman (1970), Mintz and Hicks (1984), Jencks (1985), Abelshauser (1999), Johnson (2007).

example would be the role of *expectations* of economic actors. Present-day economic actors must react much more immediately and directly to changes in economic and political conditions, or better, in the assessment of such conditions by a variety of groups participating in discourse about economic affairs today, than was the case in the 1930s. Economic conditions today are much less *robust* and recalcitrant than a few decades ago. In other words, economic actors are much more certain today that the future is uncertain, and that disappointments are common and occur more frequently. Rumors, rapid changes in sentiments and opinions, and fluctuating expectations about future developments are highly characteristic dimensions of economic affairs which, from time to time, have a decisive effect on economic developments.[33] But as the conviction among economic actors that economic conditions lack robustness becomes common knowledge, and as the belief that prompt and rapid responses are the only meaningful and effective reaction to rapid changes in conditions becomes widely entrenched, the very lack of the recalcitrance of the economy is only reinforced and compounded.

Finally, the enumeration of some of the reasons which could be responsible for a decline in the practical usefulness of Keynesian economic thinking in the 1970s and 1980s for economic policies cannot ignore the distinct possibility that the very success of Keynesian policies eliminated any future effectiveness of such policies. Keynesian economic policies may well represent a peculiar case of self-elimination. That is, Keynes could not have anticipated that his theories would become part of economic common sense. Nor was he able to foresee the transformation of economic realities as the result of the wide practice of economic policies inspired by his ideas throughout the world. One of the conditions for the very effectiveness of economic policies suggested by Keynes, for example, is the capacity to influence demand. But once economic actors anticipate attempts by the state to influence demand – for instance, with the aid of fiscal policies in order to bring about a reduction in unemployment rates – such policies can be undermined by inflationary pressures (e.g. Scherf 1986: 132). However, the extent to which the possibility of any successful employment of Keynesian

---

[33] Robert Heilbroner's response to the question of why economists today have much greater difficulty anticipating future economic developments is linked to a similar diagnosis of the growing lack of recalcitrance of the structure of economic phenomena: "It may be that this (prediction) is less possible than it was, because the economy itself now is so much more a creature of decision making, and so much less the outcome of sheer interplay of impersonal forces, that prediction becomes inherently more difficult" (quoted in Greene 1974: 64).

policies has been undermined by the success of Keynesian policies themselves is probably the result of a much more fundamental structural change. This is to say that it cannot merely be attributed to the cognitive anticipation of state-initiated economic policies by various economic actors. The fundamental structural features of the modern economy itself have changed considerably, and this transformation is, last but not least, the result of and made possible by the application of the economic ideas that Keynes developed and advocated.

Successful economic policies under present-day conditions demand economic theories that explicitly take these changes into account. As a result, Alfred Marshall's ([1890] 1948: 30–31) observation about the fate of economic doctrines is still valid: "Though economic analysis and general reasoning are of wide application, yet every country has its own problems; and every change in social conditions is likely to require a new development of economic doctrines." In a way, Keynes's self-assessment of the status of his critique of neoclassical doctrines confirms Marshall's views, for Keynes (1936: 378) indicates that his own critique is not so much a critique of certain logical or methodological problems of classical theories. His critique is based on a fundamental disagreement with the unrealistic premises concerning the structure and the nature of the modern economy with which classical theories tended to operate. And, given these unrealistic assumptions of classical theories, any economic policy derived from these premises is bound to fail. More concretely, therefore, Keynes (1936: 382) attempts to point out in his *General Theory* that

under the system of laissez-faire and an international gold standard such as was orthodox in the latter half of the nineteenth century, there was no means open to a government whereby to mitigate economic distress at home except through the competitive struggle for markets. For all measures helpful to a state of chronic or intermittent under-employment were ruled out, except measures to improve the balance of trade on income account.

Keynes's own ideas, of course, are by no means immune to this general observation.

Summary and conclusion

The case of Keynes's role in influencing policymaking is in some sense unique: here we deal with one individual who became associated with a revolution in academic thinking and political intervention into the economy. To be sure, his direct influence during his lifetime was limited; nevertheless, even during this time we witness some elements which proved to be crucial for the long-lasting impression he made.

Keynes was a member of a cultural and political elite in a country that was, and still is, politically centralized. His acquaintance with the power elite of Britain in the interwar period stretched to the highest levels, and Keynes played an important role as an advisor on government committees. Despite his presence in the chambers of power, and his great analytical and rhetorical skills, in addition to his informal and at times even formal leadership in these instances, his advice was not followed during the 1929 crisis. He did not succeed in convincing the government to abandon the pursuit of currency parity through adherence to the gold standard, nor in getting large public works programs started, nor in lowering the interest rates or increasing tax. His proposals became influential only later, after several countries had experienced a long period of economic and political crisis.

At this point, it is useful to introduce historical and political aspects. In his book *The Political Power of Economic Ideas*, Peter Hall (1989a) asks why Keynes's ideas have been taken up in some countries at certain times but not in others. Based on several case studies from various authors, Hall develops a model of three interrelated factors that aim at an explanation. These factors are *economic*, *administrative*, and *political viability*.

Economic viability is a misnomer – this term really refers to the theoretical and academic credibility and appeal that a theory has to academics, practitioners, and younger scholars. In the case of economic theory and policy, this refers to the promise to solve the most important economic problem of a nation at a given time. For Keynes, this problem was unemployment; nations that saw inflation as their prime issue were unlikely to adopt Keynesian policies. Keynesian ideas were first convincing to the economics profession and then influential on policymaking elites, above all through the institutionalization of ideas. Salant (1989) makes the point that various generations of economists have been brought up in the Keynesian paradigm. Most influential was Samuelson's textbook *Economics: An Introductory Analysis*, which was published for the first time in 1948. This is an argument about the persuasive power of ideas that set in motion a change in reality. Hall (1989b: 10) rightly cautions that this view neglects the fact that economic theories are "often only one of many considerations that went into the ultimate determination of policy."

Administrative viability refers to the worldviews of the officials within ministries. Based on their experience with past problems and policies, they make a judgment about the workability of economic policies. If state officials are concerned about budget deficits, they are unlikely to be favorably disposed toward Keynesian policies. The "relative openness of policy-making institutions to advice from outside econo-mists" is seen as the central variable to explain the differential uptake of Keynesian ideas in economic policymaking. Most notably, Margaret Weir and Theda Skocpol have developed such a view. However, as Hall admonishes, this approach tends to overemphasize the role of officials and underestimate the role of politicians.

There was an institutional manifestation of the Keynesian doctrine in the US government's Employment Act of 1946, which combined the goals of high output and high employment. Salant (1989: 51) states that from about "the mid 1930s to the end of WW2, economists in the government were ahead of those in the universities in developing the policy aspects of Keynesian macroeconomic theory and especially in its application to empirical data." The Harvard academic elite was quicker, influencing government before the doctrine had spread across universities. As Salant also points out, Keynes had "no direct influence on policy in the US and, until perhaps 1938 or 1939, very little indirect influence. His influence later was on the intellectual atmosphere, and there it was immense."

Political viability is related to the wider political appeal such ideas have in the construction of political coalitions. According to Peter Gourevitch (1984; see also his contribution in Hall's book, 1989a), Keynesian ideas will only become implemented if there is a large enough political coalition to support the proponents of these ideas. This points to the importance of interest groups in policymaking and the need to adjust policies to the anticipated reactions of such groups. However, the notion of interest is regarded as a given in such accounts, where it rather needs to be problematized. Here Hall's argument takes into account that ideas are crucial in defining one's interests, an observation also made by Barnes when criticizing Collingridge and Reeves's inter-est model (see Chapter 1).

Hall goes on to apply these mechanisms to explain the differential uptake of Keynesian policies across nations, at different times. He finds that the single most important variable affecting the adoption of Keynesian policies was the political orientation of the governing party in a country. If the ruling party had strong links to the working class and if high unemployment was the largest concern, it was more likely that such a government would look towards the implementation of Keynesian proposals. For the period of the 1930s, Hall lists the examples of the Swedish Social Democrats, the Democratic Party in the USA, and the French Popular Front. However, there were other governments (such as the German and Japanese) that did not have left-leaning policies, but an authoritarian structure and military mobilization of society. This would suggest that Keynesian instruments are not primarily dependent on the political color of the ruling party.[34] It appears that left-wing and right-wing, democratic and authoritarian regimes can use Keynesian ideas. However, Hall tries to make the most of this explanatory factor, referring especially to Scandinavia, where the countries with the strongest Social Democratic parties were those who implemented Keynesian policies most thoroughly, those with weak Social Democratic parties least (Sweden and Norway as opposed to Finland, with Denmark occupying a middle ground). Once they are proven to work, conservatives will seek the continuation of Keynesian policies, too. This is what happened in the United States, where President Nixon famously declared "we are all Keynesians now."[35] Hall also finds the power of the central bank vis-à-vis the top political decision-makers to be of crucial importance, and the influence of the civil service versus advisory boards that are appointed by government on a more temporary basis. Clearly, all these factors can be said to matter; but the array of countries and different periods in history requires an extensive reconstruction and reinterpretation of events to make such models work. Hall tries to do justice to such a task in only a few pages toward the end of his concluding chapter. Here he mentions a further variable, exogenous shocks or crises. World War II was even more important than the economic crisis of the 1930s (Oliver and Pemberton 2004).

Pierson (1993: 615) asks:

Why does "learning" sometimes produce positive conclusions and incremental policy change and at other times generate negative conclusions and reactive policy shifts? As Hall acknowledges, "It is all very well to say that policy makers are influenced by the lessons drawn from past policy experiences, but the lessons that history provides us with are always ambiguous" (p. 362). Although hindsight may lead one to say "success" encourages repetition, defining success and failure is necessarily a sociological and political process. ... Hall's account does offer some suggestions about when policies are likely to be perceived as failures. Drawing on Kuhn's concept of scientific paradigms, he argues that learning connected to third-order change (paradigm shifts) [...] is likely "to involve the

---

[34] It is somewhat odd that Hall (1989c: 376) says that of the "five main cases of Keynesian or proto-Keynesian experimentation between the wars, the only ones not directly associated with attempts to mobilize a working class constituency were those associated with military mobilization in Germany and Japan." This would mean that two cases do not confirm his hypothesis – quite a big proportion in a sample of five. But he is quick to acknowledge that "of course, social democracy is not synonymous with Keynesianism" (p. 377).

[35] A similar observation can be made with regard to Tony Blair's New Labour project. After coming to power he continued Thatcherite neoliberal policies.

appearance of anomalies ... developments that are not fully comprehensible, even as puzzles, within the terms of the [existing] paradigm."

Pierson comments that "it remains unclear whether this provides a clear guide, except perhaps ex-post, to the circumstances when policies will be regarded as failures. The complexity and multiplicity of policy interventions, combined with the uncertainty of the links between interventions and outcomes, will generally leave considerable room for dispute. The fact that policy 'success' is often contested suggests a substantial indeterminacy to the learning process."

Hall (1989c: 365) ends up offering a somewhat different account of the ultimate reason for the practical efficacy of Keynesian economic theory for economic policies. He emphasizes the rapid and unimpeded diffusion of Keynes's conception of the economy to members of the economic profession, without any endorsement from political authorities, and once his views had become the governing currency among economists it only took their migration into policymaking to achieve the kind of practical influence that Keynesian ideas enjoyed in economic policy: "The growing role of the experts in contemporary governance carried them into the heart of the policy process."

Keynes's *General Theory of Employment, Interest and Money* closes with the following, now almost classic, observations:

[T]he ideas of economists and political philosophers, both when they are right and when they are wrong, are more powerful than is commonly understood. Indeed the world is ruled by little else. Practical men, who believe themselves to be quite exempt from any intellectual influences, are usually the slaves of some defunct economist. Madmen in authority, who hear voices in the air, are distilling their frenzy from some academic scribbler of a few years back. I am sure that the power of vested interests is vastly exaggerated compared with the gradual encroachment of ideas. Not, indeed, immediately, but after a certain interval; for in the field of economic and political philosophy there are not many who are influenced by new theories after they are twenty-five or thirty years of age, so that the ideas which civil servants and politicians and even agitators apply to current events are not likely to be the newest. But, soon or late, it is ideas, not vested interests, which are dangerous for good or evil.

Hidden in these sentences is Keynes's prophetic anticipation of the fate of his own *General Theory*. At the same time – and this is of direct relevance to the topic at hand – Keynes is observing that the potential *practical influence* of scientific knowledge is propelled by the *ideas* produced by science. The ambiguous term "ideas" was probably chosen quite deliberately and signifies, among other things, that the most important practical consequences of a body of knowledge (or, for that matter, a doctrine's *lack* of practical relevance) are, after all, cultural. Keynes is indicating how knowledge may shape human affairs latently (and belatedly), without necessarily affecting discussion and decision-making about the *means*, that is, instruments, of social action – if, indeed, means and ends can be so easily separated.

To summarize the story so far: we have defined knowledge as capacity to act which enables actors to make a difference in reality. We then distinguished between knowledge for practice and practical knowledge. Knowledge for practice has potential for application; practical knowledge identifies effective tools for action. However, providing practical knowledge does not tell us if it is put into practice. In this chapter we saw how Keynes developed practical knowledge that was not taken up at the time. It was only after the political environment had changed that his advice was heeded.

We also saw that knowledge, apart from having theoretical appeal, needs to be administratively and politically viable. This directs our attention to the influence of government departments and the nature of party competition in various political systems. It is also indicated that sometimes new knowledge will only be embraced when reality has changed in unpredicted ways. Crises call for new solutions.

We shall revisit these questions in the concluding chapter where we discuss the uptake of knowledge in our remaining two case studies, to which we now turn.

3   The mentors of the Holocaust and the power of race science

National Socialism is the active and willful application of the findings of race science.

Rügemer (1938: 476)

The questions we would like to address in this chapter concern the role of "race science" in the Holocaust.[1] "Racial knowledge," as it became established and efficacious both in the scientific community and in society in the first half of the last century, relied on various established scientific fields of the time: biology, natural history, and especially anthropology. In asking about the role of "racial knowledge" and race scientists as mentors of the Holocaust, we want to address a number of specific issues of interest to us in the context of inquiring into the power of knowledge. Aside from a brief history of the intellectual origins and the nature of race science, and its successful efforts to acquire scientific authority and legitimation by linking itself to established scientific practices and methods, we are interested in the practical role that race science attempted to play; the "triumph" it enjoyed in doing so; the ways in which this was accomplished; and why its most tragic consequences played out only in Germany.

The significance assigned to racial categories in science originated well before race science become a scientific discipline, with its own university chairs, research programs, research institutes, curricula and journals in the early part of the twentieth century. We have to go back to the origins of social science itself.

[1] We would like to thank Augustine Brannigan, Robert Citino, S. N. Eisenstadt, Sander Gilman, James McKee, Martin Meissner, Volker Meja, Jack Nusan Porter, Benjamin Singer, Gerd Schroeter, David N. Smith, and Klaus Taschwer for their constructive comments on an earlier version of this chapter. Furthermore, we appreciate the technical assistance provided by Irene Knokh, Sonali Thatte, and Amir Allam. The original English version of this chapter, here heavily reworked and supplemented, is a joint work by Jay Weinstein and Nico Stehr. It appeared in *Social Epistemology* 13 (1999): 3–36.

The eighteenth century – which, according to many contemporary historians of social science, represents the era in which modern social science discourse originated – was an age in which the educated part of the population in France, Germany, and England spent enormous intellectual energy arguing about the climatic determinants of the civilizational peculiarities of entire nations (relying on such works as Montaigne's *Essais*, Montesquieu's *Esprit des Lois*, and Falconer's *Remarks on the Influence of Climate*).

As a contemporary observer was prompted to point out, there were an endless number of writers who ascribed supreme efficacy to climate. The extent to which these ideas both resonated with and influenced the understanding of nature and the effects of climate, and the importance assigned to nature and the effects of climate in and on everyday life in different cultures, still need to be examined in greater detail. Equally unexamined is the impact of common-sense understandings on scientific ideas of climate, climate change, and the effects of these processes on individuals and on society.

But at the end of the nineteenth century, in unmistakable contrast, Emile Durkheim's classic study *Suicide* (first published in 1897) put forth the argument, which soon became paradigmatic for modern sociology and anthropology, that apparently completely idiosyncratic individual actions are social phenomena, and that neither their patterns nor their distribution can be explained by invoking physical or even cosmic phenomena. Durkheim did not fail to notice, of course, that many contemporary scientists were convinced that a causal relationship did in fact exist between air, land, soil, and especially climate or weather, and the number of suicides. Durkheim's judgment is harsh. For explanations that refer to cosmic, biological, or physical phenomena, Durkheim has at best gentle consternation ([1897] 1952: 104): "To require such an hypothesis the facts must be in unusual agreement …We must therefore seek the cause of the unequal inclination of peoples for suicide, not in the mysterious effects of climate but in the nature of this civilization, in the manner of its distribution among the different countries." Precisely that is where environmental determinism ceases, and the social sciences commence.

Durkheim's epistemological views have had a spectacular career in sociology. Not least with their help, the separation of the social and the natural sciences, especially biology, was cemented and celebrated. But the victory of Durkheim's position was never complete and immediate in all branches of the social sciences.[2] Durkheim's plea to avoid,

---

[2] The persistently contentious nature of the role and legitimacy of the notion of race within the sociological community is well illustrated in the early controversy regarding

and radically surpass, the fallacy of environmental determinism fell on deaf ears, at least in some quarters of the scientific community. For the heyday of climate determinism, but also of race science and geopolitics, only reached its peak in the scientific community in the following decades of the twentieth century.

Although somewhat obscured in the history of ideas, during the nineteenth century and the early part of the twentieth century intellectual racism was a prominent, respected, and radicalizing part of Western thought. Theories of racial difference, biological determinism, and the policy science called eugenics are embedded and taken for granted in mainstream intellectual perspectives (cf. Banton 1998).[3]

Race science

No court will ever sit where the judges will sentence choice specimens of humanity to frequent parenthood and condemn the rest to sterility; though the outcome of such an experiment would undoubtedly be interesting. (Edward M. East (1929))

I really must warn my Jewish fellow citizens that they ought not to get the wind up as soon as any one begins to speak of the Jewish race. This inevitably arouses the impression that they must have some reason for fighting shy of exposition of any racial questions. Yet a tranquil and objective discussion of the Jewish problem would best serve the true interests of both sides. (Fritz Lenz (in Baur, Fischer, and Lenz [1921] 1931))

The early proponents of race science (*Rassenwissenschaft*) clearly recognized and boldly proclaimed the novel intellectual perspective and

the explanatory potential of the notion of race within sociological discourse during the first meeting of the German Sociological Society in 1910 (and later, see Schleiff 2009), for example in the conflicting statements made by Max Weber (1911; also Weber [1922] 1978a, [1922] 1978b) and Werner Sombart (1911) during the meeting of the congress.

[3] Piritim Sorokin (1928: 195–356) devotes some 250 pages in his *Contemporary Sociological Theories* to various branches of the "biological school of sociology." Sorokin (1928: 355), in a general conclusion of his discussion of the biological school within sociology, notes that the school represents "one of the most powerful currents of sociological thought." Moreover, he adds, and whether we like it or not, the "greater and more accurate the findings of biology ... the more powerful [an] influence they are likely to exert on sociological thought in the future." Any attempt to isolate sociology from biology is harmful. Sorokin's prediction, published in 1928, is both accurate and erroneous. Opening any present-day history of sociological ideas will yield little, if any, information about a "biological school" in sociology. But the summit of the influence of biological thinking on the social sciences was about to be reached only a few years after Sorokin made his prediction. In contemporary social theory, aside from sociobiology, the conspicuous exception to the Durkheimian legacy of a strict distancing of phenomena is represented by tendencies in feminist sociology to more immediately incorporate the human body into view and examination.

eminently practical nature of their work. In 1921, citing the views of the "Nordic thinker Kant" in support of his argument, Fritz Lenz (cf. Weiss 1992), the initial occupant of the first chair for racial hygiene (at the University of Munich) in Germany,[4] maintained that the field's "outlook is fundamentally new, [it] is something to which the old classifications and catchwords are inapplicable; and in its essential nature it is not pessimistic, for it, alone, points the ways towards the *sanitation* and stable advance of mankind and human civilization" (Baur et al. [1921] 1931: 698, emphasis added).[5] As Proctor (1988a: 15) pointed out, "the degeneration of the race feared by German social Darwinists was said to have come about for two reasons: first, because medical care for 'the weak' had begun to destroy the natural struggle for existence; and second, because the poor and misfits of the world were beginning to multiply faster than the talented and fit."

In 1904 Alfred Ploetz, one of Germany's leading social Darwinists, founded the journal *Archiv für Rassen- und Gesellschaftsbiologie* (Archive of Racial and Social Biology). The year after, together with the psychiatrist Ernst Rüdin, the lawyer Anastasius Nordenholz, and the anthropologist Richard Thurnwald, he founded the Deutsche Gesellschaft für Rassenhygiene (German Society for Racial Hygiene). This society was to grow rapidly over the years and decades to come, beginning with only a handful and rising to over 1,300 members in 1930.[6]

---

[4] As Fritz Lenz (1924: 227) describes the event: "Bavaria, in 1923, became the first of the German states to establish a university chair of eugenics. There was indeed no money for a new professorship; but as Germany's enemies had deprived her of tropical colonies, a chair of tropical hygiene was converted into a chair of eugenics."

[5] This and later quotations are from the English translation of Erwin Baur, Eugen Fischer, and Fritz Lenz, *Human Heredity*, which constitutes the first volume of their *Grundriß der menschlichen Erblichkeitslehre und Rassenhygiene*, originally published in 1921. The translation is based on the third German edition, published in 1927 (with additional supplements and corrections supplied by the authors during the translation, as the translators note). Fritz Lenz is the sole author of the second, untranslated volume; it deals entirely with eugenics. The origins and the career of the work are discussed in Lösch (1997: 136–52). The idea for the book, although it may have originated with one of the three authors, was strongly supported by the publisher Lehmann in Munich, who saw his role as that of a "political publisher" aiming to achieve a particular intellectual renewal after the lost war. Lehmann had already published and financed the work of Hans F. K. Günthers, *Rassenkunde* (1919), as well as the *Archiv für Rassen- und Gesellschaftsbiologie*, founded in 1904. The authors and the publisher of the Baur, Fischer, and Lenz volumes were all members of the *Deutsche Gesellschaft für Rassenhygiene* at the time, indicating the expected thrust of the intended spiritual and political renewal. The book soon attained, and retained for decades, the status of a standard and prestigious genetics textbook in Germany – and other countries. However, the intended focus of the book evidently was not so much a contribution to genetics but the promotion of the idea and practical importance of racial hygiene.

[6] An analysis of the social background of the members of the society may be found in Weiss (1987).

The reasons that an intervention by and for "civilized nations" is possible and required are outlined in the introductory paragraph to the volume on *Human Heredity* by Eugen Fischer (1874–1967), Erwin Baur (1875–1933), and Fritz Lenz (1887–1976)[7]: "Every people or nation is subject to perpetual changes in its composition ... this transformation of a people may be beneficial to it, may make it fitter, may signify a genuine advance; but it may (and most often actually does where civilized nations are concerned) denote a slow or speedy process of decay, of degeneration." Legislative interference "in matters of population and racial hygiene," unless it amounts to nothing but the "dangerous quack-salvery of uninstructed laymen" (Baur et al. [1921] 1931: 20), must be based on scientific knowledge.

It is noteworthy that the early racial hygiene movement "does not fall cleanly into Left–Right divisions. Many socialists identified eugenics with state planning and the rationalization of the means of production"; many thus found the idea of a "planned genetic future an attractive one ... as late as 1925, the leading Soviet eugenics journal published translations of articles from the *Archiv für Rassen- und Gesellschaftsbiologie*" (Proctor 1988a: 22).

The practical science that aspired to put an end to the degenerative process to which Lenz refers emerged in Germany, other parts of Europe, and the United States during the World War I era.[8] The close affinity and intersection of practical-political and scientific impulses was never a hidden element. As a matter of fact, the symbiosis between scientific and practical-applied (political) ambitions constituted a feature of the intellectual development of race science that assured its

[7] Lenz had studied medicine, had been a student of Alfred Ploetz, and was a prolific author with a commitment to the strong efficacy of race in societal life. On October 1, 1993, Lenz became the director of the section "Eugenics" (which he quickly renamed "Racial Hygiene") of Eugen Fischer's Kaiser Wilhelm Institute for Anthropology in Berlin. He joined the Nazi party in 1937. Lenz was known as one of Weimar Germany's most influential eugenicists, who remained influential in the race hygiene movement during the Nazi era. As Sheila Faith Weiss (1992: 7) emphasizes in her close examination of race and class in Fritz Lenz's eugenics, "race" for Lenz was "really little more than a projection of class prejudice – the prejudices of the German *Bildungsbürgertum* and mandarin academic elite to which he belonged."

[8] In a 1924 invited article in *The Journal of Heredity* describing the development of eugenics in Germany, Lenz appeals to the international solidarity of scientists. Lenz (1924: 223) implores that "eugenic cooperation of all nations of European race and civilization is urgently needed. The existence of the best racial elements of all these nations is already more or less directly threatened." In the fourth edition of the Baur, Fischer, and Lenz volume, published in 1936 – and therefore after the Nuremberg Laws came into force in 1935 – Lenz unequivocally stresses: "Our German *Volk* is – or, as one now happily can say, was – mainly threatened by the intermixture with Jews" (p. 766).

development, support, and resonance among the public. One of the chief architects of eugenics in Germany was Wilhelm Schallmayer (1857–1919), a practicing physician. A pamphlet he issued in 1891 carried the self-explanatory and urgent title "On the Menacing Physical Deterioration of Civilized Man." In 1903, Schallmayer took part in a competition whose aim was clearly political, and which was underwritten by Friedrich A. Krupp. It asked, "What can we learn from the theory of evolution for the internal political development and legislation of nations?" Schallmayer's treatise "Heredity and Selection in the Life of Peoples" won first prize and ranked for many years, according to Fritz Lenz's (1924: 224) judgment, as the "best German exposition of eugenics."

As the international field of race science developed through the 1920s, its practitioners both contributed to and were influenced by a general shift in Western culture from a religious to a quasi-objective, racial anti-Semitism. Here we try to advance our understanding of one of the most consequential aspects of this shift, the linkage between race science, race policies, and the Holocaust.

In the course of this discussion, we briefly review the history of the concept of "race" from its roots in evolutionary theory to its refinement in the works of the leading race scientists of the era, especially Fritz Lenz, Eugen Fischer, and their immediate associates. In addition, we examine the linkages between racial explanations and the closely related climate-based theories of geographers and social psychologists working in the same period. By expanding the scope of our investigation in this manner, we are able to forge what we believe is a more complete account of the manner in which Nazi policies of racial hygiene were formulated. That is, they were based not on ignorant prejudice or on the paranoid delusions of a madman, but rather on the findings of what was at the time considered to be rigorous and authentic scientific research conducted by highly respected professional scientists.

Thus, we seek to demonstrate that the Holocaust was, to a considerable extent, scientifically "justified."[9] The mutual, radicalizing impacts between race science and race policy, and the manner in which these in turn contributed to the pursuit of state-sponsored genocide, provides what we believe to be an especially clear, not to mention disturbing, illustration of the kinds of conditions under which knowledge is

---

[9] Burleigh and Wippermann (1991: 56) note, "Contrary to the notion that Nazism somehow corrupted and distorted the temples of learning – which of course it did – one could argue that a corrupt and inherently distorted science lent Nazism a specifically 'academic' and 'scientific' character" (cf. also Jaspers [1945] 1965: 31–40).

power, or power is knowledge.[10] In light of more recent revelations that for several decades the government of Sweden sterilized thousands of "useless" citizens (Roll-Hansen 1989; Gunnar Broberg and Nils Roll-Hansen 1996; Balz 1997), it is evident that the impulse to employ science to justify the abuse of human rights remains difficult to resist (for an earlier account, see Freiburg 1993).

From the sacred to the scientific

What National Socialism realized, by means of sterilizations, murdering the mentally ill and obsession with race, had all been formulated long beforehand in a misuse of science. (Karl Jaspers [1947] 1965: 45)

The long-standing legacy of anti-Semitism in Western culture contributed significantly to the rise of National Socialism in Weimar Germany, and to the conditions that made possible the slaughter of Jews during the years of Hitler's fascism.[11] The historian Heinrich Treitschke's slogan, *Die Juden sind unser Unglück* (the Jews are our misfortune), which later appeared on the masthead of Julius Streicher's notorious anti-Semitic rag *Der Stürmer*, methodically summarized this connection by providing (1) a readily comprehensible diagnosis of the cause of Germany's post-World War I material and spiritual malaise; and (2) an implied therapy – i.e. the creation of a Jew-free or Jew-cleansed (*judenfreie, judenreine*) nation – a therapy that was, in fact, ultimately put into practice.

It is equally evident, however, that the effective execution of the *judenrein* policy depended upon the development of a clear, readily applicable, and practical standard whereby individuals could be reliably assigned to the categories *Jew* and *non-Jew*; an operational definition, so to speak, of those who were (and were not) agents of Germany's *Unglück*. As inscribed and explicated in the "Nuremberg Laws" of 1935, the solution came via the invocation of hereditary principles elaborated in biological discourse, whereby people were categorized on the basis of the *racial* identity of their ancestors.[12]

---

[10] It is perhaps unnecessary to note that our account of race science is not intended to establish whether or not the field was/is a *scientific* form of discourse. There can be no doubt that, at the time relevant here, and in many quarters within and outside of the scientific community, race science was considered to be a prominent and exemplary scientific undertaking.

[11] As noted by Berenbaum (1993) and others, race science developed within a broader, Euro-American cultural milieu that considered anti-Semitism to be a reasonable, if not normal, point of view. Earlier general treatments of the roots of anti-Semitism in the West include Poliakov (1974); and Mosse (1978).

[12] The so-called Nuremberg Laws were issued in several installments, including the "Law for the Alteration of the Law for the Prevention of Hereditarily Diseased

It has been widely observed that this standard represents a significant departure from traditional forms of anti-Semitism (see, for example, Katz 1980; Gilman 1996: Ch. 2).[13] For nearly two millennia the Jews of Europe had been viewed as "different" (marginal, outsiders, and in many instances pariahs) because they refused to accept Christ as their Messiah and, according to Church doctrine belatedly revoked in 1968, because they were responsible for the Savior's death. Although these beliefs and the exclusionary practices based on them made life difficult for Jews, they also allowed for the possibility of exculpation through conversion. Moreover, since even a Jewish mother and father could produce a Christian child, the religion of one's parents was not necessarily grounds for exclusion, persecution, or execution. "The world without Jews" envisioned by European Christians prior to World War I was one in which all former Jews will have joined the faith – or, as in Karl Marx's (1844) secularized formulation, will have stopped behaving "like Jews."

The religious motives and rationale for the special treatment of Jews reflected the medieval worldview, in which human affairs generally (and natural events as well) were primarily interpreted and managed in spiritual terms. The Jewish problem was posed as a matter of erroneous belief that could be corrected, like other sins, through confession, repentance, and related spiritual conduct. By the turn of the twentieth century, however, natural science's growing distancing from and challenges to Church doctrine, which had begun centuries earlier and had more recently been expressed in biological inquiry via the quickly popularized Darwinian Revolution, were extended to the relations between Christians and Jews. Thus, these intellectual transformations ultimately contributed to a kind of secularization (or, more accurately, "scientification") of the relations between Jews and Christians.

Progeny" of June 26, 1935; the "Law for the Protection of the Hereditary Health of the German People" of October 18, 1935; and the "Law for the Protection of German Blood and Honor" of November 26, 1935. Although these are generally understood to be the first set of Nazi race laws, a series of related acts had already established a precedent. Among these were the "Law for the Reduction of Unemployment" of June 1, 1933; the original "Law for the Protection of the Hereditary Health of the German People" of July 14, 1933; the "Law against Dangerous and Habitual Criminals" of November 24, 1933; and the beginnings of racial registration in accord with the earlier Reduction of Unemployment Law in October 1934. From that date onwards, "social policy was indivisible from the 'selection' of 'alien' races and those of 'lesser racial value'" (Burleigh and Wippermann 1991: 48).

[13] Jacob Katz's discussion of the shift from religious to racial anti-Semitism is especially informative. His focus on the development of a more "scientific" outlook on Jewish-Gentile relations in Europe supports the characterization of academic race studies as a discipline whose time had arrived.

By the early Weimar Republic, indeed not only in Germany but throughout the Christian world,[14] it was not uncommon to define a Jew as anyone who belonged to the Jewish "race" and, by virtue of immutable biological laws – explicated, for example, by Mendel and Galton ([1898] 1962) – could produce only Jewish offspring. As evidenced by the growing concern with measuring physiognomy for classificatory purposes and other reasons (see Efron 1994), this conception implied that Jews could be identified in terms of anthropometric indices – especially nose length, size of ears, head shape, skull capacity, shape of face, inclination of the brow, degree of prognathism, and foot shape (Gilman 1991). In this manner, religious, intellectual, or "cognitive" anti-Semitism came to be increasingly displaced (although obviously never entirely replaced) by racial anti-Semitism.[15] It follows from the racial concept that the objectionable ways of the Jews, because they are lodged in the blood, are beyond repair by mere "cultural therapies." A more "material," more objective and quantifiable criterion now differentiated human groups. In this respect, a *judenfreie* nation (or continent or world) means the physical exclusion or elimination of an entire gene pool.

This dramatic shift from religious to biological anti-Semitism is one of the elements that sets the Holocaust apart from earlier instances of Jewish persecution and genocide;[16] for it automatically condemned the religious and the irreligious, the orthodox and the convert, and the dead, the living, and the unborn to a common fate.[17] The slaughter that occurred during the Holocaust was thus, in part, the result of the prevailing definitions of the intended victims, definitions that were

[14] "Racial anti-Semitic theories were not an exclusively German phenomenon. However in Germany they appear to have enjoyed especially wide currency and a high degree of political instrumentalisation" (Burleigh and Wippermann 1991: 36). For a discussion of the history of Judeophobia, see Smith (1997).

[15] In this diary entry of March 31, 1933, Victor Klemperer (1995) notes that the general boycott of stores and businesses owned by Jews in Germany will start the next day and that the proclamation of the boycott committee commands that religion is irrelevant; what counts is race.

[16] Indeed, based on an astounding compilation of information about genocide and race war through the ages, Katz (1994) argues that the innovation of a categorical approach to defining Jews makes the Holocaust *unique* in *Jewish* history. This claim, as is true of other aspects of Katz's book, is in dispute; but it does raise pertinent issues in the study of the impact of race science.

[17] The next logical step was the discovery of the *Rassejuden*. Those who carried out race policy on a day-to-day basis did not necessarily care about logical and conceptual clarity in their hatred and persecution of Jews. Rather, they often mixed naturalistic-biological and cultural conceptions of identity, for example, as they denounced those who were not *Rassejuden* but who were nevertheless critical of the regime as Jewish-Bolshevists or *Judenknechte* (cf. Rosenstrauch 1988). Many also continued to employ traditional religious anti-Semitic constructs.

now cast in categorical and inalterable "scientific" terms; although the astounding scale that was achieved was also very much a function of the application of bureaucratic procedures and mass-production techniques to the task at hand, in the context of a totalitarian regime.[18]

Moreover, since the "problem" was now viewed as one of heredity rather than creed – racial degeneracy, not false belief – it became possible to subject other perceived enemies of the Reich to similar treatment as *Entartete Rassen* (degenerate races), even those such as Slavs, Romani, and Sinti who were officially Christian (see Burleigh and Wippermann 1991: Ch. 5).[19] By equating the concept of *Volk*, one of whose definitions is "race" in the pre-Darwinian sense, with *Rasse*, the Nazis were able to claim all Aryans as *Herrenvolk* (a master race) even if they were not especially exemplary Christians in the traditional sense.

The situation is summarized succinctly in the *Yad Vashem Guidebook*'s (1995: 13–14) section on "Racism and Anti-Semitism in Germany":

Racism added new and substantial dimensions to traditional anti-Semitism. In the past, hatred of Jews had had specific grounds and certain lines of development. The hatred nurtured by ancient Christian concepts regarded the Jews as the people of Israel and the people of the Messiah, but also as the people who had rejected its Redeemer, Jesus, and thus had condemned itself to ostracism and the eternal enmity of the Christian world. The Jew had to be kept in a state of servitude, misery, and degradation. Moreover, their eternal wandering among the nations, forever at the mercy of the Christians, seemed to confirm the veracity of Christian teachings. Later, anti-Semitism was reinforced by a greater stress on economic, social and political factors. Racial anti-Semitism,

[18] Christopher Browning (1992) closely examined the extent to which racist indoctrination served to "soften" the morality of members of the *Einsatzgruppen* killing squads (see especially Chapter 18). This line of inquiry is also taken up by Daniel Goldhagen (1996), and in the considerable body of commentary generated by his book (for example, Finkelstein 1997). From these and related sources, it seems clear that the collective dehumanization of the *Entartete Rassen* rendered abusive behavior toward Jews, including their "extermination," ethically acceptable or even necessary. But it could not make the bloodier aspects of the task more pleasant. Thus, it was necessary to apply principles of complex organization and human engineering so as to depersonalize (and, thus, in the characteristic dialectic of injustice, dehumanize) the execution of race policy. Goldhagen's view that the Holocaust is explained by destructive anti-Semitism among Germans might suggest that Hitler and the Nazis were such virulent anti-Semites that they did not need race science to "justify" their deeds. Finkelstein specifically takes exception to this premise, pointing to well-established findings that suggest that scientific and other rationales were necessary so that leaders and ordinary Germans could accept, if not support, policies they felt to be otherwise objectionable. In any case, race science did exist and it was well supported by the regime. Indeed, all ruthless dictators of the twentieth century appear to need a legitimizing ideology deemed "scientific."

[19] The Racial-Hygienic and Hereditary Research Center in the Reich Health Office was established in 1936, under the directorship of Dr. Robert Ritter, in order to deal with "the Gypsy question" (Burleigh and Wippermann 1991: 54).

linked with a misinterpretation of Darwin's views of society, lent a new validity to traditional Jew-hatred. According to Nazi theorists, the danger arising from contact from the evil, perverted Jews sprang not from their mistaken beliefs or their economic role, nor even from their tendency to live as a closed social group, but from their very identity, their tainted Jewish blood.

The difference between racist policies based on religious beliefs and those based on biological race can be illustrated with an event that took place on the Crimean peninsula in 1941. When the German armies moved eastwards into Polish and Russian territory, they deployed a unique organization known as the *Einsatzgruppen*. It is no exaggeration to say that they were an extermination commando. They came into being through an agreement between the RSHA (Reich Security Main Office), the OKW (Armed Forces High Command), and the OKH (Army High Command).[20]

When one of the Einsatzgruppen reached the Crimea, its leaders did not know what standards to apply in determining whether the Krimchaks they found there should be killed or not. Very little was known of these people, except that they had migrated into the Crimea from a southern Mediterranean country, and it was noted they spoke the Turkish language. It was rumored, however, that somewhere along the arterial line which ran back into the dim past some Jewish blood had entered the strain of these strange Krimchaks. If this were so, should they be regarded as Jews and should they be shot? An inquiry went off to Berlin. In due time the reply came back that the Krimchaks were Jews and should be shot. They were shot. (www.lawofwar.org/Einsatzgruppen%20 Case.htm)

Another ethnic group, the Karaites, escaped the Holocaust. Repeated Nazi "expert inquiries" in the Crimea and elsewhere confirmed that the Karaites were not "racially" Jews. Clearly the authorities felt a need to explain why an ethnic group espousing a variant of Judaism was not being eliminated (see Tyaglyy 2004: 451 and the cited literature).

---

[20] "At top secret meetings held in Pretzsch and Dueben, Saxony, in May 1941, the Einsatzgruppen and Einsatzkommando leaders were instructed by Heydrich, Chief of Security Police and SD, and Streckenbach, Chief of Personnel of RSHA, as to their mission, and they were introduced to the notorious Fuehrer Order around which this extraordinary case has risen. Under the guise of insuring the political security of the conquered territories ... the Einsatzgruppen were to liquidate ruthlessly all opposition to National Socialism – not only the opposition of the present, but that of the past and future as well. Whole categories of people were to be killed without truce, without investigation, without pity, tears, or remorse. Women were to be slain with the men, and the children also were to be executed because, otherwise, they would grow up to oppose National Socialism and might even nurture a desire to avenge themselves on the slayers of their parents. Later, in Berlin, Heydrich re-emphasized this point to some of the Einsatz leaders" (www.lawofwar.org/Einsatzgruppen%20 Case.htm).

Race sciences as practical knowledge

Race sciences were devised to discover a lot of differences among the races that do not follow from the marks of color and structure by which we distinguish them. (Ian Hacking (2005: 104))

Nowadays there is an inclination to deny race science the attribute "scientific" and to classify it as pseudo-science, and thus to exclude it from the scientific community. This disqualification of race science and race theorists as *pariahs* of the scientific enterprise is far too easy. It inhibits our understanding of how and why it was able actually to pursue and exercise practical political power in Germany in the first half of the last century.

The central question of racial science was and is, as Weber ([1924] 1988b: 488) put it in 1912 in a comment to a lecture by Franz Oppenheimer on "The Racialist Philosophy of History," delivered during the second annual meeting of the German Sociological Association in Berlin,[21] "are historically specific politically, culturally and developmentally *relevant* differences demonstrably inherited and heritable, and what are these differences?" Weber takes the framework of Oppenheimer's lecture seriously. The question for him is just this: do racialist theories and the racialist research in general deserve the attribute "scientific"?

Weber is skeptical that one can solve the issue of the "racial problem" in a scientifically accurate and satisfactory way. He refers to his own empirically oriented attempt, which he did not find satisfactory and which was based on a narrowly circumscribed topic, published as *Psychophysik der industriellen Arbeit* (Psychophysics of Industrial Labour; Weber [1908–09] 1988a). Weber thinks that when one applies racialist premises in a much broader way, for example in the area of social history, one can prove everything and nothing. And backwards-looking research, for example about the fall of the Roman Empire, with the help of racialist assumptions, is even less likely to solve the general question of the role of inherited assets. Arbitrariness, the uncritical use of racial assumptions, and the use of unclear terms are the distinguishing features of contemporary race theory. In short, racial researchers and race theorists commit "an academic crime" (Weber [1924] 1988b: 489). They have to be marginalized.

---

[21] We will come back below to another early intervention by Weber (1911) at the first Meeting of the German Sociological Association in 1910, where he dealt with the issue of race in sociology. This was part of his reply to the paper by A. Ploetz on "Die Begriffe der Rasse und Gesellschaft."

Holocaust scholar Michael Berenbaum (1993: 31) notes that under the Nazi regime, eugenics became national policy and so-called racial sciences were taught in the universities; the teaching of medicine, biology, history, anthropology, and sociology was perverted to support the "pseudo-science" of racial theory.[22] The Nazi regime eventually established thirty-three university research institutions, eighteen university professorships, and four health divisions within the Reich Health Offices dedicated to "racial hygiene."[23] The Nazi-appointed rector of the University of Berlin (a veterinarian and member of the storm troopers [i.e. Eugen Fischer]) introduced twenty-five courses in "racial science" into the curriculum.[24] As Proctor (1988a: 285) puts it, "racial science was 'normal science,' in the sense that Kuhn has given this expression."

The granting of scientific legitimacy to the concept of *race* and its use in explaining a group's beliefs and behavior were (and remain) essential prerequisites to the legalization and promotion of eugenics and euthanasia. Such practices, in combination with hierarchical principles adapted directly from Darwin's discussion of speciation, to the effect that some species (and thus races) are well developed whereas others are degenerate,[25] turned the practice of state-sponsored genocide into a

[22] John Gray writes in the *The Guardian* (Saturday March 15, 2008): "[S]ome of the worst atrocities of modern times were committed by regimes that claimed scientific sanction for their crimes. Nazi 'scientific racism' and Soviet 'dialectical materialism' reduced the unfathomable complexity of human lives to the deadly simplicity of a scientific formula. In each case, the science was bogus, but it was accepted as genuine at the time, and not only in the regimes in question. Science is as liable to be used for inhumane purposes as any other human institution. Indeed, given the enormous authority science enjoys, the risk of it being used in this way is greater."

[23] In the early 1930s, The *German Society for Race Hygiene* exclusively adopted or returned to the usage of the term *racial hygiene* instead of *eugenics*. In the last years of the Weimar Republic, as Graham (1977: 1139) relates, "eugenics" was considered by "proto-National Socialist publications and organizations as a kind of leftist deviation." Alarmed by the growing racist sentiments of scholars interested in human heredity and their growing alliance with right-wing political parties, "a coalition of Centrist, Catholic, and Social Democratic biologists and anthropologists mounted a counterattack with the German Society for Race Hygiene with the goal of chaining its name to the German Society for Eugenics" (p. 1139). The group failed to symbolically halt the increasing crystallization of particular political values and goals to biological conceptions.

[24] These facts obviously contributed to the decisions surrounding the inclusion, placement, and design of the compelling Race Science exhibit at the United States Holocaust Memorial Museum, where Berenbaum served as director of research until 1997.

[25] "The extension of Darwin's theories to human society lent an air of scientific legitimization to the various utopias involving selective breeding which had been propounded from antiquity onwards by *inter alia*, Plato, Moore, and Campanella. Francis Galton (1822–1911) took the principle of selection further, 'in the interests of improving the

modern technological undertaking (Horowitz 1980). In this sense, race science in Nazi Germany was first and foremost a policy science, or a form of practical knowledge (Stehr 1992). Sewell (2010) traces the roots of the race hygienist movement directly to Spencer, Darwin, Haeckel, and Galton. In the years leading up to World War I, this movement

> looked like a Darwin family business. Charles Darwin's son Leonard replaced his cousin Galton as chairman of the national Eugenics Society in 1911. In the same year an offshoot of the society was formed in Cambridge. Among its leading members were three more of Charles Darwin's sons, Horace, Francis, and George. The group's treasurer was a young economics lecturer at the university, John Maynard Keynes, whose younger brother Geoffrey would later marry Darwin's granddaughter Margaret. Meanwhile, Keynes's mother, Florence, and Horace Darwin's daughter Ruth, sat together at the committee of the Cambridge Association for the Care of the Feeble-Minded, which we might nowadays regard as nothing less than a front organization for eugenics. (Sewell 2010: 54)

Although Berenbaum refers to *Rassenwissenschaft* as pseudo-science, there is good reason to resist such labels. We are not suggesting that real science is analytically indistinguishable from pseudo-science, or that truth and myth are thus cognate. Rather, we are suggesting that the entire issue, raised by Berenbaum's characterization of the field as *pseudo-science*, is not relevant to (and may even detract from) our understanding of the impact of *Rassenwissenschaft*. In fact, it was treated as, and thus behaved as, "real" science.

As Truzzi (1996: 574) pertinently notes, "The real danger to science may be from dogma rather than pseudoscience ... [and] there are other good reasons to purge the term *pseudoscience* from our disputes. It may simply prove more useful and less incendiary to speak of bad, poor, or even *stupid* theories without entanglement in the demarcation [between 'real' and 'pseudo'] problem." There, reference is, of course to Karl Popper's demarcation criterion separating science from pseudo-science: In an autobiographical account in his *Conjectures and Refutations*, Popper (1963: 9–13) relates how, in 1919, he came to understand that pseudo-science (astrology, Freud's psychoanalysis, Adler's psychology, and Marxism) lives from advancing corroborations, while science (Newton, Einstein) seeks to generate testable conjectures.

Proctor (1988a: 6) convincingly argues that biomedical scientists played an active, even leading role in the initiation, administration, and execution of Nazi racial programs. In this sense the case can be

---

biological health of the *human* race'" (Burleigh and Wippermann 1991: 29, emphasis in original). See also Marks (1995).

made that science (especially biomedical science) under the Nazis cannot simply be seen in terms of a fundamentally "passive" or "apolitical" scientific community responding to purely external political forces; on the contrary, there is strong evidence that scientists actively designed and administered central aspects of National Socialist racial policy.

Race science, and in particular the view that race is the cause of mental and behavioral traits, had by the early 1900s gained considerable scholarly legitimacy in Germany and throughout Europe and North America. The earlier conception of human nature that viewed man's constitution as more plastic and less rigid gives way, as Rosenberg (1976) has shown, to a much more robust and fixed view of human heredity (cf. Shapin [1982] 1986: 356–57). Social and natural orders converge. Representations of nature are deployed by race scientists in society and socio-cultural and socio-political resources of the day are taken in by race science. The writings of Herbert Spencer ([1862] 1873) and, especially, Arthur de Gobineau (1915)[26] had begun to influence academic and popular thinking along these lines decades before the publication of Houston S. Chamberlain's (1900) landmark work on racial differences (Biddis 1970). And whereas the line of inquiry may have been thoroughly discredited, in one form or another, racial explanations still prevail in several quarters of the *contemporary* academic establishment (see Barkan 1992).

The race scientists of Germany and other countries produced an enormous body of literature. Although there is a selective lack of data to substantiate certain claims, as well as immense leaps of faith in interpreting some of the information gathered, these works all aspired to be rigorously "scientific" and to be critically judged by the accepted scholarly standards of the day.

In their attempts to amass volumes of quantitative evidence to illustrate and justify their theories, these scholars saw their work as leading-edge science. Indeed, at first glance, the works of race scientists contain an imposing range of evidence: naturalistic, experimental, and survey-based. The level of discourse is sophisticated, the arguments apparently conform or endeavor to be close to the then-prevailing logic of science, and the conclusions that are drawn seem to be sound. Any

---

[26] The most effective reception and widespread resonance of Gobineau's ideas took place in Germany. Richard Wagner and Gobineau became friends, for example; Wagner and his Bayreuth circle did much to popularize and disseminate Gobineau's racial theories. Some of his most influential German interpreters also added an anti-Semitic twist to Gobineau's ideas, absent from his own work (cf. Weingart et al. 1988: 94).

serious criticism that is demanded of the field, so it seems, must at least meet the same standards. This is not the racism and anti-Semitism of the beer hall; it is indeed science – of a sort, and it was widely interpreted to represent the best in modern thought.

But race science is more. It always aspires to be practical; it is almost driven to engage practical contemporary problems, and it desires to formulate public policies. Its aspirations and its historical and intellectual roots are drawn from applied science, in the sense of having an inherent political agenda that addresses major social and political problems of the day. Although characterized by its proponents and pursued as a nomological undertaking, its prominence and popularity did not result from the strength of its scientific rigor. By these criteria, it was no more successful than other, competing, approaches; nor, and this is an important matter, was it probably any *less* successful. Rather, race science succeeded – to some extent wherever it was/is pursued, but especially so in Weimar and Nazi Germany – because it had practical applications that appeared to be effective and to resonate with salient public and private troubles of the day: first, in the management of the affairs of everyday life for citizens and in the foreign affairs of government; later as the centerpiece of state domestic and military policy.

In Germany, race science's practical aspirations and success were also reinforced and supported by a host of intermediary social organizations. Of perhaps greatest significance are the nationalist-*völkische* social movements that embraced race science, promoting it widely in society and championing its policy implications.[27]

As a result, in many instances the boundaries between scientific and political agendas became almost indistinguishable, as did the individual scientific objectives and the personal ideological ambitions of the race scientists.

---

[27] Prior to World War I and during the Weimar Republic, many existing organizations in Germany incorporated racial theories into their platforms and vigorously demanded political action, including laws to minimize *Rassenmischung*, that is, the biological mixing of races. In a 1913 study of the so-called "Rehobother Bastards," a group of individuals of mixed Hottentot and Boer origins in German Southwest Africa, Eugen Fischer had concluded, without the benefit of any empirical evidence, that racial mixing invariably had deleterious effects. This conclusion was later often cited in support of policies designed to outlaw *Rassenmischung*. In Fischer's contribution to *Human Heredity* (Baur et al. [1921] 1931: 183), he alludes explicitly to the harmful effects for the German nation of race mixing because, as he suggests, "the present fate of the German nation" has been caused and sealed by a different composition of races, and is therefore not unlike the fate that befell the "Greeks who trembled before the Roman emperors." In a lecture in Königsberg, only days after the Nazis assumed power, Fischer demanded that those who are racially alien and who have inherited diseases should be weeded out (see Weingart et al. 1988: 385).

Since the days of Gobineau's *Inequality of Races* (1915), race science has been (and remains) a policy-driven field. It was never merely a classificatory / explanatory framework, although Max Weber, among others, has argued the case for a "neutralist" position. During the first meeting of the German Sociological Association in 1910, an early confrontation took place between sociologists who argued in strong terms for the exclusion of any reference to race or other biological categories within sociological discourse. The race-biologist Alfred Ploetz delivered a guest lecture (Ploetz 1911), advocating precisely the relevance of race for sociological considerations. During the heated discussion, it was Max Weber (1911) who most vigorously opposed any such argument. He made clear what is at stake when sociologists oppose racial approaches. Weber's intervention exemplifies the basic theoretical decisions that were taken by those theorists who nowadays belong to the sociological canon. It is noteworthy that Werner Sombart participated as chair of this discussion, and took a much more "conciliatory" position toward the speaker than Weber; that is, Sombart was not prepared to close the door entirely, and hoped for joint and additional research on the relation between racial attributes and social processes (cf. Sombart 1911). At the beginning of the twentieth century and under the dominance of the biological paradigm, sociology tried hard to gain its own professional profile and identity. In order to succeed, the "founding fathers" wanted to draw a clear distinction between this new academic discipline and all its competitors. To be sure, Weber does not exclude a priori racial explanations of human behavior or social structures. But he stresses the fact that there is no such evidence available. Between the lines we grasp his conviction that there will never be such an explanation available. He rejects such approaches for two reasons: One is to be sought in his attempt to give sociology a professional profile of its own, the other in his general political outlook. Weber developed his own theory in sharp contrast to naturalistic or biologistic concepts.

The field of race science is meant to explain why people behave as they do, but in such a way that practical measures can be set into motion in order to control or rectify behavior. True to its base in Darwinian natural science, it is concerned with the effects of breeding, and thus establishes the crucial linkage between heredity and social conduct. As confirmed by Fritz Lenz (in Baur et al. [1921] 1931) and later by the US geneticist Thurman Rice (1929), the entire racial issue would be without any significance whatsoever if racial differences were confined to anatomical differences. Decisive, therefore, are the "spiritual" attributes of the races; that is, attributes that cannot, as Lenz admits, be measured with the same technical devices employed to quantify organic features.[28] Nevertheless, as Eugen Fischer (in Baur et al. [1921] 1931: 181) summarized the position of this group, "the various races of man differ from one another to an extraordinary degree in mental respects no less than in bodily." And, as Lenz (in Baur et al. [1921] 1931: 655) categorically summarizes the matter of mental gifts, "the Nordic race marches at the very front of mankind."[29]

It took Fischer some time to embrace the concept of Nordic superiority which was to become a touchstone of Nazi race science. One day before Hitler's *Machtergreifung*, he delivered a speech to the Kaiser Wilhelm Gesellschaft, "maintaining that the racial mixing of Nordic with non-Nordic peoples of Europe ... was not only not harmful but was in fact responsible for many of the spiritual achievements of present-day peoples. He even maintained that 'where it has remained most pure, the Nordic race has brought forth no great cultural achievements'" (Proctor 1988a: 40). After being denounced, he was replaced as head of the Society for Racial Hygiene and ousted from the *Archiv für Rassen-und Gesellschaftsbiologie*. He bounced back to a powerful position during the same year, when he became rector of Berlin University.

As practical knowledge, the understanding of this relationship between heredity and "spiritual" attributes is driven by an interest in population control; the rise and decline of civilizations; progress; "the quality of people," health and energy: that is, the preservation of the "best" social traits through selective breeding. "Just as scientific therapeutics is impossible without a thorough grounding in human anatomy, physiology and pathology," notes Erwin Baur (in Baur et al. [1921] 1931: 10), "so there must be a broad foundation of natural science for the study of human sociology, for any fruitful attempt to solve the problems of population, and for our endeavors to promote racial hygiene (eugenics)." And it comes as no surprise that the most prominent proponent of modern climate determinism, the Yale geographer Ellsworth Huntington, was also the author of *Tomorrow's Children: the*

---

[28] The essential ambiguity of Lenz's position was evident, but it does not lead him to abandon his assertion concerning "spiritual" characteristics. The conviction that these are truly racial attributes is linked to a value-based conception of race ("*Rasse als Wertprinzip*," see Lenz 1933). The spiritual (or mental) features of the races are thus taken to be self-evident, and are derived quite independently of any scientific exploration of race. Indeed, the value conception of race justifies both (1) this special convergence of ideology and science (cf. Weingart et al.1988: 102–03) and (2) the strategic alliances between scientific and non-scientific associations willing to support and push for a realization of the political agenda of race science. Nonetheless, the social scientists in the already exiled *Zeitschrift für Sozialforschung* continued to express the hope that race science as a valuable natural science could be immunized against race science as a pure ideology (cf. Landsberg 1933: 388).

[29] We have changed the translation slightly to better reflect the original meaning.

Goal of Eugenics (1935), and served as the president of the American Eugenics Society from 1934 to 1938 (see also Hankins 1926).

The interest among race scientists in asymmetries and hierarchies was also the product of practical concerns, as identified by popular writers such as Hans F. Günther, often called the canonical race theorist (e.g. Günther 1927; also see Kolnai 1977). Not only can the differences in the way people act be traced to their varying genetic heritages, but it was clear to the race scientists that lineages differ according to how well adapted they are to their environments, including their socio-cultural environments when behavior is factored in. It therefore follows that at a particular time and place, some races will be more advanced than others. This is generally operationalized in terms of cultural, economic, and/or political relations of domination-subordination; one group or nation rules over, is wealthier than, or is larger in size than another by virtue of natural (i.e., racial) advantages.

When northwestern Europe was experiencing its greatest era of imperial prosperity, the task remained for race scientists from Gobineau to Fischer to explain (and justify) why this was the case: because the region was populated by the most advanced races. When conditions began to deteriorate at home and abroad, these same explanations served to provide (1) a rationalization: inferior races were exercising undue influence on public policy, and their genes were mixing too freely with those of the more advanced races; and (2) a solution: social control and, when necessary, euthanasia for the living and genetic control for the unborn. The audiences whom the race scientists addressed did not need to establish, nor did they inquire into, the validity and reliability of these views. They were offered secularized and sanitized arguments (worldviews), couched in terms of the most trusted discourse of the day, namely scientific discourse.

Despite the apparently impeccable scientific rigor and other intrinsic scholarly properties of the manner in which race discourse was framed and executed, these attributes were by no means sufficient for the granting of extraordinary academic legitimacy to the study of race; nor, in Nazi Germany, for its elevation to a unique position of societal prominence and its translation into practical knowledge. Rather, its acceptance was the result of three features *extrinsic* to the academic discipline: (1) It provided continuity between traditional conceptions of national character – *Volksgeist* – and acknowledged, modern naturalistic theories and methods of establishing facticity.[30] (2) Its accounts resonated with

---

[30] Here and in several other respects, Benoit Massin's (1996) historical study is crucial to the understanding of the intellectual and social forces that led to the rise of Fischer

common-sense perceptions of the physical and behavioral differences between groups. (3) It had direct practical applications (initially realized in the Nuremberg Laws).

The Holocaust was the result of public policy decisions made in the presumed interests of benefiting the German totalitarian regime. These decisions were science-based, and the scientific discourse was nurtured by decision-makers with a level of complementarity rarely achieved in any political regime.[31] "According to Nazi theory, humanity is not a homogeneous unit, and the human race has no common denominator. Those who spoke of the unity of the human race were intent on falsifying the truth, and they denied the existence of races and refused to recognize the constant conflicts between them. Phrases about the common destiny of mankind were ridiculous, as absurd as talk of a partnership between men and insects" (*Yad Vashem* 1995: 14).[32] In race science terms, this doctrine was known as *polygeneticism*, and it had become the dominant approach of physical anthropologists, especially in Germany, by the mid 1920s. In this context, the concept of *Lebensraum* is uniquely illustrative of the intimate meshing of physical anthropology, *qua* race science, and politics in Germany.

The scientific and political meanings of *Lebensraum*

Like other regimes with imperial aspirations, Hitler's Germany deemed it necessary to reclaim or claim anew sovereignty over, and to colonize, territory not within its national boundaries. For most of history such policies had been justified by what has become known as versions of *Realpolitik*, that is, some combination of political, economic, religious,

and his school. Gilman (1996: 77–84) cites a related work by Andrew Lyons (1974) that covers an earlier, but overlapping, period.

[31] This science-policy complementarity is reflected in several ways, including the facts that not only were most of the academic scientists Nazis, but many were also SS members (including Fischer); relevant government bureaus in the areas of education, racial hygiene, and medicine were staffed by race scientists; and courses in racial hygiene were required in all civil and military training programs. Burleigh and Wippermann (1991) and Lerner (1992) provide considerable historical detail on the race science/race policy interface.

[32] At least some race scientists assumed that the capacity to understand race effectively was itself genetically determined. Thus, some kinds of science (e.g. monogeneticism) are Jewish and thus "corrupt," whereas others are Aryan, anti-Semitic, and therefore "true." Moreover, as the German race scientist Joachim Haupt (1933: 2) observed in 1933, "Race theory and the *völkische* idea provide research with a generally valid value concept based on results achieved by way of the methods of natural science. Such a concept reestablishes the basis for the hierarchical ordering of scientific work which had been lost in the epoch of liberal science, merely concerned with the collection of empirical evidence."

and cultural interests – as was the case in the making of the British Empire. By the end of the nineteenth century, however, imperialism and colonialism had developed a social Darwinian superstructure, after the fact: the then-current world order was understood to reflect the outcome of evolutionary selection. Chamberlain's account is formative in this regard. When Germany at last "awoke" to the prospect of imperial expansion, its policymakers simply took the new rationale to the next level. Annexation and colonization were deemed to be racial imperatives.

In the case of German expansionist policies, these principles were applied in two distinct phases. First, prior to the invasion of Poland in September 1939, each case of Nazi territorial conquest was justified as a step toward the consolidation of the dispersed German population / Aryan race. It was argued that the German natural *ecumene* had unfortunately been dissected by artificial national boundaries, and that what appeared to the outside world as imperialism was actually the restoration of Aryan living space.

The period that began with the opening of the Polish campaign marks a major policy shift. From that point until the end of the war, the notion of *Lebensraum* was adduced as the ideological principle in support of expansion *beyond* the then-current *ecumene*. As first argued by Hitler in *Mein Kampf* (with surprising cogency, as we know), if a particular race is the fittest to survive and to rule over other races, then it must ensure that it has domain over sufficient territory to satisfy evolutionary imperatives. We stress here that this claim – in contrast to traditional arguments that emphasize benefits that pertain to the substructure of society, enlargement of a religious community, and the like – is subject to scientific resolution. It appeals not to greed nor to spiritual passion, but to reason.

The truth and the efficacy of *Lebensraum* as a policy principle were not, as with other justifications for expansionism, manifestly arbitrary. Rather, its appeal and efficacy depended on how one defines *race* in practice: what physical and mental characteristics are understood to be associated with racial differences, what determines fitness, how much territory is sufficient, and so forth. During the three decades that preceded the writing of *Mein Kampf* in 1924–25, highly respected researchers and scholars in geography, biology, anthropology, and other fields had been addressing and wrestling with these very concerns (see Gilman 1996: 30–42; Lerner 1992, especially his discussion of Konrad Lorenz).

The classic work by Erwin Baur, Eugen Fischer, and Fritz Lenz, *Menschliche Erblichkeitslehre und Rassenhygiene*, was published in

1921.[33] In 1928, Eugen Fischer was appointed director of the Kaiser Wilhelm Institute for Anthropology, Human Heredity Teaching, and Eugenics.[34] Hitler had developed close personal ties with Germany's leading race scientists, many of whom were Nazi Party members, years before becoming chancellor.[35] These included Fischer, who was appointed rector of Berlin's Humboldt University in 1933 (Wistrich 1988).[36] Thus, by 1935, when the race-territory connection began to be inscribed into the legal code, race science was already well established:

The two main associations of racial hygienists were "coordinated" in the summer of 1933. This included the German Society for Racial Hygiene, which at the time had 1,300 members and twenty local groups. Many of its members were academics, including some who were also functionaries in the Racial Political Office of the NSDAP. From this time onwards, the association and its periodical, *Archiv für Rassen- und Gesellschaftsbiologie,* served to "enlighten" others about the racial policies of the regime. The German Society for Anthropology, renamed the German Society for Racial Research in 1937, fulfilled a similar function. Moreover, members of both societies took part, either as individuals or as members of research institutes, in the drafting and implementation of racial policy measures. The most important academic research institute was the Kaiser Wilhelm Institute

---

[33] This and the following section rely heavily on the Baur, Fischer, and Lenz volume. As is clear from its bibliography, and from the listing of other editions in the book's series in the original German version, this is just one of numerous items published on race science during the field's brief history. Nevertheless, it is *the* definitive text, divided into sections for which one or the other principal author draws on scores of published and unpublished reports. Lenz (1931: 303) writes appreciatively that Hitler embraced the ideas of race science, reporting that he has been told that Hitler read the second edition of the Baur, Fischer, and Lenz volume while in jail in Landsberg.

[34] An informative description of the rise and fall of the influential Fischer Institute during the Nazi era may be found in Weingart et al. 1988: 413–24 and in Lösch 1997.

[35] As Garver and Garver (1991: 1112) note: "After 1933, when the Nazis came to power, the zeal of young physicians to identify themselves with Nazism increased to the extent that they became the largest professional group in the party. As the Nazi party began to promulgate its ideas concerning racial hygiene, many physicians readily endorsed the movement and accepted the mission of changing their role from doctor to the individual to 'doctor of the nation.' During the years after the Nazi ascension to power, there was a change in attitude of these physicians, from that of recognizing all life as valuable to that of life not being worth living. The early biological and intellectual racial hygiene movement in Germany developed into a political/racial hygiene movement designed to demonstrate a supposed difference in value of the various population groups."

[36] Proctor (1988a: 292) claims that many race scientists wanted to be seen as standing above party politics (*überparteilich*), and thus were reluctant to join the Nazi party. Lenz, Ploetz, and Rüdin joined in 1937, Fischer and Verschuer in 1940.

for Anthropology, Heredity and Eugenics, which was established in 1928 under the auspices of the Kaiser Wilhelm Society (KWI). The KWI's directors, Eugen Fischer, Fritz Lenz, and Otmar Freiherr von Verschuer, were willing and enthusiastic conformists (Burleigh and Wippermann 1991: 52; Lösch 1997).

Henceforth, Germany's foreign policy was guided by principles verified and endorsed by the nation's leading scientists. The early and close affinity between race scientists, anthropologists, geographers, sociologists, and other social scientists who were proponents of racial doctrines in Germany – and yearned to see their science translated into applied science – indicates clearly that it was not necessary for the Nazis, once in power, to falsify or corrupt the knowledge that emanated from academic race science (see also Weingart, Kroll, and Bayertz 1988: 381–89). In fact, once the Nazis had assumed power, social scientists who had already displayed an ideological affinity to the Nazi doctrines began to quarrel among themselves over who should be credited with originating the doctrine. The case of Werner Sombart, for example, is documented in Lenger (1994: 365; also see Lenz 1933).

The principles of race science

By the early days of the Third Reich, it was widely presumed that race science had demonstrated the following six principles, derived from Lenz and other race scientists (see Burleigh and Wippermann 1991; Lerner 1992; Rushton 1995).

1. Several distinct human racial groups had evolved over the course of millennia, with traits that reflect variable adaptations to distinct environments. In this respect, every race has an ancestral territory to whose natural conditions its traits are best suited. As we shall discuss below, contemporary social psychologists and geographers such as Hellpach and Huntington considered climate to be the principal environmental engine in this process.
2. Interbreeding had resulted in considerable variations among individuals, but dominant physical and behavioral traits are still identifiable. Thus, it is possible to place individuals within racial categories (with reasonable accuracy) through observation of anatomical and social-psychological characteristics. These observations, in combination with archeological findings and historical records, also aid in identifying the region to which individuals properly belong.
3. Some physical traits are progressive and make a positive contribution to the survival of the species, whereas others are regressive and

pose a threat to humanity's future. For example, effective hand-eye coordination is an evolutionary advantage over congenital neuro-logical disorders that affect this capacity.

4. "Spiritual" or mental/behavioral traits are similarly associated with or constitute behavioral or intellectual manifestations (*Äußerungen*)[37] of the essence of race, and hence with survival prospects. "Dealing with the human race as a whole, we can with a high degree of prob-ability infer that an individual with frizzy hair will have a dark skin; and, in like manner, we can with considerable probability infer that certain bodily characters will be accompanied by particular mental traits. But certain bodily characters appear also to warrant direct conclusions regarding mental endowment. Thus the size of the fore-head and the size of the head are to some extent racial characters, and we have shown that mental gifts are associated with these bodily characters" (Lenz, in Baur et al. [1921] 1931: 687–88).[38]

5. Furthermore, under prevailing economic and political conditions in Europe and the world, the races clearly vary in their capacity to sustain a modern civilized lifestyle (as signified by the *Naturvölker/ Kulturvölker* dichotomy, for example). Prior to the Industrial Revolution, such matters may have been of little consequence; but since then, the presence or lack of this capacity has had a crucial impact on inter-group and international relations. Moreover, the fact that the Industrial Revolution occurred in northwestern Europe indicates that its native races are the most highly evolved (this is a direct extension of the Gobineau/Chamberlain thesis).

6. Methods exist that allow for intervention in the process of natural selection, so as to maximize the positive and minimize the negative traits in a national population. That is, through selective breeding

---

[37] The German term *Äußerung* is likely chosen with deliberate care by Lenz, since it has the rhetorical advantage of multiple meanings, including "utterance, expression, observation, manifestation and demonstration," which in conjunction signify the idea that race works and speaks for itself in specific observable behavioral acts, as well as cognitive expressions. The latter are derivative of the former, and exemplify the dominance of race.

[38] In a review of Spengler's *Untergang des Abendlandes*, in the "light of racial biology" as the title indicates, Lenz (1925) is particularly irritated with the emphasis on the role of culture he encounters in Spengler's book. Spengler simply has the wrong causal factor. Instead of culture, he should have emphasized race. Race is essential; culture is superficial. And this can be demonstrated, as Lenz argues (p. 298), in the case of musical ability, because in the example of music it becomes most clear that hereditary traits – or what amounts to the same, racial dispositions – are much more essential than the sharing of a specific culture. "Culture is always ephemeral in comparison to race" (our translation). In addition, Lenz does not share Spengler's pessimism and fatalism. Lenz declares that the decline of a civilization is not inevitable. It is possible to intervene and arrest the "death of a race" (p. 309).

(including euthanasia where prescribed), races can be "pruned" and "purified" in such a way that a nation's survival prospects are materially improved. The same methods can also be employed in combination with colonization to satisfy the advanced races' requirements for living space. This notion of practical intervention – the application of scientific principles to population policy – is the special contribution of the racial hygienists.[39]

Stipulations five and six are pivotal in race science's successful forging of the link between scientific observation and public policy. The former assertion, that the races and cultures of northern Europe are the most advanced, was supported by a long line of scholars, from Spencer and Gobineau, to Ellsworth Huntington, Edward East, Hans F. K. Günther, Willy Hellpach, and the German physical anthropologists of the 1900–30 period – both monogenists and polygenists, as Massin notes (1996: 97–100). Later, in the work of Fischer and his colleagues, this association was taken for granted to be accurate. As a whole, Nazi race science was increasingly concerned with the technologies of intervention featured in stipulation six. As Fritz Lenz urges in the conclusion to *Human Heredity*, "If we [the members of the Nordic race] continue to squander that biological mental heritage as we have been squandering it during the last few decades, it will not be many generations before we cease to be the superiors of the Mongols. Our ethnological studies must lead us, not to arrogance, but to action – to eugenics" (Baur et al. [1921] 1931: 699).

The claims that Lenz and his colleagues advance are especially credible because they simply extend tried and tested, even common-sense, notions and experience with selective breeding in plants and animals into the human sphere. Thus, Fischer (in Baur et al. [1921] 1931: 173, n.1) observes – responding to those who might object to the application of the concept of domestication to humans, since the essential characteristic of "domesticated animals is that in respect of their breeding they are subjected to the will of man" – that "domesticated man comes to

---

[39] These principles had all been adumbrated by Friedrich Nietzsche (1880: 189; passage translated by Burleigh and Wippermann 1991: 34) as early as 1880: "Satisfaction of desire should not be practiced so that the race as a whole suffers, i.e., that choice no longer occurs, and that anyone can pair off and produce children. The extinction of many types of people is just as desirable as any form of reproduction. Much more so: marriage only 1) with the aim of higher development; 2) in order to leave behind the fruit of such persons. Concubinage is enough for all the rest, with measures to prevent conception. – We must do away with this crass lightheartedness. These geese must not marry! Marriage must become much less frequent! Go through the towns and ask yourself whether these people should reproduce! Let them go to their whores."

resemble the domesticated animals, with the same result, that marked variability ensues. That is why I have spoken of man as, biologically considered, being subjected to the influences of domestication."

In order to make "proper" use of the findings of race science, at least three conditions are required, one practical and two epistemological: First, in the practical realm, there must exist a profession that is equivalent to occupations based on human agronomy or husbandry. This condition was, of course, to be satisfied by the racial hygienists themselves, with programs coordinated at the Humboldt University of Berlin and the Kaiser Wilhelm Institute.

Second, in the realm of knowledge, it must be assumed that natural selection prevails over Lamarckian processes – a contentious area of inquiry throughout the race science movement.[40] If traits could be acquired as the result of changes in the geographical environment or through socialization, and subsequently genetically passed on to future generations, then selective breeding would be an ineffective and otherwise doubtful technical application. Such a position, supported by Lester Frank Ward and others in the United States, was effectively excluded from German race science during the early 1920s (see Massin 1996). By 1933, even the most remote suggestion that racial characteristics could be significantly altered through environment or education was considered to be, *ipso facto*, unscientific.

Third, "pruning" and "purifying" a national population is a viable policy only if races have a concrete and identifiable existence. Means must be available to operationalize race according to clear, measurable

[40] The rejection of Lamarckian principles was extremely important to the race scientists, who justified their zeal on the grounds that any appeal to hereditary mechanisms other than pure Darwinian natural selection was unscientific. As a matter of fact, we know that socio-cultural traits (one might even say "mental capacities") are routinely acquired during the course of one generation and transmitted to subsequent ones, not genetically, of course, but through enculturation. For example, a man and a woman born in Italy and speaking Italian from a very early age can readily migrate to an English-speaking country, such as the United States, acquire the English language later in life, marry, have children, and raise their offspring in a household in which only English is spoken. The children would thus have inherited (in the socio-cultural sense) an acquired characteristic. To equate this situation with the imagined case of, say, giraffes that stretch their necks to reach the leaves on tall trees and then pass the long-necked trait to offspring is the height of sophistry. Yet this is precisely the line of argument taken by Fischer and his colleagues in their refutation of Franz Boas's allegedly Lamarckian bias (Lenz, in Baur et al. [1921] 1931: 689–90). Despite the profound differences in the way they deal with group-based "mental capacities," Boas is classed along with the Marxist materialists *and* Marx's idealist critics as "in truth warring brethren, being children of one father, Lamarck" (Lenz, in Baur et al. [1921] 1931: 697). Herbert Spencer's insights on cultural acquisition continue to be dismissed on similar grounds (see Ashley and Orenstein 1995: Ch 5).

criteria. Thus, fields such as anthropometry, hematology, and comparative anatomy must be developed to a fairly high degree. Significantly, all
three conditions were present in Germany by 1935.

Race science, text, and context

Race science took a distinctive turn in Germany between 1927 and
1933, although it had been practiced since the late nineteenth century in several countries, including England and the United States.
Although several scientific disciplines contributed to this field of study,
a remarkable consensus existed among the various scholars on the
principles explicated above, and on a range of related matters as well.
For example, Eugen Fischer's hereditary classification of races, which
was accepted at the time as definitive – i.e.: Neanderthals, Negroes,
Mongoloids, and the "four great races of Europe," Mediterraneans,
Orientals, Near Easterners, and Nordics[41] – is virtually identical to that
of Knox, Edward East (1929: 186), and Frank Hankins (who refined
Gobineau's scheme).

The theories of the race scientists were well known to, and generally
respected among, members of the educated public, with entries in the
Encyclopedia Britannica of the 1920s and early 1930s on race and related
topics written by leading proponents of the field. This is to say that,
in a profound sense, it was common knowledge; and its proponents
wanted it to be common-sense knowledge that race "matters" in human
affairs.

The main intellectual problem faced by the race scientists was to
explain certain observed variations in what most referred to as "mental
traits." Eugen Fischer (in Baur et al. [1921] 1931: 181) argues, for instance,
that

the racial composition of a people is, in all circumstances, decisive (in conjunction with other conditions) as to its cultural and mental functional efficiency.
Of course we must not overlook the fact that the rise and fall of a nation in history is dependent on a number of external factors ... Unquestionably, however,
in addition to these, racial endowments play a mighty part. The various races
of man differ from one another to an extraordinary degree in mental respects
no less than in bodily. Some races are highly gifted as regards imagination,
vigor, intelligence, etc., these qualities being variously combined, hereditary,
and inalienable. Just as the environment modifies physical qualities paratypi-
cally, there can be no doubt that, as in the individual, so in the nation consisting of thousands upon thousands of individuals with their special racial

---

[41] The "Teutons" were classed as a branch of the Nordics (cf. Lenz, in Baur et al. [1921]
1931: 627–65).

endowments, the circumstances of life must modify in many ways the development of the hereditary mental equipment. But the endowments are themselves provided by heredity once and for all; and inasmuch as the nations are racially different, their mental gifts must also be different.

In fact, the object of these investigations ranged widely, and usually included behavioral traits and socio-cultural characteristics as well – as indicated by Fischer's matter-of-fact equation between cultural and mental "functional efficiency." Whatever these traits are, they would now be termed, in the mundane language of social research, the *dependent* variable(s), or as the *work* that race presumably does.

If race membership is taken to be essentially fixed, natural, and altered over time only through "hybridization" (the common clinical term for race-mixing), then eugenics policy is the appropriate means of managing variation in the dependent variable. If climate can affect genetic traits, as some modern climate determinists maintain, then policies enforcing a geographical division of labor are the more viable policy alternative. Of the two approaches, only *Rassenwissenschaft* entails race war. Nevertheless, both climate determinists and race scientists support the notion of *Lebensraum* and endorse expansionism scientifically.

Climate and race

The great deliberation about the relative influence of nurture and environment did not bypass the discussions about the effect of climate on human history and society. The famous French naturalist Georges Buffon (1707–88), for example, was convinced of the unity underlying the diversity of the human races, thereby expressing a rather modern idea. But according to Buffon, the observable diversity was due to effects of a purely physical and external nature. In particular, he considered the human races as varieties that evolved from an original white race under the influence of climate (cf. Boas 1935).

During the period under consideration, later contributions are written under the strong influence of Darwinian views, while discussions prior to the turn of the century were also influenced by neo-Lamarckian conceptions. Contributions that were indebted to a Lamarckian conception – for example, the views associated with physical anthropology in Germany during the 1880s and 1890s – suggested that as humans are transplanted into a different climate, their physiology would actually change; and that the organic consequences of acclimatization could then be inherited by subsequent generations.

In the end it does not really matter whether it is an exclusively Darwinian, a Lamarckian, or an evolutionary perspective that ambivalently mixes the two approaches[42] and that provides the biological foundation for climate determinism, because these perspectives share the prior commitment to the idea that the natural climate is a basic environmental force that accounts for different manifestations of human success or failure.[43]

The physician and anthropologist Rudolf Virchow ([1885] 1922: 231), for example, who espouses a neo-Lamarckian perspective on climate and was writing at a time when colonial expansion was on the political agenda, is convinced that the fertility of individuals who migrate to regions of the world in which climates prevail that are different from their "native" climate will suffer, and that they will experience a dramatic, constant decline in numbers.[44] At least in the short run, the population of colonizers is bound to decrease, and can only be sustained as a result of a constant influx of new individuals.[45]

---

[42] Herbert Spencer (1887: 349–50) shares such ambiguity, which appears to be typical of contemporary discourse; for example, with respect to the importance of climate, he expresses the view that "men having constitutions fitted for one climate, cannot be fitted to an extremely different climate by persistently living in it, because they do not survive, generation after generation. Such changes can be brought about only by slow spreadings of the race through intermediate regions having intermediate climates, to which successive generations are accustomed little by little. And doubtless the like holds mentally. The intellectual and emotional natures required for high civilization, are not to be obtained by thrusting on the completely-uncivilized, the needful activity and restraints in unqualified forms: gradual decay and death, rather than adaptation, would result" (see also Huntington 1907: 15).

[43] See the account of the racial myth underlying the settlement of Southern California at the end of the last century in Starr (1986: 89–93); Starr describes the conviction of many in contemporary Southern California that it represented the "new Eden of the Saxon homeseeker," and that the Anglo-Saxon stock – weakened by an overlong confinement on the crowded and chilly British Isles – would be reinvigorated and reinforced as a result of the healthy climate in the Southland.

[44] There was a long-standing debate during colonial rule about the prospects and dangers of white persons' adaptation to a tropical climate and the question of what "acclimatization" exactly means. There was a wide range of positions and expertise; Virchow and others warned about the dangers of the tropics (cf. Sapper 1932). The opposite view held that there was no reason to believe that "the North European would not be able to colonize tropical regions permanently" (Bormann 1937: 11). However, there was concern about the "'low cultural level' of European settlements in tropical regions which was barely higher than the natives" (Bormann p. 112). Based on this observation, Bormann revokes his positive account of the Europeans' adaptability. We can speak of successful adaptation (Bormann calls it "permanency of the master race") not only when there is demographic survival, but also when we see a "dynamic rise of a people."

[45] Ellsworth Huntington ([1915] 1924: 6) concurs with Virchow and claims, referring to the "poor whites" who have settled in the Bahamas, that "when the white man migrates to climates less stimulating than those of his original home, he appears to lose in both physical and mental energy." A more explicit statement that resonates closely with Virchow's observations can be found in a sociology reader to which Huntington (1927: 257) contributed: "If the white man tries to reside permanently on

In general, of course, neo-Lamarckians have a more "optimistic" out-look, in that they are convinced that climate can be conquered almost perfectly by way of adaptation and then inheritance. Darwinians are resigned to the fact that inherited climatic dispositions cannot simply be altered from one generation to another, but at best in a long-term process of natural selection.

Darwinian climate determinists will stress the extent to which climatic conditions attract and pull in some, while rejecting others. Similarly, climatic conditions will assert their superiority and drive out cultural practices that are not in accord with them (cf. Huntington 1945: 610). In the long run, as Huntington (1927: 165) observes, "ill health, failure and gradual extinction are the lot of those who cannot or will not adapt themselves to the climate, but before that happens many migrate to other climates better adapted to their physiques, temperaments, occu-pations, habits, institutions and stage of development."

Leading early twentieth-century proponents of climate studies, including the geographers Ellsworth Huntington ([1915] 1924) in the United States and the social psychologist Willy Hellpach (1938) in Germany, shared the race scientists' interest in using evolutionary principles to explain inter-species ("sub-specific") variations in *Homo sapiens*. In particular, they sought to demonstrate that distinct regional groupings, often (but unsystematically) termed races, exist and can be identified by physical and "mental" traits that presumably reflect adap-tive responses to the particular environmental conditions that prevail in the region. Among these formative geographic conditions, climate is granted a preeminent role. Huntington's ([1915] 1924: first edn. 270) own opus is best summed up in the following conclusion: "No nation has risen to the highest grade of civilization except in regions where the climatic stimulus is great." In 1911, Ellen Churchill Semple (1911: 1–2) opened her widely cited study on the control of the natural environment over human affairs with the following general declaration:

Man is a product of the earth's surface ... the earth has mothered him, fed him, set him tasks, directed his thoughts, confronted him with difficulties that have strengthened his body and sharpened his wits, given him his problems of

the equatorial coasts of Africa, and to work there as at home, he can scarcely succeed unless his physique is different from that of the average of his race. He must be more leisurely than at home, he must pay more attention to health, his wife and children must often live in more bracing climates if they are to preserve their health. His ideals of public service, of social and scientific progress, and of democratic government may remain unchanged, but lack of surplus energy, even without specific disease, gener-ally causes him to be relatively inactive along such lines. Thus although the outward forms of society may remain the same in a tropical climate as in more bracing regions, the actual mode of life is almost certain to be decidedly different."

navigation and irrigation, and at the same time whispered hints for their solution ... Man can no more be scientifically studied apart from the ground he tills, or the lands over which he travels, or the seas over which he trades, than polar bear or desert cactus can be understood apart from its habitat.

For Huntington ([1915] 1924: 363–64), as for the race scientists, these insights into the profound effect of environmental conditions on human affairs constitute much more than merely scientific observations. These are matters of practical urgency:

A race or nation can apparently be made by natural selection. Mere numbers count for nothing: in many cases a dense population is the greatest of curses, as it has been in Ireland, China, Japan and Germany. Quality is what counts and what quality is can be obtained only by diminishing the number of people who inherit low moral and mental capacities and increasing the portion who inherit the high qualities which lead to racial dominance. In the past, without man's conscious intervention, natural selection has been actively at work, sometimes for good and sometimes for ill. The only question is whether a race or a nation will control such selection so that it will always act beneficially as in the first and greatest days of ancient Greece and Iceland, or will permit it to continue to work haphazard [sic] and perhaps toward great unhappiness, as in China or in Greece of later days.[46]

Arguments that establish the connection between climate and race are no longer based on pure conjecture, as was the case for centuries in related reflections on the efficacy of climate on human affairs. Rather, these scholars employ a large body of quantitative environmental, sociological, and anthropological data to make their case scientifically convincing. But, in essence, modern climate determinism still asserts – as did Plato, Montesquieu, or Hegel – that a particular climate (for instance, that which we find in contemporary northwestern Europe) is conducive to the survival of some genetic features (light skin, fair hair, long legs, etc.) but also to specific cultural, economic, and political accomplishments. Individuals with the more advantaged characteristics are more likely to survive and reproduce, and thus to determine the composition of the future gene pool. Ultimately, this process of selection creates a group in which unsuitable traits have been eliminated. Group/regional differences are thus the outcome

[46] Clearly, these principles, and the practical implications they represented, were by no means confined to German race science. These comments also suggest a critical, comparative – but unexplored – line of investigation; that is, to specify the social, political, and intellectual conditions that limited the impact of race science on public policy in the United States (in light of the fact that race policy was incorporated into the Constitution, and has been part of legislation to this day). Significantly, Huntington's ideas failed to advance from the stage of "science knowledge" to practical knowledge, and thus into the political-legal arena.

of long-term interaction between climatic conditions and genetic processes.[47]

Formulated in this way, formidable obstacles exist to any effective method of factoring out relevant dimensions and attributes. The claims are filled with operational complexities (e.g. how does one define "inhabitant?"). In addition, no mechanism is specified whereby variations in climate can "produce" the supposed cognitive and behavioral variations, with the result that a curious and ambivalent mixture of both Darwinian and Lamarckian evolutionary principles is invoked (cf. Stehr 1996).

Similar issues emerged in the field of race science, especially as it came to fruition at the Humboldt University in Berlin under the leadership of Eugen Fischer. Whereas climate-based explanations require race or a similar concept to account for intergenerational continuity of mental and behavioral traits, race-based explanations need to identify the causes of sub-species formation. In the latter case, "environmental conditions" play this role through their impact on reproductive capacity. This line of argument is especially evident in the several instances in which Fischer (in Baur et al. [1921] 1931: 173–74) and other race scientists explicitly discuss climate. For instance,

let me remind the reader of the variations in the tint of the skin and the color of the eyes, in the stature, and in the shape of the nose. As an example, I may refer here to the origination of the so-called white skin and of fairness. It is a matter of common observation that comparatively fair individuals appear from time to time in all races. Under natural conditions, however, a fair skin is dangerous to dwellers in the tropics, so that in those regions persons exhibiting such a variation are eliminated by natural selection. The tropical sun is so harmful to the human body when unprotected by clothing or by an ample supply of pigment that a fair and blond race can only arise in temperate regions. The fact that the blond inhabitants of northern Europe exhibit a general distribution of pigment, above all in the iris, exactly like that of the fair domesticated animals but quite unlike that of animals belonging to the polar zone, is plain proof that we have to do here with a form resulting from domestication which is able to maintain itself in temperate climes, whereas similar idiovariations have always been eliminated in the tropics by natural selection and are still so eliminated there whenever they arise ... Nature, therefore, perpetually sees to it that the race shall remain at the acme of efficiency.

In a similar vein, Lenz (in Baur et al. [1921] 1931: 657) observes that "[t]he Nordic environment was not one which allowed human beings

---

[47] Huntington (1926: 76–78; cited in Gilman 1996: 51) does not attribute Jewish traits, including their fabled cleverness, to climate. Rather, in a fairly typical excursion into racial explanation, he links this mental trait to the selective survival of the mentally capable but physically weak after the Jews' defeat at the hands of the Romans in 79 AD.

to dwell in great communities. In view of the scarcity of food, only small kinships could outlive the northern winter. The result was that in the Nordic race there was fostered by selection an inclination towards isolation." Indeed, climate, race, belief and behavior were routinely conflated by a diverse range of authors between the late nineteenth century and the World War II era, including Ellsworth Huntington, who was the subject of devastating critique by P. A. Sorokin on this matter (Sorokin 1928). The parallels among these writings are not coincidental, as evidenced by abundant cross-referencing and co-citation. Rather, climate determinism and race science were complementary approaches to "explaining" why hierarchy and inequality are inevitable, and why certain peoples do or should dominate others.

Race, measured intelligence, and crime rates

In comparison to the climate determinists, the race scientists were less directly concerned with the effects of climate on genetics, on the distribution of human races, or on civilizational transformations. Rather, they were more interested in the impact of genetics on individual "mental traits." Thus, they self-consciously remained more faithful to pure Darwinian principles. Central to this program was their use of IQ test results to operationalize the impact of race on mental ability (see Baur et al. [1921] 1931: Part III).[48] Measuring intelligence and linking it to "race" is, of course, an issue that continues to fascinate and divide.

The position taken by the race scientists of the 1930s is that the anatomy and physiology of the nervous system, and the brain in particular, are shaped by heredity and tell us something about the cultural significance of race. For example, Lenz believed that "there could be no doubt whatever that mental racial differences exist. In each race we find

---

[48] Amidst the controversy generated by the publication of *The Bell Curve* (Herrnstein and Murray 1994), little notice was taken of the fact that the use of IQ scores to measure the dependent variable had been employed several decades earlier by the race scientists and that then, as now, this practice was commonly tied to the promotion of eugenics policy. But even in the 1920s and 1930s, and earlier, the voices of scholars who considered the link between biological and mental traits to be highly suspect were quite strong: Franz Boas (1935: 34), for example, concludes in no uncertain terms in his essay on race in the *Encyclopedia of the Social Sciences* that the only safe conclusion to be drawn is "that careful tests reveal a marked dependence of mental reactions upon conditions of life and that all racial differences which have been established thus far are so much subject to outer circumstances that no proof can be given of innate racial differences ... A positive answer to the claim that racial descent determines mental characteristics would require proof that without regard to cultural environment and to location the same type must always produce the same mental characteristics."

that there are average values in the structure of every organ, the brain included; and therefore for each race there must be an average kind of mental equipment" (Baur et al. [1921] 1931: 633). Later he reasserts this view in the form of a convincing metaphor: "No one can get out of his own skin or rid himself of his own mind, and minds are racially differentiated quite as much as are the tints of the skin" (p. 690).

If one were to assume, as the race scientists did, that performance on IQ tests is a direct measure of brain capacity and functioning, then differences in scores between individuals reflect authentic, hereditary differences in "mental equipment." The final step in the argument was to demonstrate that systematic group-based differences do in fact exist in the IQ performance of the various races, which East, Fischer, and the others believed they had done (see, for example, Lenz, in Bauer et al. [1921] 1931: 629–34). The conclusion, drawn without recourse to Lamarckian mechanisms, is thus straightforward: the races have inherently different mental capacities that can be ranked from high to low, just as species have different, more-or-less advanced traits. Fritz Lenz explicitly emphasizes this advantage of *Rassenwissenschaft* over the climate studies approach: "Thus, race is to a degree the product of environment, but it is not the direct product of environment in the Lamarckian sense of the term, inasmuch as selective process is involved" (Baur et al. [1921] 1931: 656).

Further substantiation of this important link is offered for race scientists by way of comparative crime statistics, with the understanding that a race's level of mental development/IQ is directly correlated with the number of offenses for which members are officially charged: "The *frequency* with which the members of the various races are guilty of *criminal acts* throws some light on the mental differences between these races," asserts Lenz (in Baur et al. [1921] 1931: 678), and, "in the United States, there is much more criminality among the Negroes than among the immigrants from Europe and their descendants. This is obviously due to the fact that the Negroes have less foresight, and that they have less power of resisting the impulses aroused by immediate sensuous impressions."

Whereas present-day social researchers are inclined to be highly skeptical and circumspect about taking such bold leaps among levels of discourse, from (a) genetics to (b) brain anatomy and physiology to (c) psychology (lack of self-control), and thence to (d) criminality, the race and climate scientists were untroubled with such a "transdisciplinary" discourse. In this and related matters, they found support in a rich literature on "criminal body types," including the classic works of Lombroso. When they did take exception to the then-prevailing theories of deviant behaviour, it was, characteristically, to demonstrate that the physical traits associated with criminality are not randomly distributed among all nations, but rather are actually race-specific. Moreover, the supposed associations among mental capacity, behavior, and race by no means end with the explanation of crime. Rather, a broad range of other racial-mental effects are cited throughout the race science and climate studies literature, to which we will return presently. For the moment, however, let us shift our attention to race as such, the *independent* variable in the formulations of *Rassenwissenschaft*.

The reality of race

We now understand that the entity referred to as *race* by race and climate scientists is in fact a *post hoc* construction. Perhaps the more contemporary and more appropriate way to describe it is as a relatively isolated set of geographically proximate populations. Moreover, as the mapping of the human genome indicates, the concept of human races has to be "denaturalized." Human races are not a biological, but a cultural phenomenon. Genetically speaking, there is but one human race.

This has several important consequences. For one thing, because the location of populations and the judgments as to what constitutes "relatively isolated" and "proximate neighborhoods" are all known to vary over time, so-called race is a construct that is variable and contestable. It is not an immutable category beyond the control of all. A population (that is, a naturally occurring human population) is an aggregate of individuals with three essential properties: (1) It is relatively endogamous; (2) it shares a bounded territory; and (3) it shares a social structure that includes (a) rules of endogamy/exogamy and (b) a definition of the population's territory. Members of a specific population resemble one another, within and between generations (and they differ systematically from members of other populations), by virtue of inheritance. However, two distinct and separable types of heritage operate in population dynamics, the one genetic and the other cultural.

The observations of the race scientists, to the effect that individuals who are anthropometrically similar also think and behave alike, are thus accurate; but they are entirely explicable in terms of this dual inheritance. That is, members of a population inherit physical traits through genetics and mental-behavioral traits through enculturation. Included among these culturally inherited propensities are the "power of resisting the impulses aroused by immediate sensuous impressions," as Lysgaard and Schneider (1953) have since established, and the probability of being apprehended and booked for criminal activity *ceteris paribus*, as contemporary criminologists know well.

For the race scientists, there were no essential differences between the evolution of species and that of races. "We may say, indeed," observes Eugen Fischer, "that the formation of species is at the same time the formation of races" (in Baur et al. [1921] 1931: 171). But a population is quite unlike a true species, in fact, because it is only relatively endogamous and its gene pool is thus open. In addition, in human populations, breaches of the rules of endogamy and the consequent alteration of genetic material can occur not only through incidental contact but also by design. No doubt, such transgressions always carry some type of stigma; proscribed exogamy is, after all, deviant behavior. However, not only is marriage between members of distinct populations possible, it has been routinely practiced as long as *Homo sapiens* has existed. Moreover, it is the basis of the formation of "races."

A thought experiment allows us to stipulate the existence of a population that is perfectly isolated from all others; there would be no opportunity either for exogamy, and thus for hybridization, nor for acculturation, whereby members would come to share mental and behavioral traits of others. A population free from external contacts would have all the characteristic features associated with a "race": members would look alike and act alike in ways that clearly distinguish them from members of other populations; and it would be difficult not to conclude that the former is the cause of the latter. If, at some imaginary point in history, the human species consisted only of a number (say one hundred) of such pure populations – all of whom were absolutely cut off from one another, for whatever reason – then there would be one hundred "races."

In reality, such isolation is only possible in a thought experiment; for every human population has experienced sufficient contact with another, geographically proximate, population to produce a discernible level of both hybridization and acculturation. Moreover, the degree to which this has occurred generally varies directly with the distance or degree of accessibility between the populations' respective territories. The result is that at a given moment, within each relatively isolated region of the world, one can find several populations that have observable physical and cultural affinities, whereas substantial differences exist between such regions. These regionally bound population groupings are identical with what the anthropologists, geneticists, and climate scientists of the early twentieth century labeled *races*.

Significantly, the number of such "races" varies with time, depending on how many regions happen to lack access to each other. For example, by this standard one could argue that, in an increasingly mobile world, there are bound to be fewer even moderately "pure" races today than in the past. That is: (a) members of populations within regions are interacting and interbreeding with greater frequency and, at the same time, (b) inhabitants of the various regions are establishing routine contact with one another.

On the other hand, at the dawn of the Age of European Exploration in the early sixteenth century, vast oceans and mountain ranges still divided the world into regions so isolated from one another (although obviously not absolutely so) that each could sustain distinctive, identifiable inter-population gene pools and cultures. It is in this context that the conception of a humanity consisting of five distinct major racial groups gained ascendancy: Caucasians in Europe (subdivided into the four "great European races," see above), Negroes in Africa, Australoids in the Pacific, Mongoloids in Asia, and (their cousins) the Amerinds of the New World. This categorization was codified as, during the latter part of the nineteenth century, exploration and discovery gave way to the need for explanation (and justification). Such an explanation was provided by the early anthropologists, sociologists, and geographers, and ultimately was reified and elevated as the most efficacious variable in the race scientist's repertoire.

However, the archeological record makes it clear that within at least the first four of the five world regions, the predominant population grouping ("race") had been formed from earlier contacts between previously isolated populations (that is, isolated prior to the technological innovations that made access possible). Thus, at some point not long before 1500, the number of then-isolated regions, and thus the number of "races," most likely exceeded five; and prior to the Bronze–Iron Age transition, some five to ten thousand years ago, there may well have been scores or even hundreds of so-called sub-species of *Homo sapiens*. Over the long course, "racial" barriers are routinely broken down (and in theory at least, can be consciously or inadvertently constructed), because they do not really exist. Rather, they reflect a combination of demographic, historical, legal, and technological conditions that are highly dynamic and, in principle, partly under human control.

Much of this is common-sense knowledge. Yet the appeal of the concept of race is apparently very subtle, one that easily yields to the simpler idea that biology and genetics determine both belief and behavior. Perhaps it is because the realities of population, culture, and dual inheritance are so complex that those championing their use as key explanatory variables lost out to racism in the internal struggles in Weimar-era anthropology – and elsewhere. However, the true cause of race science's ascendancy is more likely to be found in its compatibility with Draconian public policy priorities. It is difficult to justify campaigns to secure *Lebensraum* and to achieve a *judenfreie* world if we must deal with "geographically proximate, historically variable population groupings." However, if one proclaims oneself to be secure in the knowledge that individuals are the way they are because of deep, natural, and unalterable genetic forces, then race hygiene has a very important role to play in statecraft.

Race works

In this section, we return for a closer look at the alleged work race does. We have noted that race scientists construed race-based "mental capacities" or "mental traits" to be the outcome of observed variations in inherited physical characteristics, including genetic determination of the anatomy of the brain and "internal secretions" (i.e. hormones). Viewed in this manner, there is much that contemporary social and biological scientists would find sound in this association. Undoubtedly, our nervous and endocrine systems are as subject to the principles of genetic inheritance as are the colors of our eyes and hair. To the extent that the demographic preservation and alteration of gene pools occurs as discussed above, one could properly conclude that the different "races" (that is, geographically proximate population groupings at a given moment in history) do have distinct somatic endowments in this respect.

However, what sorts of "mental capacities" are presumed to result from such endowments? We have already seen that (a) intelligence, as measured by IQ score, and (b) morality, as measured by official crime statistics, were especially strongly emphasized by leading race scientists in Germany and the United States. The apparent reason for this preference is that these quantitative indicators were readily available at the time, and were considered to be eminently reliable and valid by contemporary standards. Today we know better, and understand that these are essentially contested indicators.

Although the debate over the link between IQ scores and "race" continues to rage (and will likely be sustained by the remnants of the modern eugenics movement and others), by their very nature these scores must, to some as yet unknown degree, reflect learned characteristics of a very narrow type (that is, narrow in comparison to what we mean less formally by "intelligence"). No method has yet been devised to discern the mental capacities of a newborn infant; and even if one existed, it could not discern between neurological and hormonal traits that are directly genetically determined and those resulting from pre-partum conditions – such as the diet of the mother, the kinds of drugs or medication she ingests during or just prior to pregnancy, and the like.

If there are, indeed, systematic "racial" differences in IQ scores, they cannot be wholly (or even substantially) explained by genetics. People learn to exercise the skills for which IQ tests award points just as surely as they learn to read and write. As for crime rates, not only are they known to be socially constructed, but there are even greater obstacles to their use in racial explanations. For here the case is even clearer that people's enculturation experiences and social backgrounds are decisive in determining not only their propensity to commit crimes, but also the probability that they will be processed as criminals, whether or not they are actually guilty.

It is entirely possible that all "races" are equally inclined to immoral behavior, whether or not official crime rates adequately measure these propensities. But it is most difficult to move beyond selective public perceptions and the prejudices of some scientists. Race scientists such as Lenz contrasted the presumed inherent deviancy of "Negroes" to the evident law-abiding character of "Nordics." But was it not the Negroes who were the victims of kidnapping, slavery, and starvation during the colonial era, and was it not Nordics who planned and carried out the Holocaust? What is immoral, what is criminal, after all?

Notwithstanding the difficulties that attend the use of intelligence and criminality measures as indicators of the work race is presumed to do, race scientists did not hesitate to venture into even more uncertain territory in identifying mental capacities with several other traits. It is significant that, in contrast to their treatment of intelligence and morality, their assertions concerning racial variations among these other factors uniformly lack quantitative support. Instead, their empirical "proofs" consistently rely on common-sense knowledge, accounts of travelers, and quotations from classic and contemporary poets, philosophers, and the like. Indeed, one finds a remarkable discontinuity among the race scientists in their concern for the accuracy and quantifiability of the independent variable, IQ and crime on one hand, and their decidedly ambiguous and non-quantitative approach to the (crucial) "mental traits" on the other.

Among these unmeasured characteristics, one of the most commonly cited (among race scientists, climate determinists, and others) is the capacity to conceptualize beyond immediate sense experiences. This cognitive trait is understood to be formative, and to be closely associated with several other characteristics, including the ability or propensity to defer impulse gratification, level of energy, industriousness, and (of course) a high IQ. Systematic variations in this trait are assumed to be inherent, immutable, and hierarchically ordered in relation to survival adaptability.

Thus, proponents of *Rassenwissenschaft* correlated the ability to imagine, to think abstractly, and to defer impulse gratification with the hierarchical classification of the living races of *Homo sapiens*. The Australoid peoples, whom Lenz refers to as "Australian Blackfellows," and who are deemed to have "mental characteristics closely akin to Neanderthal man" (Baur et al. [1921] 1931: 627), are the least developed in these respects. "Attempts to teach them agriculture and to make them settle down have been a complete failure. The chief cause of the inability of these primitive races to attain a higher degree of civilisation would seem to be their lack of imagination." Moreover, he warns, "Those who hold a more favorable view of the possibilities of such primitive races should be reminded that these latter have had just as long a time as we [Nordics] ourselves have had in which to develop a higher civilization."

At the other extreme from the Australian Blackfellows are nature's favored Nordics, who in respect of mental gifts, as we have seen, "march in the lead of mankind" (Lenz, in Baur et al. [1921] 1931: 655). These gifts, according to Fischer (1913: 150), include "great energy and industry," "vigorous imagination," and "high intelligence. Conjoined with these," he continues, "are foresight, organising ability, and artistic capacity."

Lenz and his colleagues identified numerous other "mental traits" that were presumed to be racially/genetically determined (some of which are identified in our Appendix). Significantly, although these include all sorts of "capacities" and "propensities," the race scientists attempted to connect each one with what they understood to be the fundamental cognitive abilities; that is, imagination, etc. Indeed, the fact that the race scientists attributed a kind of master role to imagination and deferred gratification has additional implications for analyzing their concept of racial hierarchy, in general, and the place they assigned to the Jews, in particular:[49]

1. First, it helps us see why these images had such popular appeal, to appreciate the ease with which they could be comprehended because they resonated with common experiences: their "elective affinity" with

---

[49] The Marburg psychologist Erich Jaensch (1930) has been credited with providing the formative theory of the Jewish mind, although his major work appeared several years after the publication of the sections of the Baur, Fischer, and Lenz volume cited in the text (see Jaensch 1927).

Nazi race policy. The races are depicted as representing different levels of development, in both the evolutionary and the life-cycle senses of the term. Just as newborns cannot cope with complex environmental conditions, the less-advanced races are incapable of mastering the challenges of modern civilization. Racial "toddlers" cannot control themselves. Like infants, they are ultimately dependent, and at best a source of amusement (because they like to play and sing). In contrast, the most mature of the races has the capacity – if not the obligation – to control the destiny of all others. Moreover, armed with the advanced knowledge of race hygiene, the Nordic people have the means rationally to effect the healthy maturation of humanity.

The discourse of race hygiene thus allows one to set the process of natural selection in motion in order to maximize the aggregate propensity to defer gratification, to imagine, and thus to succeed under civilized conditions. "Self-control is, perhaps, the most distinctive among the characteristics of the Nordic race, and upon this depends in large measure the Nordic gift for civilisation. Races lacking in self-control are unable to be guided by long views and to pursue remoter ends" (Lenz, in Baur et al. [1921] 1931: 656).

2. Second, whereas some races are as easily controlled as human infants, those at intermediate levels of advancement ("teenagers") display a difficult combination of advanced and infantile traits. Although lacking the complete capacity for deferred gratification and rational behavior exhibited by Nordics, these peoples are "clever" enough to resist the kind of disciplined subjugation to which Negroes, Blackfellows, and Mongoloids appear to have adapted effectively. Included in this category are the Orientals and the Near Eastern race – at whose juncture lie the Jews (and Slavs, etc.). Because they are neither children nor adults in the phylogenic scheme of things, they require "special treatment." The Jews are thus understood to be a prime example of a degenerate race, but not because they are consistently "lower." Rather, their degeneracy stems from the fact that they reflect an especially dangerous moment in the evolutionary process, at which intelligence and immaturity freely comingle.

Classifying the Jews

Our final section on the nature of race science considers the manner in which practitioners approached the "Jewish problem." From the preceding commentary, it may already be evident that the project of explaining the hereditary mental capacities of this group was at once extremely important and rife with problems exceptionally difficult for the race scientist to resolve. Whereas official Nazi doctrine was clear and unequivocal (that is, Jews are a degenerate form whose mental and behavioral traits are inimical to social and political progress), the academic race scientists were less inclined to draw such definitive conclusions.

Rather, the extensive commentary that Lenz, Fischer, East, Stoddard, and others offered represents a curious mixture of respect, admiration, and mistrust for distinctively "Jewish ways," an attitude clearly drawn from the extensive literature on the Jewish mentality that had accumulated in the preceding decades (see Gilman 1996).[50] The race scientists and their colleagues argued that the Jewish race represents a uniquely heterogeneous mixture of genetic material, and therefore of associated mental characteristics. This was understood to be the outcome of their fabled wanderings, and thus due to (a) a combination of several discrepant, formative climatic factors and (b) frequent hybridization.

Notwithstanding these rampant impurities, the definitive analyses of Fischer and Lenz classed Jews as a branch of the Near Eastern race, "into whose racial composition the Oriental [itself a branch of the Mediterranean] stock enters very largely." Thus, "a Jew can usually be recognized at once by his bodily appearance. In North Germany it is hardly possible to mistake a Jew. But the mental racial peculiarities of the Jews are more marked even than the bodily, so that we might speak of the Jews as a 'mental race.' The fundamentals of the Jewish mind are those already described as characteristic of the Near Eastern race ... but even more strongly developed" (Lenz, in Baur et al. [1921] 1931: 667).

Eugen Fischer, in particular, made a special effort to unpack the complexities of Jewish genetics by way of a long historical account in his chapter "Description of the Races of Man (Anthropography)." This discussion is distinguished by the author's explicit concern with the interaction between Oriental and Near Eastern components,

---

[50] As Gilman indicates, one can discern a kind of triple stereotype developing in Europe and the United States, as the influence of Darwinian thought spread throughout and beyond academic circles: (a) Jews are *genetically* different; (b) this difference is associated with their superior intelligence; and (c) there may indeed be a sinister side to their extraordinary wits. The body of literature on the subject of Jews and Jewish "mental traits" upon which the formal race science of the Weimar and Nazi eras was based is thus extensive (see Gilman 1996: 33–40, 53 – where Lenz is cited, and 211–14, nn. 1–16). It includes works by Galton (1892; 1962) and, in the United States, Mark Twain ([1895] 1985; also Gilman 1993). Jewish writers at the peripheries of the academic establishment even created a "positive" race science, in which supposed Jewish physical and "mental" traits were viewed as the most advanced (see Efron 1994; Gilman 1996, 63–71).

his reference to the distinction between Sephardic and Ashkenazi Jews, and his insistence that, all of these complicating factors aside, Jews and Teutons are fundamentally different types of human beings. Thus, a considerable section of this account may be worth repeating:

If from among the Semitic people, the Hebrews are to be singled out as especially interesting, I may say that these also are the products of the same general racial intermixture, the Near Eastern and the Oriental races being the fundamental stocks. If to-day among the Jews we distinguish two main branches, the Sephardim and the Ashkenazim, ethnological study shows that among the former the Oriental racial admixture predominates, and among the latter the Near Eastern. The differences among the Jews in Europe are to be accounted for by their mingling with the peoples among whom they respectively dwell. The southern Jews, the Sephardim, have been largely crossed with Mediterranean blood, whereas the eastern Jews, the Ashkenazim, have been crossed with Alpine and Mongoloid blood. We may suppose that at the very beginning of the diaspora, the Jews who had been more strongly influenced by a Near Eastern admixture in northern Palestine must have tended to migrate northward, whereas the Jews of southern Palestine, in whom there was a large infusion of Oriental elements, must have inclined to sail westward across the sea into the countries of southern Europe – so that the two main branches began to become sundered in those very early days. The Sephardim and the Ashkenazim represent different racial mixtures. After what has been said it is almost superfluous to insist once more that we are just as little entitled to speak of a "Jewish race" as of a "Teutonic race," inasmuch as the Jews, no less than the Teutons, are the outcome of particular racial minglings. Nevertheless, we can describe the main racial characters of the Jews and of the Teutons, respectively, distinguishing them clearly from one another [evidently a very important project]. (Fischer, in Baur et al. [1921] 1931: 202)

This notion of "minglings" also dominates the race scientists' characterization of how race works in the case of Jewish mental traits. Many of the geneticists, geographers, and anthropologists of the era busily contributed to this account; in Germany, Fritz Lenz took the lead in this regard – as he did on questions of racial psychology in general.

As measured by the quantifiable indicators, IQ and criminality, Jews were actually understood to exhibit markedly *superior* traits. "Some of the Near Eastern and Oriental elements among the Jews are fully equal to the Nordics in many domains of intellectual life, and are superior to them in some" (Lenz, in Baur et al. [1921] 1931: 655). Lenz also notes that "the Jews greatly excel in intelligence and alertness," that "Jews are precocious," and that "the Jews have produced noted scientists in the domains of physics, mathematics, medicine, and psychology ... their strength lies in their highly developed sense for numbers, and in their gift for formal logic. It is to these same hereditary factors, doubtless, that the Jews owe their remarkable skill at chess. Most of the great masters of the game have been Jews" (Lenz, in Baur et al. [1921] 1931: 670–71).

The American geneticist Edward East (1929: 212) relates Jewish genius to heredity, with strong praise for what he claims is their "selective breeding": "Among the leading hundred scientists [in J. M. Cattell's 1915 study], 7 were Jewish, 6 of them having been invited [to the United States] to fill scientific positions. This fact speaks well for the race as a whole." Nevertheless, he does leave open the possibility that degeneracy and intelligence are not mutually exclusive:

The degenerate product of a bad genetic combination is not saved by the record made by others of his race. Greatness is an individual matter. There are no uniformly great races. Historically the Jews are great. They have wandered over the earth and have mingled their blood with the blood of other peoples. Contrary to general belief, they form one of the most variable groups on earth, as Fishberg has shown. Starting as a mixed race, they have become more mixed. In every country they have produced exceptional individuals, and these exceptional individuals have usually married well, whether within or without their faith. Stringently selective breeding, therefore, has brought forth individuals celebrated in nearly every line of endeavor. (East 1929: 178–79)

Associated with the Jews' high level of intelligence is an admirable degree of sobriety and a remarkably peaceable nature. "The sobriety of Jews, their power to resist the seductive charms of alcohol, might set an example to the Germans. Obviously, their sobriety is based on their hereditary mental endowment"; and "the greater frequency of assaults among Christians than among Jews is, presumably, due not to religion but to race" (Lenz, in Baur et al. [1921] 1931: 674, 680).

Despite these favorable traits, it was nevertheless evident to the race scientists that there is a darker side to Jewish intelligence and morality, and that the "positive" attributes did not exculpate the race: For example, "Jews show comparatively little interest in concrete natural objects, their chief concern being with all the factors of mental activity" (Lenz, in Baur et al. [1921] 1931: 671). "The visualizing and technical abilities of the Jews are comparatively small" (p. 672). Indeed, this lack of concreteness and preference for the abstract – "the abstract gift of Jews" (p. 654) – are claimed to underlie several other hereditary Jewish traits, including their choice of occupations.

Similarly, the Jews' propensity for fraud and for the obscene ought to condition our interpretation of their apparently low crime rates, and our understanding of several related aspects of their business and cultural practices. Lenz (in Baur et al. [1921] 1931: 681, quoting E. Wulffen) observes that

if we are to reach an objective judgment concerning the criminality of Jews, we must compare Jews, not with the non-Jewish population in general, but with those sections of the non-Jewish population which occupy a similar social position to the Jews. My own impression is that when this is done it will be found that deeds of violence are no more frequent in the non-Jewish than in the Jewish population, but that fraud and the use of insulting language really are commoner among Jews ... It is said that Jews are especially responsible for the circulation of obscene books and pictures, and for carrying on the White Slave trade.

A related mental trait also figures prominently in the race scientists' account of the Jew. This is variously referred to as "empathy" and "sociability." It seems to stem from the Jewish propensity for the abstract, and is presumed to explain a great deal about why they behave as they do. "The Jew is more often importunate than the Teuton, and is more sensitive; but even when he has been mortified by a repulse, he will usually return to the charge; for by nature he is eminently sociable" (Lenz, in Baur et al. [1921] 1931: 668).

Significantly, this quality is associated with the Jews' presumed talent at manipulating others. "Jews are characterised, not only by shrewdness and alertness, by diligence and perseverance, but also by an amazing capacity to put themselves in others' places (empathy) and for inducing others to accept their guidance" (p. 668). Here we also gain an insight into why Jews apparently dominate certain occupations and avoid others. "In part [their] devotion to medicine may doubtless arise from the circumstance that the Jew dreads pain, illness, and death more than does the Teuton; but a powerful factor may also be that the success of the physician so largely depends upon his capacity for exerting a mental influence over his fellow human beings" (p. 672).

Such occupational selectivity appears to extend well beyond medicine, and even to the much-feared job of making social revolutions. "A strikingly large proportion of celebrated musicians have been Jews [p. 646] ... The Jewish talent for living among purely imaginary ideas as if they were concrete facts is advantageous, not only to the actor but also to the barrister, the trader and the demagogue ... In revolutionary movements, hysterically predisposed Jews play a great part, being able to give themselves up unreservedly to utopian ideas, and therefore able with a sense of inward sincerity to make convincing promises to the masses" (p. 673).

Armed with such an understanding, the student of race science is thus able, in a single formulation, to explain (a) why Jews are successful;

(b) why they are not to be trusted; and (c) why so many of them are doctors, musicians, *and* revolutionaries. This formulation also provides the foundation for one of the most important of the race scientists' concerns: explaining the evident economic success of Germany's Jews, the "well known business ability of Jews" (Lenz, in Baur et al. [1921] 1931: 644). For detailed commentary on this trait, Lenz refers his reader to the political economist and sociologist Werner Sombart, who "has given a brilliant description of the Jewish talent for economic life" (p. 669; see also Stehr and Grundmann 2001).

Most important, perhaps, one must note whence this talent came, for "the quality is not peculiar to the Jews, being shared by other Orientals and especially with the Greeks and Armenians" (Lenz, in Baur et al. [1921] 1931: 644). This is the capacity to be middlemen, intermediaries, and to excel at occupations that emphasize this talent. Given these roots, "they naturally turned to commerce and similar occupations. The result was that, in the main, only those Jews could found a family who had special aptitude for acting as intermediaries in dealing with the goods produced by others, and in stimulating and guiding others' wishes" (p. 667).

Through the mechanism of natural selection, these circumstances ultimately produced the familiar association between certain lines of work and Jewishness: "the professions they especially choose, and practice with advantage to themselves, are those of merchant, small trader, money-lender, journalist, author, publisher, politician, actor, musician, lawyer, and medical practitioner" (p. 668). Moreover, "The theatres are for the most part in the hands of Jews; in the United States exclusively so, according to Henry Ford [citing *The International Jew*].[51] The same is true of the movies. A large proportion of daily newspapers and other periodicals are issued by Jews, edited by Jews, and provided with articles by Jewish journalists" (p. 668).[52]

---

[51] Henry Ford was well respected in Nazi Germany and played an especially prominent role in popularizing anti-Semitism there as well as in the United States; he is also one of the few Americans cited by Lenz, and the only one cited by Hitler in *Mein Kampf*. Leading US *academic* race scientists of the era included Madison Grant and Lothrop Stoddard. See, for example, Grant (1918) and Stoddard (1924). A brief but thorough account of the connection between US race science and Nazi race policy, via the eugenics movement, is provided by Kühl (1994). Gilman (1996: 233, n. 1) observes that "The association of the Jew with 'intelligence' is an old American trope."

[52] As always, Adolf Hitler was far more blunt in making essentially the same point. In a communication with Himmler in 1942, he observed that "the discovery of the Jewish virus is one of the greatest revolutions that has taken place in the world. The battle in which we are engaged today is one of the same sort as the battle waged, during the last century, by Pasteur and Koch. How many diseases have their origin in the Jewish virus! We shall regain our health only by eliminating the Jew. Everything has a cause,

In addition to accounting for their "well-known" business acumen, the Jews' empathic/manipulative nature presumably contributes to their most sinister and mysterious racial trait: their ability to blend into any social milieu. This assertion, to the effect that Jews have a special capacity to assimilate wherever they find themselves, was presumed to be common-sense knowledge by the race scientists. Indeed, this characteristic, in particular, had been anticipated in earlier, prescientific studies of race, such as that of the French historian, Anatole Leroy-Beaulieu (1895; cited in Gilman 1996: 50). Because, according to Leroy-Beaulieu, the Jew has a special "faculty for assimilating," he "responds more rapidly than ourselves to the influences of his environment and times." Lenz updates this observation with an illuminating discussion of this talent, in which he compares the Jew in relation to the Gentile with the Viceroy butterfly in relation to the Monarch (whom the Viceroy imitates to an uncanny degree).

If the peculiarities of Jews are less conspicuous in the bodily than in the mental domain, this may arise from the circumstance that Jews whose bodily aspect was markedly exotic were less successful than those whose bodily type resembled their hosts. The instinctive desire not to look singular would also operate by sexual selection, by a preferential choice of a partner in marriage who did not look too much unlike the hosts. The adoption of Gentile names by many Jews is likewise a manifestation of the wish not to be recognisable as Jews. Insofar as the type has become less conspicuous thanks to the working of such a process of selection, we have to do with the mimicry which is familiarly observed wherever a living creature gains advantage in the struggle for existence by acquiring a resemblance to some other organism. Thus we find different species of animals which are very closely alike, and which may be akin, but which are sharply distinguished each from the others in manner of instinct. Among butterflies I know many such species. The great resemblance here is obviously due to the fact that the mimicry has been advantageous to one of these species in their struggle for existence. (Lenz, in Baur et al. [1921] 1931: 667–68)

While an advantageous trait for the Jew, this ability to mimic can be potentially disastrous to the host population. The danger is especially great when combined with a talent for empathy and manipulation, a tendency toward hysteria, and an inclination to foster revolutionary demagoguery. If we add to this the fact that the race in which such gifts are most developed also dominates in business, science, the press, entertainment, and other key positions of social influence, the potential threat to other races is evident. Lenz's readers are left to draw their own conclusions concerning the racial-hygiene implications of

nothing comes by chance" (Cameron and Stevens 1988: 332; cited in Burleigh and Wippermann 1991: 107).

this syndrome, but within the decade that followed the publication of his "findings," the circle was closed in the form of *judenrein* policy. Significantly, a great deal of effort was expended by those who formulated the policy to establish reliable (genealogical, anthropometric, etc.) criteria for "unmasking" Gentile-appearing Jews.

Although well developed for scientific and business activities, music, and the like, the Jewish mind appears to suffer from a type of closure, most probably the result of its preference for the abstract. In discounting the feasibility of a Zionist solution to the Jewish problem, Lenz (Baur et al. [1921] 1931: 669) invokes this incapacity: "Owing to their deficient talent or inclination for the primary work of production, it would seem that a State system consisting exclusively of Jews would be impossible." In any case, there are clear limits to expanding Jewish intellectual horizons. "Jewish authors seem to have a preference for quoting one another rather than Gentiles, and this may be mainly attributed to their finding the thoughts of their co-nationals more congenial" (p. 667).

In connection with this account of the recalcitrance of the Jewish mind, Lenz makes a remarkable observation, mentioning it not once but several times in the course of debate with his critics. Obviously concerned with establishing that racial characteristics are indeed genetically determined and immutable, he derides explanations that suggest that traits such as empathy, business acumen, and preference for certain trades may be acquired during the life of an individual. Employing the logic that typifies the *Rassenwissenschaft* approach, he classes all such explanations as "Lamarckism," and dismisses them as unscientific. But he goes even further, suggesting that a preference for the doctrine is itself a race-based mental trait, especially prevalent among Jews!

This commentary forms part of a long and extremely interesting polemic by Lenz (in Baur et al. [1921] 1931: 674), which concludes with a telling remark: "I drew attention to the fact that most of the Lamarckians are Jews, not in order to give the mercy stroke to Lamarckism, but in order to illustrate the psychology of Jews."

Thus, the race scientists raised a final, fatal doubt concerning the Jewish mind. Not only is this otherwise intelligent race prone to guile, deception, manipulation, and lofty ambition, it is constitutionally incapable of accepting the well-founded conclusions of race science. "This inevitably arouses the impression that they must have some reason for fighting shy of exposition of any racial questions" (p. 674).

Judaism is a faith that, like Christianity, had special historical appeal to various peoples who ultimately settled in Europe. One can convert into the faith, and one may convert out of it. And, also like Christianity, it has spread to and been accepted by minority groups on all the continents. The dark-bearded, caftan-wearing man who, as reported in *Mein Kampf*, so shocked Hitler during his days of awakening in Vienna, and who later became the stereotyped symbol of the Eternal Jew of anti-Semitic lore, was almost surely an Ashkanazi: a Jew of Central and Eastern European ancestry. But one wonders about what Hitler's reaction would have been if he had just happened to run into a Mongoloid Chinese Jew, an Oriental Bene Israeli from Bombay, or a Negroid Jew from Ethiopia. These "minglings" were as unknown to him as they were to any ordinary Austrian citizen; and if the race and climate scientists were aware of such Jews, they were never mentioned in their accounts – perhaps because *to them* they represented inexplicable anomalies.[53]

In their catalogue of the physical and mental traits of the Jewish race, the race scientists were in fact arguing from ignorance. The object of their studies (until it was for all practical purposes decimated) was actually a set of ethnic sub-populations within Germany and several other European populations who were substantially more like their fellow Europeans than their fellow non-European Jews. Yet the category and its attributes were good enough, familiar enough, to evoke a favorable response among the public that mattered. Whether or not it was accurate down to the last detail, it proved capable of isolating "undesirable" elements in society and providing the means to eliminate them. As was the case in its treatment of the other races, race scientists employed Jewish ethnic stereotypes as the dependent variables in their explanatory scheme, and as a justification for the practice of eugenics, euthanasia, and at last murder. Whatever its scientific merits, it was nevertheless a science that "worked" – or at least very nearly so.

The association we have explored suggests that the Holocaust might not have occurred, or at least that things would have turned out quite differently, if this new form of anti-Semitism had lacked the support and scientific legitimation afforded by Lenz and his colleagues. That is, Hitler's road might still have led to Auschwitz if race science had never existed; but it would have been far more difficult, "technologically" and politically, to have undertaken the slaughter of Jews and members of other "degenerate races" that began in the 1930s without the academic respectability that *Rassenwissenschaft* provided to Hitler's final solution.

[53] The Jewish Museum of Amsterdam has an exhibit of photographs of Jewish women from all parts of the world that beautifully illustrates the "racial" diversity of the Jewish peoples. The contrast between the first photo, of a Polish-born Israeli girl dressed in blue jeans and T-shirt, and the last, a black girl from sub-Saharan Africa in tribal dress with the "chai" symbol on her neck, is especially striking.

Knowledge and power

This discussion of race science has focused on the conditions under which scientific *knowledge* comes to be translated into action. In the context of a general theory of social action, knowledge can best be defined as a faculty or *capacity for action*. Alternatively, it can be understood as the ability to describe, in the case of a particular thing or process, how that thing is generated or set in motion. Therefore, from a social action perspective, knowledge is underdetermined. This suggests that knowledge may remain unused or dormant; and, in any case, that it is by no means assured that knowledge will be employed in any optimum sense. And, as we have seen, of course, knowledge can also find its application for the purpose of highly irrational ends. Knowledge as a capacity for action does not prejudice its use, nor does it predetermine the ways and the circumstances in which it may find application. Knowledge is not a *deus ex machina*. The uses to which it is put and the impacts that follow from its application depend on local conditions and contexts (cf. Stehr 1994: 91–120).

Thus, our observations also are offered with a sense of some urgency, since, as we have tried to show, the power of scientific knowledge does not necessarily derive from its faithfulness to the truth. This reminder is especially pertinent today, following the discovery that Sweden had a long-standing, state-sponsored eugenics program, as noted above, and in view of a renewal of social scientific interest in race (cf. Lieberman and Reynolds 1995; McKee 1994; also Weinstein 1997: 47, nn. 2–4), in the hereditary bases of behavior, and in the momentous effects of climate on character and society (see, for example, Rushton 1995; Lerner 1992). Paradoxically, in this age of globalization, *race* and apposite concepts are experiencing a period of considerable cultural resonance, as is evident from the frequency and intensity of debate on the subject played out in the mass media, in political forums, and in academic circles.[54] A range of academics, including social scientists, natural scientists, and some self-identified "critical" scholars, have increasingly granted race and/or climate a central explanatory role in accounting for inequalities or group differences.[55] Based on the case study we have documented,

[54] Daryl Michael Scott (1997) provides an insightful discussion of the race concept and race policy in the United States. Two historical works, one an essay and the other a collection, that relate specifically to Nazi Germany, Mason (1993) and Crew (1994), are noteworthy, as is the above-cited monograph by Rushton (1995).

[55] In Germany today, race science is by no means absent from teaching and research in the university setting, nor is it simply dormant. An article in *Der Spiegel* (May 12, 1997) refers to ongoing controversies in the University of Hamburg and its Institute for Anthropology, which is dominated by race scientists and their students. In addition,

it is evident that such an approach can acquire considerable power in practice quite independently of its "objective" merits.

Conclusion

The link between scientific knowledge and public policy was provided through a network of personal and ideological affiliations, with a worldview at its basis that centered on racial ideas and concepts. These ranged from popular ideas to scientifically founded frameworks. Race science was, after all, a respected academic discipline before the Weimar Republic and Hitler's rise to power, also outside Germany. It became a deadly tool of legitimation in Germany when the ruling party sought to implement a policy of ethnic cleansing combined with imperial expansion. Racial doctrines were especially appealing because they resonated with beliefs deeply held by the public, politicians, and scientists themselves. We have argued that the Hitler regime did not pervert science; that race science was a science. It is perhaps astonishing to see how a shared cultural outlook (which was largely anti-Semitic) could be turned into a seemingly scientific justification for the enhancement of the Aryan race. In so doing, its proponents were confident to enroll the power of science for their purposes. As they never tired of repeating, it was scientific truth, not prejudice, that drove their policies.

We concur with Proctor (1988a: 286), who describes the use of science by the Nazi regime as follows:

The Nazis took major problems of the day – problems of race, gender, crime, and poverty – and transformed them into medical or biological problems. Nazi philosophers argued that Germany was teetering on the brink of racial collapse, and that racial hygiene was needed to save Germany from "racial suicide." Racial hygiene thus combined a philosophy of biological determinism with a belief that science might provide a technical fix for social problems. Harnessed to a political party mandated to root out all forms of racial, social, or spiritual "disease," the ideology of biological determinism helped drive the kinds of programs for which the Nazis have become infamous.

there are at least two other anthropology units, at the Universities of Mainz and Kiel, where subjects with intellectual affinities to race science continue to be practiced. This is not all that surprising, considering the relative ease with which race scientists, race hygienists, and their assistants from the Nazi era, including Fritz Lenz in 1947 at the Universität Göttingen, were able to retain their posts, or found themselves appointed after the war in West Germany to university chairs and as heads of research institutes in Human Genetics, Anthropology, Population Science and Psychiatry (see Kühl 1997: 176–81; Ash 1999). The emergence of a kind of neo-climate determinism is in turn critically discussed in Stehr and von Storch (1997).

This could serve as a cautionary tale when considering other, more benign cases of public policy. Here, too, people have defended specific courses of action with reference to scientific truth, disregarding the fact that it is largely a public choice to identify and implement sound and just policies. In other words, even if findings from race science were "true," it would not follow automatically that different races should be treated differently (let alone be exterminated). However, if such a position had been firmly grounded in society, the Nazis' race extermination policy would have been much more difficult to justify through science alone.

Appendix

Race works: some other cognitive and affective consequences

In addition to the imagination/deferred-gratification syndrome, the race scientists identified a wide range of other characteristics presumed to reflect the races' respective mental gifts – again with their character- istic lack of interest in measurement. Although these are typically pre- sented unsystematically, they tend to cohere in what might be termed "packets of stereotypes": bits of common lore concerning how certain kinds of people are supposed to behave.

Because the general context of the commentary establishes a close and easy connection among several formative traits, principally the abil- ity to defer impulse gratification, intelligence, maturity, mental health, and "Nordicness," no effort is made by the commentators to indicate precisely which of these traits gives rise to other specific differences.

Emotionality is discussed frequently in this context. For instance, Lenz contrasts "the Negro" who "vacillates between a cheerful indifference and a hopeless depression" (in Baur et al. [1921] 1931: 629) with a typ- ical member of "the Nordic race," who "has little taste for superficial sociability and superficial cheerfulness, but the current of his feeling runs strong and deep. In warm cordiality the Nordic race is inferior to none" (p. 660). Thus, what we would today label "bipolar disease" (manic-depressive psychosis) seems to the race scientists clearly to be correlated with genetic inheritance along racial lines, in association with lack of intelligence and criminality. Notwithstanding the continuing uncertainty about the causes of this fairly common affliction, the reader is presumed to understand how and why this somewhat astounding var- iety of personality and cultural characteristics go together: because the "good" ones are more advanced/Nordic/white, whereas the "bad" ones are regressive, un-Nordic, and black.

In some cases the imputed association is evident. Sexual behavior, for instance, obviously reflects a degree of maturity and the propensity to delay gratification: "We may suppose ... that the notorious lack of sexual control manifested by Negroes is not so much due to any exceptional strength of the sexual impulse as to general childish lack of the power of restraint" (Lenz, in Baur et al. [1921] 1931: 634). Predictably, in contrast, "The Nordic is fastidious in his love, but never cold. Frenssen, the Norse poet, who is well acquainted with the Norse mind [and thus, one supposes, is to be accepted as a scientific authority on the subject] lays frequent stress upon the vigor of the sexual temperament among the Nordics, and is right in so doing" (p. 660).

In other cases, however, the connection is less direct. While seemingly remote from the realm of biological drives, the ability to create complex organizations, too, is understood to be a racial mental trait. "The organizational and political faculties are very poorly organized in the Negroes. They have never produced any kind of social structure worthy to be compared to those in Europe and Asia" (Lenz, in Baur et al. [1921] 1931: 634). However, "In the Mongol, it is above all the hereditary factors tending to promote an aptitude for social life which are well developed" (p. 635).

Standing somewhere between these sorts of biological and social capacities in Lenz's catalogue of hereditary mental traits are what we might term aspects of character, or even taste. These include:

1. Honesty: "[E]very Chinaman lies, even when he seems unlikely to gain anything by it" (Lenz, in Baur et al. [1921] 1931: 637, citing "a medical practitioner who has lived for many years among the Chinese"). Also, "The southern European has less sense of truth and honor than the Nordic" (p. 641). On the other hand, "In the Nordic lands, one can trust the word of a manual worker ... Such honesty and straightforwardness are, to say the least of it, by no means the rule in southern lands" (p. 660).
2. Frugality: "The Mongol's most powerful weapon in his competition with persons of other races is his frugality" (p. 637).
3. Appreciation of music: "Near Easterners are extremely musical; indeed, I think the Near Eastern is the most musical of all races" (p. 645). "For music, which expresses the emotions of the soul, I do not consider the Nordic race to be especially gifted" (p. 661). Lest one suspect that this renders the latter race somehow inferior, Lenz quickly adds, "Although it is true that a great many among the most distinguished composers are mainly of Nordic blood, it seems to me [*QED?*] that what they owe to their Nordic heritage is rather their mental creative faculty than their musical endowment proper."
4. Capacity for work, creativity, business acumen, and the like: Whereas the Negro is "clever with his hands, is endowed with considerable

technical adroitness, so that he can easily be trained in mental crafts"
(p. 629), "no other race can compare with the Mongoloid in its capacity for sticking to primitive and monotonous labor" (p. 637). The
Oriental race, in contrast to both of these less advanced groups, "is
distinguished alike for its shrewdness and for its energy and enterprise" (p. 643). But, above all, "The great scientific discoveries, the
most important inventions, and other mental [sic] acquirements of
the present day are almost all derived from the north western part of
Europe ... or from North America" (p. 650).

This list by no means exhausts the entirety of the race and climate
scientists' set of dependent variables. It does, however, strongly suggest the kinds of human characteristics they believed to be manageable
under a regime of race hygiene, the traits that would and should be
selected into or out of future gene pools. Once more, we wish to stress
that this compilation of widely accepted racial stereotypes was never
subjected to critical scrutiny, to the tests of scientific validity and reliability. Evidently, the grain of truth contained in them was sufficient to
support the credibility of the entire project. Indeed, because "everyone
knew" these to be racial differences, such scrutiny was unnecessary.

Far more important in understanding the appeal of the doctrine were
its practical implications. And in this regard the attraction is obvious:
Applied race science, based on the assumption that the propensity to
defer gratification – along with the other traits – does vary as proposed
by Fischer and his colleagues, had at its disposal the means to maximize
the civilization-promoting, good features of humanity and to minimize
the uncivilized and the bad. Whether ultimately right or wrong in its
faithfulness to the true facts of human variability, if effective, such a science would inevitably work to benefit the good (that is, it would promote
Nordic qualities). This, indeed, is policy science *in extremis*.

4   Protectors of nature: the power of climate change research

From climate research to climate politics

Climate change has been constantly covered in the mass media in recent years, and this coverage has grown at a phenomenal pace. At the time of this writing, there is virtually no single day that there is not a report on this subject. Policymakers and most of the public deal with it, and the reactions show awareness and concern. The climate debate raises fundamental questions about the future of society, its natural environment, and appropriate policy decisions.

Again, we need to emphasize the role of scientific knowledge in the public debate about climate change. Scientists have brought the issue to the attention of the media and decision-makers, and it is fair to say that we would not worry about changes in the climate system without their warnings. There had been early studies conducted in the nineteenth century, most notably by Fourier (1824), Tyndall (1863), and Arrhenius (1896). However, none of these implied that there was a need for action, and many of these early works were not built upon in later studies. Modern climate change discourse did not emerge before the mid 1960s, when two research fields merged that had been separate before: carbon cycle research and atmospheric modeling. The first was conducted by researchers such as Roger Revelle and Hans Suess, the second by John von Neumann and others. This new research field tried to estimate the atmospheric response to increasing CO_2 concentrations in the air. This was the birthmark of the field, which revolved (and still largely revolves today) around modeling. In the mid 1960s, the common perception among the research community was that we were conducting a large-scale experiment with planet Earth, but that this did not pose a threat and required no political action. Revelle stated in 1966 that "our attitude toward the changing content of carbon dioxide in the atmosphere ... should probably contain more curiosity than apprehension" (quoted in Hart and Victor 1993: 656). The President's Science Advisory Committee (PSAC) considered as early as 1965 the "deployment of reflective material in the atmosphere as a technological fix to counter rising CO_2" (Hart and Victor 1993: 656).[1] In 1970 and 1971 two reports were published, the "Study of Critical Environmental Problems" (SCEP) and the "Study of Man's Impact on Climate" (SMIC). These subsequently fed into the United Nations Conference on the Human Environment, held in 1972 in Stockholm. At this conference it was agreed to establish a global atmospheric monitoring network. Several participants realized that a long-term orientation was needed, plus appropriate leading champions. The following quote highlights this insight:

In a letter to Maurice Strong, the chairman of the Stockholm conference, Carroll Wilson wondered "... how and in what ways one might develop a kind of network of the rather limited number of *key influential people* in a certain number of countries around the world who are globally conscious and who have a vision extending to the end of this century and beyond and who have a deep concern for the environment in its broadest sense." (Quoted in Hart and Victor 1993: 664, our emphasis)

In the United States, climate scientists received more clout in the years to follow: there was a fourfold increase in funding over the period 1971–75. The research community developed a sense of urgency and a concern about climate change, not least because severe weather anomalies occurred during this period. The then "Secretary of State Henry Kissinger called for better international research on climatic disasters, and indicated that the US was willing to take the lead. With a little help from Mother Nature, then, climate change research reached the agenda of top US policy-makers" (Hart and Victor 1993: 665).

As we shall see, this pattern was to be repeated in the following decades, especially the evocation of weather anomalies as evidence for climate change. Climate change is "one of the most complicated scientific and hottest political debates in recent history" (O'Donnell 2000). This is the case because facts are uncertain, values in dispute, stakes are high, and decisions urgent (Funtowicz and Ravetz 1993). The knowledge base has been contested, and it could well remain controversial (Hulme 2009).

---

[1] Hart and Victor (1993: 656) comment that such visions "reflected the optimism of other proposed 'mega-projects' (such as vast civil engineering works using nuclear explosives) that were driven by Cold War competition. Such proposals diminished in the late 1960s, just as the intellectual climate outside of science changed and the greenhouse effect emerged as an important scientific priority." Now such proposals are back with a vengeance: In 2009, the Royal Society in the UK published their report *Geoengineering the Climate: Science, Governance and Uncertainty*, in which various options are discussed.

Knowledge producers and brokers are important and can play different roles. There are pure scientists who care little about political decisions (in the case of climate science this is perhaps the exception), there are scientists who argue for particular policy positions on climate policy (so-called advocates or activists), there are scientists who are honest brokers (see Pielke 2007), and there are policy entrepreneurs, as analyzed by Kingdon (1984). All these roles can be exercised by scientists or by so-called "experts" (see Stehr and Grundmann 2011). The role of policy entrepreneur is often carried out by science managers who have worked for the government and therefore know how to act in a political environment. It is useful to note at this point that there is a type of scientific activity that is usually overlooked. Pielke (2007: 7) describes this as hidden partisanship, or *stealth advocacy*:

So when a scientist claims to focus "only on the science," in many cases the scientist risks serving instead as a Stealth Issue Advocate. For some scientists stealth issue advocacy is politically desirable because it allows for a simultaneous claim of being above the fray, invoking the historical authority of science, while working to restrict the scope of choice. The stealth issue advocate seeks to "swim without getting wet." Other scientists may be wholly unaware of how their attempts to focus only on science contribute to a conflation of scientific and political debates. One way for scientists to avoid such conflation ... is to openly associate science with possible courses of action – that is, to serve as Honest Brokers of Policy Alternatives.

As we will show in this chapter, the case of climate change provides several examples of stealth advocacy.

In their account of the early history of climate science and policy from a US perspective, Hart and Victor (1993) point to the crucial role played by policy entrepreneurs, who managed to exploit a policy window in order to put the issue on the agenda, to boost funding, to create networks, and to influence policymaking. Hart and Victor argue that members of the scientific elite used policy windows to promote their specific research fields. This was a process influenced by their own interests, but also by the appeal to the pursuit of "pure science." Mission-oriented research was not seen as a good way to promote their research fields.

The two crucial scientific disciplines, carbon cycle research and atmospheric modeling, arose as concerns after nuclear testing suggested that there were changed weather patterns that needed study. Scientists did not find that weather was influenced by radioactive fallout; US federal agencies (the Atomic Energy Commission, the Office of Naval Research and the Department of Commerce), however, stimulated interest in carbon cycle and global atmospheric circulation (Hart and

Victor 1993: 648). Hans Suess and Roger Revelle, two of the pioneers in the field of carbon cycle research, concluded in the 1950s that some, but not all, of the carbon released by burning fossil fuel was absorbed by the oceans. This meant that rising consumption of fossil fuels in combustion would lead to a rise in carbon dioxide concentrations in the air. Revelle did most of his research at the Scripps Institute, which became the world leading institution in this research area. The Scripps Institute later ran the monitoring station at Mauna Loa on Hawaii, which has the most comprehensive dataset of global carbon dioxide concentrations worldwide and established one of the few undisputed facts on climate science, i.e. that carbon dioxide emissions are rising steadily.

The second research field, atmospheric modeling, was initiated by John von Neumann during wartime, when he was funded by the Navy for a Numerical Meteorology Project at the Institute for Advanced Studies in Princeton. Later, this group of researchers became the Geophysical Fluid Dynamics Laboratory (GFDL).

The two fields did not combine until after 1965. Hart and Victor argue that this was not the outcome of an increase in knowledge, or a loss in the faith that climate change could be controlled. Instead, so the argument goes, the leaders of these research fields became more entrepreneurial, as a window of opportunity opened that "allowed them to pose their work as a basic science problem, rather than as the subject of a Federal mission. Such positioning made it possible for Revelle and his colleagues to pursue heartily larger funding and the more thorough integration of carbon-cycle research and atmospheric modelling" (Hart and Victor 1993: 657). Scientific research into the issue was seen as crucial for providing a rationale for action. In 1973 it was thought that the science basis would be complete by 1980 (NAS, 1973, quoted in Hart and Victor 1993: 679). However, despite this desire to develop climate research, many political initiatives were not rooted in scientific advances.

Commenting on the postwar period of early climate research in the United States, Hart and Victor write: "Atmospheric modeling, with its roots in numerical weather prediction and its original military sponsorship, seems to have followed the pattern of post-war physics in establishing and maintaining relative autonomy. With this margin of comfort, modellers could comfortably swim in their own science 'stream,' to use Kingdon's term. The great 'experiment' of the greenhouse effect was an interesting scientific problem, but not one that demanded a political effort on their part" (1993: 654). Moreover, the developing research did not provide unambiguous answers to pressing questions: In 1968, for instance, a *Time* magazine essay, "The Age of

Effluence," used the dispute between warming and cooling theories to exemplify the difficulty of obtaining useful scientific advice on policy issues. "It seems undeniable that some disaster may be lurking in all this, but laymen hardly know which scientist to believe." Such competition within science seems more likely to stimulate efforts of devotees of a particular hypothesis than to deter them (Hart and Victor 1993: 656). In the mid 1960s, the US Federal Weather Modification Program supported most of the relevant research. It both stimulated these arguments and "proved to be the biggest barrier to efforts to integrate and expand carbon-cycle and atmospheric modeling research. Bureaucratic and Congressional opposition frustrated the entrepreneurship of the oceanographic and atmospheric science elites in this arena. Beginning with the experiments of Nobelist Irving Langmuir in the late 1940s, the heart of federal weather modification efforts was precipitation enhancement (especially rain-making by seeding clouds in the Western states), which had little to do with climate change on a global scale" (Hart and Victor 1993: 657). At the time, weather modification was a far more exciting area compared to "inadvertent weather and climate modification." Funding figures show that the former nearly doubled between 1966 and 1971, the latter declined by about 20 percent: "In a period of technological optimism, 'inadvertent climate modification' lacked the glamour of weather modification" (Hart and Victor 1993: 660).

Hart and Victor interpret the early history of US climate research as an instance of the "garbage can" model where science, policy, and politics are loosely coupled and windows of opportunity open which can be exploited by policy entrepreneurs. Opportunities to advance the policy agenda often resulted unpredictably from previously unrelated areas. These were usually not the outcome of new scientific research. Rather, leading scientists, with entrepreneurial and other skills, "shaped the beliefs of policy makers and the public when such opportunities arose." They conclude their study with a remarkable statement:

We find it difficult to imagine that the "weight of scientific evidence" would have inevitably moved both policy and science in the directions that they went without elite entrepreneurship and the windows opened by the environmental movement ... *The same scientific case can yield quite different policy results in different circumstances.*" (Hart and Victor 1993: 667–68, our emphasis)

One of the policy entrepreneurs who deserves special attention is James Hansen of NASA. Back in 1981 Hansen contacted a journalist from the *New York Times*, Walter Sullivan, and sent him a report he was about to publish. Sullivan wrote an article on the front page of the paper, writing about issues related to the environment for which he later became a champion. In his piece he warned that there could be unprecedented warming, causing a disastrous rise of sea level. Under the headline "STUDY FINDS WARMING TREND THAT COULD RAISE SEA LEVELS," the article reported on dire warnings from seven federal scientists who claimed to have "detected an overall warming trend in the earth's atmosphere extending back to the year 1880. They regard this as evidence of the validity of the 'greenhouse' effect, in which increasing amounts of carbon dioxide cause steady temperature increases." The article continues that according to these scientists, there would be global warming of "almost unprecedented magnitude" in the next century. "It might even be sufficient to melt and dislodge the ice cover of West Antarctica, they say, eventually leading to a worldwide rise of 15 to 20 feet in the sea level. In that case, they say, it would 'flood 25 percent of Louisiana and Florida, 10 percent of New Jersey and many other lowlands throughout the world' within a century or less" (*New York Times*, August 22, 1981, p. 1). An editorial followed a week later, declaring that "their study finds that the warming predicted by various computer models of the greenhouse effect is consistent with worldwide temperature readings since 1880 – and with observations from Venus and Mars. That gave them confidence that the effect is real and that the models can predict it." The editorial was certainly right in its prediction that "other scientists will challenge their assumptions, methods and conclusions." It was also right to foresee the argument made by some "that the greenhouse effect would be beneficial to world agriculture." Most important, perhaps, was the prediction that "conclusive observations may not be available for decades. But it is significant that a respected team of scientists has now joined the group warning of possible catastrophe." It concluded thus: "The greenhouse effect is still too uncertain to warrant total alteration of energy policy. But this latest study offers fair warning; that such a change may yet be required is no longer unimaginable" (*New York Times*, August 29, 1981, p. 22). Within the wider government administration, Hansen's activity was not welcome. The Department of Energy tried to withdraw research funding promised to him, and he had to sack five people from his institute (Weart 2003: 144).

Nevertheless, this early warning signal remained undetected by the US and world media attention for years to come. Things changed in the mid 1980s, probably after the discovery of abnormally low ozone concentrations above Antarctica, later dubbed the *ozone hole*. The discovery was made in the early 1980s by the British Antarctic Survey, published in 1985 (Farman et al. 1985), and confirmed a year later by NASA scientists (Stolarski et al. 1986).

There was a sense of a global environmental emergency, which fed into the closely related field of climate change. Public concern about disruptions to the climate system followed almost immediately. In August 1986 the German weekly *Der Spiegel* featured Cologne cathedral on its cover page, partly submerged by water, adorned with the headline *Klimakatastrophe*, or "climatic catastrophe" (Weingart et al. 2000). It was Hansen again who in June 1988 made a testimonial statement to the US Congress. He famously stated he was "99%" certain that global warming was real (O'Donnell 2000). He said that "in my opinion the greenhouse effect has been detected, and it is changing our climate now," and was even more emphatic when he told a *New York Times* reporter, "It is time to stop waffling so much and say that the evidence is pretty strong that the greenhouse effect is here" (*New York Times*, June 24, 1988: A1).

The fact that he spoke during a major drought was very effective. The timing of his appearance before the Congress committee was no coincidence, but rather carefully staged. US Senator Tim Wirth had organized the hearings on global warming (see Andresen and Agrawala 2002: 44). This context was ideal to dramatize the issue. As before, adopting such a visible role got Hansen into hot water, as the attacks that were to ensue showed. Skeptical "contrarians" described the climate issue and Hansen's pronouncements as a "global warming scare." Patrick Michaels, a professor of environmental sciences at the University of Virginia and senior fellow at the conservative Cato Institute, Washington, DC, attacked him as being the only scientist to claim that there was a cause–effect relationship between "current temperatures and human alterations of the atmosphere" (*Washington Post*, January 8, 1989: C3).

This exchange epitomizes what is at stake for individual scientists who act as advocates – they want to appear to be as objective or scientific as possible, and to avoid the impression of being driven by political or other motives. Hence Michaels's insinuation that Hansen does not fit within the mainstream of scientific opinion as being "the only scientist" to claim a relationship between current weather and long-term trends. Conversely, prominent scientists brandished contrarians like Michaels as "only a handful" of dissenting individuals. Hansen himself countered Michaels's claim by saying that "the scientific community is convinced that we are headed for substantial climate changes in coming decades if greenhouse gas emissions continue to grow, as discussed by several reports by the National Academy of Sciences and by prestigious international organizations" (*Washington Post*, February 11, 1989: A23). Both scientists have to be classified as "activist" scientists; it should be noted that their activism is practiced openly and not hidden.

Steve Schneider told *Discover* magazine in an interview about the perils of this:

> On the one hand, as scientists we are ethically bound to the scientific method, in effect promising to tell the truth, the whole truth, and nothing but – which means that we must include all the doubts, the caveats, the ifs, ands, and buts. On the other hand, we are not just scientists but human beings as well. And like most people we'd like to see the world a better place, which in this context translates into our working to reduce the risk of potentially disastrous climatic change. To do that we need to get some broadbased support, to capture the public's imagination. That, of course, entails getting loads of media coverage. So we have to offer up scary scenarios, make simplified, dramatic statements, and make little mention of any doubts we might have. This "double ethical bind" we frequently find ourselves in cannot be solved by any formula. Each of us has to decide what the right balance is between being effective and being honest. I hope that means being both. (Schell 1989: 45)

Schneider received a lot of criticism for his candid view, mainly from climate skeptics. However, one must not forget that he made this statement as an individual scientist. Things are different when institutions such as the IPCC show such a partisanship.

Global governance

In 1992 the United Nations Framework Convention on Climate Change (UNFCCC) was opened for signature at the UN Conference on Environment and Development in Rio de Janeiro, also known as the "Earth Summit." The framework document was signed by 154 nations, which committed signatories' governments to a voluntary aim of reducing atmospheric concentrations of greenhouse gases, with the goal of preventing "dangerous anthropogenic interference with Earth's climate system" (United Nations 1992).[2] These actions were aimed primarily at industrialized countries, with the intention of stabilizing their emissions of greenhouse gases at 1990 levels by the year 2000.

---

[2] Contained in article 2, which states as the aim of the Convention: "The ultimate objective of this Convention and any related legal instruments that the Conference of the Parties may adopt is to achieve, in accordance with the relevant provisions of the Convention, stabilization of greenhouse gas concentrations in the atmosphere at a level that would *prevent dangerous anthropogenic interference with the climate system*. Such a level should be achieved within a time frame sufficient to allow ecosystems to adapt naturally to climate change, to ensure that food production is not threatened and to enable economic development to proceed in a sustainable manner" (http: //unfccc.int/ resource/docs/convkp/conveng.pdf, our emphasis).

The parties agreed in general that they would recognize "common but differentiated responsibilities," with greater responsibility for reducing greenhouse gas emissions in the near term on the part of developed/ industrialized countries, which were listed and identified in Annex I of the UNFCCC and thus referred to as "Annex I" countries.

The framework convention entered into force in March 21, 1994 after more than fifty countries had ratified it. Since then, the parties have been meeting annually in Conferences of the Parties (COP) to assess progress in dealing with climate change and, beginning in the mid 1990s, to negotiate the Kyoto Protocol to establish legally binding obligations for developed countries to reduce their greenhouse gas emissions.

In his book *The Discovery of Global Warming*, Spencer Weart makes an impressive attempt to trace the various scientific activities that led to our current understanding of the issue. It is worth taking a close look at how he understands the relation between knowledge and action, and the relation between scientific understanding and political decisions. In the preface to the book he states:

The question has graduated from the scientific community: climate change is a major social, economic, and political issue. Nearly everyone in the world will need to adjust. It will be the hardest for the poorer groups and nations among us, but nobody is exempt. Citizens will need reliable information, the flexibility to change their personal lives, and efficient and appropriate help from all levels of government. So it is an important job, in some ways our top priority, to improve the communication of knowledge and to strengthen democratic control in governance everywhere. The spirit of fact-gathering, rational discussion, toleration of dissent, and negotiation of an evolving consensus, which has characterized the climate science community, can serve well as a model. (Weart 2003: 201)

Weart conjures a context of healthy scientific skepticism and critical discussion in democratic societies that could stand as a model for coping processes that lie ahead. Thus he writes: "We have hard decisions to make. Our response to the threat of global warming will affect our personal well-being, the evolution of human society, indeed all life on our planet ... By following how scientists in the past fought their way through the uncertainties of climate change, we can be better prepared to judge why they speak as they do today. More, we can understand better how scientists address the many other questions where they have an important voice. How do scientists reach reliable conclusions?" (Weart 2003: viii). Within these few lines we are told that we have hard decisions to make and that it is important to understand the scientists' pronouncements as they have an important voice. We should listen to scientists because they have reliable conclusions on offer. So far, this sounds like the usual story, told a million times, that we rely on science for its reliable knowledge, which we can take for granted without questioning or understanding. Because science works in practical contexts we, as lay people, do not need to understand it. Its instrumental success convinces.

However, this is not how Weart continues his line of thought. Reading on after the last sentence in the above quote, we are told that "our familiar picture of discovery, learned from the old core sciences like physics or biology, shows an orderly parade of observations and ideas and experiments. We like to think it ends with an answer, a clear statement about what we can do. Such a logical sequence, with definitive results, does not describe work in interdisciplinary fields like the study of climate change (actually, it often doesn't describe the old core sciences either)."

Let us pause and note that, according to Weart, new interdisciplinary fields do not come up with answers and clear advice on what to do. Even the core sciences are affected by this predicament of answers that are ambiguous and recommendations that are not clear. Of course, this is staple food for thought for anyone who is vaguely familiar with science studies. It is noteworthy that such a view comes from an author who has training in physics and is known for his historical works.

However, Weart (2003: ix) sees the lack of certainty in climate research as a result of the object of inquiry, which is a complex one. Thus he states, "The story of the discovery of global warming looks less like a processional march than like a scattering of groups wandering around an immense landscape ... The tangled nature of climate research reflects nature itself. The Earth's climate system is so irreducibly complicated that we will never grasp it completely, in the way that one might grasp a law of physics."

Here we see the traditional line of thought emerging again, stressing the distinctive difference between the laws of physics, which are certain, and other forms of knowledge, which are tangled, complicated, and "reflecting nature itself" (Weart 2003: ix).[3]

Weart concludes, "These uncertainties infect the relationship between climate science and policy-making. Debates about climate

[3] Traditionally, the social sciences are juxtaposed in this way to the natural sciences. Their object of research (society) is said to be so complex that no reliable and operational knowledge could be produced. Weart applies the same line of thought to the natural sciences in stating that they, too, confront high levels of complexity in their object of research. As we show in Chapter 2, this argument rests on a fallacy: Keynes was able to identify a few actionable variables, albeit economy and society are infinitely complex.

change can get as confusing as arguments over the social consequences of welfare payments" (Weart 2003: ix). Here we reach the nub of the problem. Does the uncertainty surrounding climate research inhibit policymaking? Would a less ambiguous knowledge base facilitate political actions? Clearly these are fundamental questions to be asked, and troubling questions they are, too – not only for policymakers and citizens, but for scholars as well.

Weart seems to suggest that we should aim for certainty and get rid of confusing arguments – and who could contradict him? As part of our dominant rationalistic culture, it is nearly impossible to step outside these basic assumptions. And yet we should ponder some implications of this approach, as it reveals an important point central to our endeavor in these pages.

As a result of the distinction between scientific (hard-core) knowledge and less certain forms of knowledge, we are led to believe several things. First, that physics could offer certain knowledge, if only the complexity of the matter could be managed. Second, being in possession of certain knowledge would increase our capacity for action. Third, it seems to imply that the certainty of physics is partly due to the fact that it does *not* reflect nature (presumably because it makes simplifications that aim to reduce complexity). However, as Weart demonstrates, climate scientists cannot operate under the traditional model of physics. This means that their knowledge cannot be certain; they are caught in the complexity of nature. Political decisions have to be taken under similar conditions, in which social or economic policies operate. And we need to be aware of the problem of identifying knowledge that is actionable.

Weart goes on to state that the problem of uncertainty has been addressed by "climate scientists [who] created remarkable new policy mechanisms" (Weart 2003: ix). The important novelty is the formation of the Intergovernmental Panel on Climate Change (IPCC), which was set up in 1988 by two United Nations organizations, the World Meteorological Organization (WMO) and the United Nations Environment Programme (UNEP). Weart is absolutely right in stating that the IPCC is a novelty in terms of organizing policy advice. It is also an exception, for better or worse. The following pages will try to evaluate this institutional innovation.

The Intergovernmental Panel on Climate Change: global governance and science

The role of the IPCC is to review and assess the published scientific literature on climate change, its costs and impacts, and possible policy responses. It also plays a role in assessing scientific and technical issues for the UNFCCC. It is to assess the state of knowledge and to ensure that global governance is made easier by representing important stakeholders in the assessment process.

The IPCC is a scientific body. It reviews and assesses the most recent scientific, technical and socio-economic information produced worldwide relevant to the understanding of climate change. It does not conduct any research nor does it monitor climate related data or parameters. Thousands of scientists from all over the world contribute to the work of the IPCC on a voluntary basis. Review is an essential part of the IPCC process, to ensure an objective and complete assessment of current information. Differing viewpoints existing within the scientific community are reflected in the IPCC reports.[4]

From around the world, more than two thousand scientists have contributed to these reports. The IPCC is the international authoritative body pronouncing scientific expertise on the issue. However, some "contrarian" scientists and other critics think that the IPCC misrepresents the state of knowledge and exaggerates the size and urgency of the problem. While some accuse IPCC scientists of being environmentalists in disguise ("stealth advocates"), others point to the processes of exclusion of specific social groups representing different knowledge claims (Boehmer-Christiansen 1994a, b; Miller and Edwards 2001). Recent scandals have lent credibility to such claims, which were dismissed in the past as propaganda of the fossil fuel industry.

The main architecture of the IPCC consists of three Working Groups (WGs), which have been reorganized over time. This reorganization has only affected Working Groups II and III. Working Group I assesses the scientific aspects of the climate system and climate change. Working Group II assesses the vulnerability of socio-economic and natural systems to climate change, negative and positive consequences of climate change, and options for adapting to it. Working Group III assesses options for limiting GHG emissions and otherwise mitigating climate change.

In addition, there are several ad hoc task forces. IPCC assessments are to be based on the available published scientific literature (although in reality unpublished work could be influencing the assessments, and some large research projects are possibly undertaken in order to influence future IPCC assessments). The IPCC publishes its assessments in a five- to six-year cycle.

There is a complex governance structure ruling the tasks, activities, and responsibilities of various bodies within the IPCC. The "scientific

---

[4] www.ipcc.ch/organization/organization.htm.

core" of the working groups provides the assessments, with the Working Groups plenary and the full panel plenary accepting and approving this work (Skodvin 2000: 107). There are different levels of acceptance and approval, ranging from reports being accepted by WGs (this applies to assessment reports and methodologies); through reports being approved by WGs and accepted by the IPCC (these are summaries for policymakers and executive summaries); to reports approved by the IPCC. The last category comprises the so-called Synthesis Reports. "An 'approved' report has been subjected to detailed, line-by line discussions in a plenary session of the relevant WG" (Skodvin 2000: 107).

The Working Groups recruit and assign lead authors, contributing authors, and reviewers for specific chapters of reports. The lead authors and contributing authors are nominated by governments; the chair and vice-chair of each WG select lead authors from lists provided by governments. Contributing authors are often invited on the basis of their geographical location. Over the years, representation from developing countries has increased.

Over time, the rules governing the composition of Working Groups have changed, leading to an effective abandonment of the idea of a "core membership." Initially, the idea was to keep the group size manageable (13–17 members, see Skodvin 2000: 110). However, because these are UN bodies, there is in principle no limitation to participation. As a consequence, the Working Group plenaries are now dominated by government officials (most of whom are scientists working in government agencies).

In the procedure for approving the Summaries for Policy Makers (SPMs), these are submitted to the full plenary for acceptance. "A synthesis of the reports of all three WGs, prepared by the chairman of the IPCC and the chairs and vice-chairs of the WGs, is also submitted to the panel plenary for approval" (Skodvin 2000: 111). This then goes through a line-by-line discussion before it is approved by the panel. The IPCC says this about itself:

Full reports are accepted during the Working Group's plenary, while for each report a Summary for Policymakers is approved line by line. The SPM therefore represents the point of agreement: participating governments acknowledge that there is enough scientific evidence worldwide to support the document's statements.[5]

The scientific community is represented at full plenary sessions through the chair of the IPCC and the leaders of the WGs. However, the panel

[5] www.ipcc.ch/press_information/press_information_fact_sheet1.htm.

plenary is dominated by government officials. No doubt, the formalization and complexity of the IPCC activities have grown over time.

Skodvin describes the process of developing drafts of summaries at workshops and regular meetings between contributing authors and the lead authors. Although the teams of lead authors (responsible for individual chapters) in WG1 are appointed by the IPCC Bureau based on government nominations, the actual working practice seems to reflect the norms and procedures of normal scientific endeavor (Skodvin 2000: 112). The IPCC Bureau provides scientific and technical support to the Chair of the IPCC and the Co-Chairs of the Working Groups.[6] Once a draft report has been written, this will be submitted to both "expert" and "government" reviews. This two-tier system was introduced in 1993, when expert reviewers were selected on the basis of their scientific merit; but governments also fed back their comments. Skodvin suggests that there is no undue political pressure or influence at this stage, as the complexity of the science prevents non-experts from participating in a meaningful way. There seems to be no clear notion about the aim of reaching a consensus view in the scientific core. Skodvin reports (on the basis of interviews with lead authors) that most do not think consensus should be a requirement in the IPCC process. However, recent revelations after the email scandals show that some orchestration of consensus has taken place (Montford 2010; Tol 2010). This indicates that Skodvin's interviewees may have been painting a rosy picture.

Shackley and Wynne (1995) have observed that these different parts of the IPCC process can be seen as forming a knowledge pyramid, with WG I standing at the top. Shaw and Robinson (2004: 110) argue that a core-set group of modelers has established conceptual hegemony, and crucially "influences what information becomes tangible, relevant, and knowledgeable both in the natural and social worlds of investigation and response." These scientists typically develop Global Circulation Models (GCMs), which are based purely on physical measurable variables and parameters. Despite some attempts at flattening the hierarchy between the three working groups, most notably through the development of Integrated Assessment Models (IAMs), the reality of the IPCC process is determined by the dominance of GCMs developed in WG I.[7]

---

[6] www.ipcc.ch/meetings/session29/new-ipcc-bureau.pdf.
[7] Shackley and Wynne (1995: 122, 123) describe the IAMs as follows: "Integrated assessment models represent the first steps along a hugely ambitious research trajectory. If they are even partly successful what they offer is nothing short of a set of reliable methods for probing and hence designing the future. Much of the cultural, political and institutional is highly variable, ever changing and uncertain, or possibly, indeterminate and unpredictable. It does not lend itself to ready quantification in an integrated modelling framework. It is probably for these reasons that integrators have

Over time, the IPCC reports have become more dramatic in tone. While this is officially attributed to the advances in knowledge over the years, others see it as a skillful dramaturgy in order to achieve politically desirable objectives. In its first report, the IPCC stated that continued GHG emissions would enhance the greenhouse effect. In its second report, it said that there is "inadequate data to determine whether consistent global changes in climate variability or weather extremes have occurred over the 20th century." However, "the balance of evidence suggests a discernible human influence on global climate." This is the detection of global warming.

In its Third Assessment Report (TAR), it noted that over the last century, the Earth has warmed by 0.6 degrees Celsius, and the increase is at least partly due to the anthropogenic release of GHGs. This is the attribution of causes of global warming. The TAR also started making claims about "unprecedented" warming:

Globally it is very likely that the 1990s was the warmest decade, and 1998 the warmest year, in the instrumental record (1861–2000) ... The increase in surface temperature over the 20th century for the Northern Hemisphere is likely to have been greater than that for any other century in the last thousand years.

In its Fourth Assessment Report (AR4), the human role in changing global climate is described as "very likely." In addition, the report states that

the warmth of the last half century is unusual in at least the previous 1,300 years. The last time the polar regions were significantly warmer than present for an extended period (about 125,000 years ago), reductions in polar ice volume led to 4 to 6 m of sea level rise.[8]

Critics see such statements as scare-mongering, unsupported by empirical evidence. The focus of the criticism is the assertion that it has never been as warm on planet Earth as it has been in recent decades. This statement is based on temperature reconstructions (paleoclimatic proxy data) of the past. This has ignited a massive controversy, which has already found its way into the history of science as the Hockey Stick controversy. It was at the center of the email scandal at the Climate Research Unit (CRU) at the University of East Anglia, which made worldwide headlines in November 2009. It is far beyond the scope of

not attempted to incorporate them at this stage; by contrast they use similar concepts, techniques and methods as modellers from biology, economics or atmospheric chemistry. (The one IAM group which is now attempting to take account of culture, is using a rather determinist theory of cultural diversity.)"

[8] www.ipcc.ch/publications_and_data/ar4/wg1/en/spmsspm-a-palaeoclimatic.html.

this book even partially to examine the ramifications of the debate; the following brief remarks are thus intended to link the story to our topic, the relation between knowledge and power.

Man(n)-made global warming?

Back in 1998, Michael Mann, a climatologist then working in the United States at the University of Massachusetts, Amherst, published an article with co-workers (Mann et al. 1998), in which they claimed that greenhouse gases are the dominant climate-forcing factor during the twentieth century. They state that "Northern Hemisphere mean annual temperatures for three of the past eight years are warmer than any other year since (at least) AD 1400." This claim was based on a time series analysis of so-called "proxy data," going back to the year 1400. Because modern temperature records only exist for ca. 150 years, paleoclimatic data was used as a source, with tree rings playing a major role. In 1999, the same authors published another analysis of proxy data, this time going back to the year 1000. Again, the claim is made that the warm period experienced in recent years is warmer than the warmest years in the so-called "Medieval Warm Period." Until then, it had been widely accepted in paleoclimatic research that there was a Medieval Warm Period (MWP) from the eleventh to the fourteenth century, followed by a Little Ice Age (LIA) from the sixteenth to the eighteenth century. Mann's paper included a graph that became known as the "hockey stick" (and the group propagating it proudly called itself "the hockey team") and gave global warming theory an iconic vehicle. It was sarcastically described as the IPCC's "poster child" by skeptics (Figure 2).

The work of these climatologists was parallel to work performed by scientists working at East Anglia's CRU, above all Phil Jones, Keith Briffa and Tim Osborn. Jones, together with Kevin Trenberth, was the coordinating lead author of the relevant chapter for the IPCC Third Assessment Report (TAR), published in 2001. In this report, the hockey stick was printed in six different locations, clearly emphasizing the importance for the overall storyline. The IPCC TAR says:

As with the "Little Ice Age," the posited "Medieval Warm Period" appears to have been less distinct, more moderate in amplitude, and somewhat different in timing at the hemispheric scale than is typically inferred for the conventionally-defined European epoch. The Northern Hemisphere mean temperature estimates of Jones et al. (1998), Mann et al. (1999), and Crowley and Lowery (2000) show temperatures from the 11th to 14th centuries to be about 0.2°C warmer than those from the 15th to 19th centuries, but rather below mid-20th century temperatures. (Houghton et al. 2001: 135)

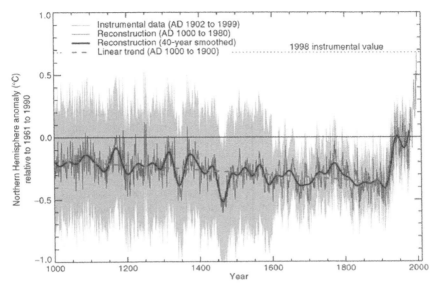

Figure 2: Mann et al.'s temperature reconstruction in TAR.

It is precisely this claim that has been vigorously opposed by other scientists. One of the crusaders in this battle is Steve McIntyre, who together with Ross McKitrick wrote a paper in which they reported that they could not replicate the findings of Mann et al. McIntyre and McKitrick had requested datasets and software programs from Mann and Jones in order to do a reanalysis of their work. However, neither of the latter was very helpful in fulfilling this request. As the East Anglia emails document, there were many attempts to fob them off for varying reasons by an *inner circle* or *core set* around Mann and Jones.[9] According to Collins, core sets of research are to be found at a few prestigious institutions and laboratories, and are linked to other networks at prestigious institutions. Leadership personalities in these groups control the access to key resources of research such as labs, publication opportunities, and finance (cf. also Hagstrom 1965; Traweek 1988). They also decide in which

[9] Various terms have been used to describe Mann, Jones et al.: "clan"; "tribe"; the "hockey team" (or simply: "the team"); "clique"; "cabal"; or "gang." Sociologists of science in the past (e.g. Price 1963; Crane 1972) have used labels such as "invisible college," taking up a notion that Robert Boyle had coined in the seventeenth century, and which refers to "past and present informal collectivities of closely interacting scientists limited to a size that can be handled by inter-personal relationships" (quoted in Merton 1995: 407). H. M. Collins (1985) speaks of "core sets" in science.

direction the field will move, and where the boundary between science and non-science has to be drawn (Jasanoff, 1990; Gieryn 1995).

In the run-up to AR4, CRU's tree ring expert Keith Briffa said that when it came to historical climate records, there was no new data, only the "same old evidence" that had been around for years:

There have been many different techniques used to aggregate and scale data – but the efficacy of these is still far from established. We should be careful not to push the conclusions beyond what we can securely justify – and this is not much other than a confirmation of the general conclusions of the TAR. We must resist being pushed to present the results such that we will be accused of bias – hence no need to attack Moberg. Just need to show the "most likely" course of temperatures over the last 1300 years – which we do well I think. Strong confirmation of TAR is a good result, given that we discuss uncertainty and base it on more data. Let us not try to over egg the pudding. (email 1140039406)

What is puzzling is that Briffa (and others who expressed reservations of some kind at some point) kept quiet when it came to the important work of communicating research findings to a wider public, and even within the IPCC. When claims such as the "warmest for 1,300 years" were published in 2007 in the IPCC's fourth report, there was no sign of disagreement. This would have been inconvenient to the IPCC core set, because there were no massive sources of greenhouse gases in the Middle Ages, yet the Earth was arguably still slightly warmer than in the late twentieth century. If there was "groupthink," it may have prevented proper scientific scrutiny.

In preparation for the TAR, Jones was working on the hockey stick reconstruction. Here Briffa's work was crucially important. Briffa knew what was expected for the report, saying:

I know there is pressure to present a nice tidy story as regards "apparent unprecedented warming in a thousand years or more in the proxy data" but in reality the situation is not quite so simple. We don't have a lot of proxies that come right up to date and those that do (at least a significant number of tree proxies) [show] some unexpected changes in response that do not match the recent warming. I do not think it wise that this issue be ignored in the chapter. (email 938031546)

However, others were more concerned about being careful which story to present to the public, as frank discussions of problems with temperature reconstructions could dilute "the message rather significantly." Mann especially was anxious that if uncertainties were admitted in the IPCC report, "the sceptics [would] have a field day casting doubt on our ability to understand the factors that influence these estimates and, thus, can undermine faith [in them] – I don't think that doubt is

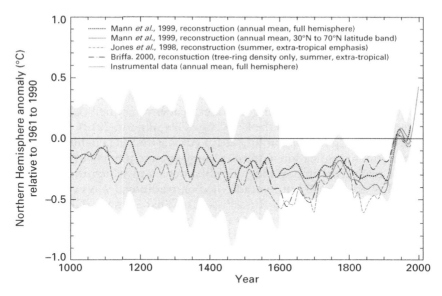

Figure 3: The IPCC hockey stick (Note: tree ring data in Briffa 2000).

scientifically justified, and I'd hate to be the one to have to give it fodder!" (email 938018124).

Briffa changed his story in the end, aligning it more with temperatures of earlier centuries, and cooling the data significantly. But this only led to other, more serious, problems. The dataset now showed a fall in temperatures after 1960, thus contradicting the observed record of thermometer measurements. The question now was: If tree rings were not reliable after 1960, to what extent were they reliable for the last centuries? Too big a question to ponder for public consumption, or so the core group thought. This is where the famous "trick" comes in. In the "spaghetti diagram" of the IPCC report, the inconvenient data showing up after 1960 was simply omitted. This was an artful technique, as it was applied to a graph which showed various overlaying curves in different colors. The tree ring curve that started to give lower temperatures after 1960 was replaced with actual temperature readings, which showed an increase. Figure 3 shows the "spaghetti diagram" in the IPCC report (tree ring data is in Briffa 2000).

There is ample evidence that the "hockey team" tried to apply tactics in order to keep the outsiders … *out*. The recognition of who counted as an expert in the field was done by the inner group. They defined who counted as a scientist and who did not, who should get data and who should be prevented from getting access. There is very little evidence of engaging on a substantial level with the arguments of their critics. Instead, rebuttal is done "via proxy" – instead of arguing specific points, we read things like: "these are bad papers," "the paper is crap," "they are the baddies," etc.

In 2010 six investigations about alleged malpractice took place, among them the Muir Russell and the Oxburgh reviews in the UK which looked at CRU's practices, and the Inter Academy Council (IAC) which looked at the procedures of the IPCC (see Grundmann 2012). The Muir Russell review (published in July 2010) emphasized the changed nature of science communication in the electronic age and points out that CRU did not realize the importance of public debate in which rhetoric and credibility are crucial but instead relied on traditional ways of publishing research results (Muir Russell 2010). What is more, CRU seems to have dismissed critical inquiries all too quickly, which was problematic and counterproductive. The IAC found that the IPCC needs more transparency and a better management structure: "The IPCC should complete and implement a communications strategy that emphasizes transparency, rapid and thoughtful responses, and relevance to stakeholders, and which includes guidelines about who can speak on behalf of IPCC and how to represent the organization appropriately" (IAC 2010). The Oxburgh review came to the conclusion that there was "no evidence of any deliberate scientific malpractice in any of the work of the Climatic Research Unit and had it been there we believe that it is likely that we would have detected it. Rather we found a small group of dedicated if slightly disorganised researchers who were ill-prepared for being the focus of public attention. As with many small research groups their internal procedures were rather informal" (Oxburgh 2010: 5).

While these reviews examined alleged malpractice, earlier investigations looked at the scientific merit of the hockey stick. These took place in the United States in 2006 where two Senate congressional hearings were held, one by the National Research Councils Board of Atmospheric Sciences, the other by the National Academy of Sciences' (NAS) Committee on Applied and Theoretical Statistics. The first report was published in 2006, and a number of statements were issued supporting Mann's arguments; for example, that during the late twentieth century temperatures were considerably higher than the average of the prior four centuries. However, the report also said that average temperatures between AD 900 and 1500 were more difficult to establish, and thus more error-prone. While this report vindicated Mann et al. against the critics overall, the second report, known as the Wegman Report, highlighted and upheld McIntyre's criticisms of the "hockey stick," emphasizing the flawed statistical methods of Mann et al., which led to erroneous temperatures. Because the Wegman Report was commissioned by Senator Barton, a Republican with links to Exxon, Mann and his supporters not surprisingly dismissed the findings.

The Wegman Report touches upon the issue of insider–outsider constellations mentioned above, and this impinges on the production of knowledge. It says:

In our further exploration of the social network of authorships in temperature reconstruction, we found that at least 43 authors have direct ties to Dr. Mann by virtue of coauthored papers with him. Our findings from this analysis suggest that authors in the area of paleoclimate studies are closely connected and thus "independent studies" may not be as independent as they might appear on the surface.

This sheds new light on the often heard argument about the scientific consensus as presented by the IPCC. When we are told that more than two thousand leading scientists produce that consensus, it is often overlooked that behind central claims like that of the unprecedented temperatures, only a handful of scientists was involved in assessing the published research, at times giving the impression of closing themselves off from any criticism, or so the suspicious critics argue. Under these circumstances, not only skeptics ask how robust the underlying knowledge base is. If the email affair and its aftermath have not proved malpractice, they did potentially, if not actually, undermine trust in climate science.

The IPCC: scientific or political?

Is the IPCC a scientific or political body? We indicated that the IPCC was founded by two UN organizations, the WMO and UNEP. Membership in the IPCC is therefore open to members of these two organizations.

On its website, the IPCC stresses its policy-neutral standpoint: "Thanks to the depth of its scientific work and to the value of its intergovernmental nature, IPCC work is very much policy relevant. Its assessment reports played a decisive role in inducing governments to adopt the United Nations Framework Convention on Climate Change and the Kyoto Protocol. However, IPCC is neutral with respect to policy and its assessment reports are not policy prescriptive."[10]

Skodvin (2000: 106) remarks that the IPCC "constitutes the scientific body of the climate change regime, while the Conference of the Parties to the Climate Convention (COP) constitutes the political or regulatory body." But one would be led astray in believing that things can be separated out so tidily. Skodvin explains that "the Executive Council of WMO

[10] www.ipcc.ch/press_information/press_information_fact_sheet1.htm.

and the Governing Council of UNEP established the IPCC as an inter-governmental organization under UN auspices. Being a UN body, the IPCC is submitted to the traditional UN procedures governing most UN bodies. Thus, one main characteristic feature of the IPCC is that it has a scientific mandate, while it is organized within a political institutional framework." It operates "in the interface of science and politics. The distinction between science and politics within the IPCC constitutes a zone rather than a clear-cut border" (Skodvin 2000: 106). This institution is thus unique, in that it comprises scientists and government representatives. It is a hybrid or "boundary organization" (Miller 2001).[11]

The first chairman of the IPCC, Bert Bolin, explained that the IPCC was designed in order to boost trust in science among nations: "Right now, many countries, especially developing countries, simply do not trust assessments in which their scientists and policymakers have not participated. Don't you think credibility demands global representation?" (quoted in Schneider 1991: 25). This conviction was one of the initial ideas for the intergovernmental organizational set-up of the IPCC and the governmental approval mechanism (Skodvin 2000; Siebenhüner 2003).

The architects of the IPCC attempt to reach an overall consensus view on the scientific aspects of global climate change, and this was seen as necessary for obtaining policy decisions based on best available knowledge. There is a complex process designed to achieve this. The line-by-line approval of SPMs is particularly central to this aim. This was based on lessons drawn from another case that preceded climate change in time: the experience of ozone layer politics seemed to provide a powerful argument for the creation of a consensus view in order to achieve international cooperation. Had not the emergence of such a consensus view led to stopping the proliferation of many, partly contradictory, assessments? Had it not led to the successful Montreal Protocol? The short answer is No. This international treaty specified targets and timetables for the phase-out of ozone-depleting substances. It has been hailed as a paradigmatic case, and many have set their aims to emulate it, especially in climate change politics. Let us therefore see where both cases diverge.

---

[11] The notion of the IPCC being a hybrid makes reference to Latour's (1993) analysis of two complementary processes, hybridization and purification. This is to say that the more scientists engage in politics, the more they will stress the validity of their knowledge claims. Conversely, the more politicians engage in science debates, the more they will claim that they make decisions based on the best available knowledge. Knowledge is therefore the central reference point for actors from both fields. This does not mean, however, that knowledge claims are translated directly into political decisions, or that scientists would be the ultimate power-holders. Quite the contrary, it is the governments that decide which policy to develop and which knowledge to use for its legitimation (see Grundmann 2009).

Ozone layer protection

In June 1974, two chemists of the University of California at Irvine published an article in *Nature*, in which they put forward the hypothesis that CFCs could damage the ozone layer (this section draws on Grundmann 2001). This so-called Molina–Rowland Hypothesis called for a revision of the long-believed harmlessness of CFCs, which were very popular with both producers and consumers of many domestic and industrial appliances, since they seemed to be chemically inert, non-toxic, and non-corrosive. According to the Molina-Rowland-Hypothesis, CFCs could deplete stratospheric ozone and hence lead to an increase in UV-B radiation, which in turn would have severe effects on biological systems (skin cancer in humans, crop damage, algae diminution) and on global climate. Rowland and Molina can be described as "issue advocates," in that they advocated one specific course of action: the limitation in the use and application of CFCs.

From the beginning, there was controversy between the proponents of this hypothesis and industry. The proponents were supported by other scientists, environmentalists, and policymakers. They believed that although little was known, it was enough to warrant controls. Following the wait-and-see principle, those against CFC controls demanded more time for scientific research before addressing the question of controls. Needless to say, vested interests were backing this position, as well as some scientists and decision-makers.

On June 30, 1975, the DuPont Company ran a full-page ad in the *New York Times* declaring: "should reputable evidence show that some fluorocarbons cause a health hazard through depletion of the ozone layer, we are prepared to stop production of the offending compounds." In the following years, DuPont took great pains to make this point, namely that *reputable evidence* was not available. In the same ad, the company spelled out the program for the coming decade: "Claim meets counterclaim. Assumptions are challenged on both sides. And nothing is settled." A fight for scientific authority and credibility ensued, which put industry on the defensive.

DuPont's statement gave scientific research an important role in the whole process. After the discovery of abnormally low ozone levels over Antarctica (later known as "the ozone hole") in 1985, more and more actors (including scientists) were convinced that something had to be done quickly – even in the absence of scientific proof. DuPont's statement also had a self-binding effect: in 1986 the company signaled that it would no longer oppose international controls. However, it has to be borne in mind that the reputable evidence was the observed damage of the ozone hole (and its potential catastrophic consequences), which ultimately convinced DuPont.

The ozone hole was clearly a focusing event that symbolized the crisis and created a sense of urgency. Furthermore, it allowed policy entrepreneurs, including scientists, to offer solutions that they had been developing before the crisis struck. An early opponent of CFC regulations, James Lovelock, acknowledges with hindsight the role played by advocate scientists, especially by Rowland:

> If Rowland hadn't been so missionary about this it would never have developed to this point. If it would have been treated objectively, scientifically, as I would have liked to have seen it done, it probably would never have been treated as a serious issue by the public and by politicians. If he hadn't stirred up the Greens and the politicians . . . He must have spent an enormous amount of his time and effort going around lecturing, talking. He really barnstormed. He went to every little town and every little community, delivering his speech. I thought this isn't the way to do science, but I think he was probably right, because he believed in it. (Grundmann 2001: 198)

A problem arises for the scientific advocates: they are accused of betraying the ideals of science. Their public role entails "popularizing" scientific findings, taking sides in a political controversy, and making policy recommendations. However, none of the scientists active in this field of research could avoid asking (or being asked) questions such as: Who has the burden of proof? What is a reasonable evidence of damage? Who should make judgments on these issues? How should one weigh "worst case" scenarios? What weight should be given to social or economic benefits when considering regulation? (Brooks 1982). Those were also the questions which had to be answered when political options were formulated – scientists and politicians alike had to find responses.

Many of the scientists who were involved in the CFC controversy "found themselves unable to avoid making explicit or implicit judgements about almost every one of these essentially non-scientific value questions, no matter how much they tried to 'stick to the facts'" (Brooks 1982: 206). At hearings before a Congress subcommittee, Rowland gave priority to ecological concerns when asked to rank them with economic interests: "I think that the economic dislocations need to be given minimal weight compared to the maximum weight to the possible harm to the environment" (quoted in Grundmann 2001: 73).

The advocacy scientists succeeded in presenting the case in a convincing way in public discussions, in school classes, during parliamentary hearings, and in media broadcasts. They also put forward a kind of "political strategy" for the protection of the ozone layer. In the 1970s it was the proposal to replace CFC in spray cans that led to a supportive reaction on the part of both consumers and lawmakers in the United States. This would be followed by a call for a ban on all CFCs after 1985. This pragmatic strategy was based on a realization of political realities and economic opportunities. It should be seen as practical knowledge as we define the term in this book. First, they proposed substitutes for non-essential applications of CFCs, particularly as a propellant in spray cans. For the United States that would already produce a reduction in emissions of about 50 percent. The proposal was based on the fact that substitute products were available (for example, pump sprays, propane/butane mixtures as propellants) or that they could quickly be developed. Other applications, for example in refrigerators and air conditioners, would be spared for the time being. This line of argument was successful and found its way into the regulations. Moreover, they argued, in making this decision under uncertainty, the potential benefit for the planet, should new findings prove the danger to be less than had been assumed, was incomparably greater than any potential harm. In the mid 1970s, more than half of the annual world production of approximately 700,000 tonnes of CFC 11 and CFC 12 went into aerosol propellants. In the United States, most of this was used in personal hygiene sprays (Grundmann 2001:114).

In view of the uncertainties in the model calculations, there was indeed no purely scientific method to decide whether CFCs should be regulated – and if so, how strictly. One of the crucial questions was whether the uncertainties of the computer models represented an argument for or against regulation. An error factor of two in the models meant that the problem could be either half as big or, just as easily, twice as big, as the atmospheric scientist Ralph Cicerone stressed at the Congress Hearings. Uncertainty cuts both ways. As we shall see, dealing with uncertainties is another issue which distinguishes the cases of ozone and climate.

The Clean Air Act of 1977 institutionalized a precautionary approach by banning CFCs in "non-essential applications" (e.g. spray cans). Of central importance was the proviso that "no conclusive proof ... but a reasonable expectation" was sufficient to justify taking action. This move was going to define US policy for the international negotiations as well (Betsill and Pielke 1997). At the time, no scientific theory about ozone depletion had become consensual, nor had actual measurements of ozone been carried out. The "spray can ban" was enacted on the basis of a scientific hypothesis and model calculations about future ozone loss. No actual data on atmospheric change had been available at the time. Industry relentlessly pointed out that it was fundamentally opposed to the idea of regulating an industrial product on the basis of "pure theory."

At the beginning of the 1980s, ozone depletion entered the agenda of international environmental policymaking. Until 1986, the opponents of regulations repeated their position that too little was known to justify regulations. More scientific research was deemed necessary to remedy this lack of understanding. They were right in stating that little was known about the atmosphere; this became clear when the Antarctic ozone hole was discovered, since no theoretical model had predicted this phenomenon. It took more than two years until it could be explained scientifically. But is (relative) ignorance or scientific uncertainty an excuse for inaction? This was the real question underlying all the controversies over whether regulations were justified or not.

It is telling that many scientists active in the field of ozone depletion held a view about precautionary policies like the following: "I always thought that in the face of uncertainty one could take a prudent course of action just as a form of insurance, just like you are buying a fire insurance, you are not predicting that you'll have a fire, but if there is a possibility for fire you can take out an insurance" (author interview with US scientist, November 1995; note that this scientist did not act as an advocate; on the contrary, he argued for some time against theories of anthropogenic causes of the ozone hole).

The discovery of the ozone hole was an alarm signal that completely changed the perception of the problem. As Rowland put it, "The big loss of ozone over Antarctica has changed this from being a computer hypothesis plausible for the future to a current reality and cause for concern" (*New York Times*, December 7, 1986). Although it was officially not a topic during the international negotiations culminating in the Montreal Protocol, it did in fact have an influence on the negotiations (Christie 2001; Grundmann 2001). Media attention rose sharply after the ozone hole had been represented as a scientific fact.

The colored picture of the ozone hole has become an icon, symbolizing the threat to the ozone layer and life on Earth. Before the "ozone hole" metaphor came up, experts and laypersons from the mid 1970s to the mid 1980s were concerned merely with a possible future "thinning of the ozone layer." The difference between the two metaphors is evident. While the *thinning* metaphor evokes the picture of a threadbare tissue, the *hole* metaphor evokes the picture of a punctured balloon exploding or losing its air, or an organism infected by a disease. This metaphor was clearly designed to capture the element of drama. Before 1985, everyone expected an ozone loss of maybe 10 or 20% in one hundred years (Benedick 1991: 13).

In sum, it should be evident that scientific consensus was not instrumental for the establishment of the Montreal Protocol. Rather, the role of advocate scientists as policy entrepreneurs needs to be highlighted. They were able to develop practical knowledge that culminated in concrete, actionable political recommendations, such as the spray can ban and the phase-out of CFCs. Of course they were helped by the advent of a genuine crisis that no one expected or predicted. Key to their success was the credibility they had gained during the controversy. When the unexpected ozone hole appeared, they were in a position to bolster their pro-regulation position most convincingly.

The catalogue of measures in the Montreal Protocol set a freeze on production totals for the year 1990, a reduction of 20 percent for the year 1994, and a further reduction by 1999; a 50 percent reduction altogether of CFCs relative to 1986. Moreover, the Protocol contains the following important clauses:

- a ban on moving production into non-signatory countries;
- a ban on importing from non-signatory countries;
- the signatories are to represent two-thirds of global consumption in 1986;
- an ongoing scientific reevaluation.

The control measures listed in the Montreal Protocol make it plain that it was above all a treaty for limiting the *production* of ozone-depleting substances. Such controls are not available in climate change politics. It is obvious that the Montreal Protocol was the role model for the Kyoto Protocol; however, despite the many parallels, there are decisive differences. One is that the production of greenhouse gases (GHGs) is closely tied to the functioning of modern societies. Modern societies need huge amounts of energy for their smooth operation. Of course, we could imagine a future where less energy was demanded. But in the meantime, we need to find ways of doing what we do with less carbon intensity. An immediate and radical cut in the production of GHGs would lead to the collapse of the economy. No country could even contemplate reducing the production of GHGs in the next five years by 50 percent – which was the case with CFCs. The boldest policies mention 80 percent GHG reductions by 2050. Even then, it is unclear how the target could be achieved (see Pielke 2009).

Climate change is different from ozone politics in another aspect. This difference has to do with the different drama in the two cases. As described above, in the case of ozone politics there was a sudden, "hot" crisis after the ozone hole was discovered which was a shocking surprise. All experts and policymakers at the time were convinced that immediate action was required. With climate politics, such a hot crisis has not materialized. Instead, many controversial discussions revolve around the question of whether signals or harbingers of such crises can be seen. Science activists, who answer this in the affirmative, are accused of exaggerating the evidence. This points to a third significant difference. While in the case of ozone politics, activist scientists were operating visibly and ultimately convinced others to follow their line, in climate politics we see *stealth advocacy* (Pielke 2007: 7).

This means that scientists are narrowing the range of options, although this is poorly suited to their official role as honest brokers. At least this is the familiar image that is portrayed by the IPCC, a body that mainly represents the authority of science.

IPCC under attack

With the growing role played by the IPCC, a dynamic has set in that complicates the simple antagonism so apparent in the ozone case. The IPCC takes great pains to demonstrate that its assessments are based on the best available science, and not on advocacy. One of its former chairs, Robert T. Watson, states:

The IPCC, which began in 1988 as an intergovernmental process, has strong expert and government peer-review, and has been highly influential on the policy process, not only within governments, but also within many parts of the private sector as well. For example, many multinational companies, including British Petroleum, Shell, Dupont, and Toyota argue that, based on the conclusions of the IPCC, the issue of climate change should be taken seriously by the private sector – this is the kind of impact a good scientific assessment should have. (2005: 474)

The IPCC aspires to a role that Roger Pielke, Jr. has labeled the "honest broker." How well the IPCC actually fulfills this role is debated, and will be discussed in the remainder of this chapter. Some sceptics argue that IPCC science is "junk" and political rather than scientific. Others have criticized its over-reliance on models (Oreskes et al. 1994), and its overselling the state of knowledge (Pielke 2007). Such critics claim that despite advances in climate science, we still face major uncertainties, which are systematically downplayed by the IPCC; and that instead a consensus is "orchestrated" (Elzinga 1995; Oppenheimer et al. 2007).

As in the case of ozone depletion, there is a widespread perception that science is the final arbiter in the climate change debate, and that science will ultimately prescribe policy.[12] Any criticisms leveled at the

---

[12] The IPCC stresses its political neutrality: "Because of its scientific and intergovernmental nature, the IPCC embodies a unique opportunity to provide rigorous and balanced scientific information to decision makers. By endorsing the IPCC reports,

work of the IPCC are seen as attempts to undermine the political project of curbing greenhouse gas emissions. During the so-called Lomborg controversy, several eminent scientists attacked Danish social scientist Bjorn Lomborg for his "bad science," with strong overtones suggesting he was the target because of a fear of political diversion (see Lomborg 2001; and the discussions in *Environmental Science & Policy*, special issue on Lomborg, 2004, and in *Scientific American*, 2002 (286)1). This is a direct outcome of the linear view held by these scientists (a view that Lomborg incidentally shares with his opponents), which culminates in the belief that if there is still scientific uncertainty, carbon emission reductions would not be legitimate.

No other than Al Gore summarized this view, when he said that "more research and better research and better targeted research is absolutely essential if we are going to eliminate the remaining areas of uncertainty and build the broader and stronger political consensus necessary for the unprecedented actions required to address this problem" (cited in Sarewitz and Pielke 2000).

Al Gore's advice has three problematic, and even dysfunctional, side effects. For one, it tends to marginalize other viewpoints that do not belong to the scientific mainstream represented in the IPCC process, or that deviate in other ways. Second, it makes science the battleground for politics. And third, it obscures the important lesson from the ozone case, i.e. that there is no need for scientific proof in order to act. If decision-makers and the public agree that it is "better [to be] safe than sorry" and that it is prudent to "take out insurance," then there is no need to place such exaggerated hopes on science.

While the target of climate stabilization (i.e. maximum 2 degrees Celsius global warming) was defined politically, this rests on scenarios which have a built-in normative preference. Who would like to embark on a path that leads to dangerous climate change? The focus on CO_2 as the most relevant GHG is a political choice, and not at all politically neutral. There are many other anthropogenic causes of global warming that are omitted by the IPCC focus. Roger Pielke, Sr. et al. (2009) articulate this charge against the IPCC:

Unfortunately, the 2007 Intergovernmental Panel on Climate Change (IPCC) assessment did not sufficiently acknowledge the importance of these other human climate forcings in altering regional and global climate and their effects on predictability at the regional scale. It also placed too much emphasis on

governments acknowledge the authority of their scientific content. The work of the organization is therefore policy-relevant and yet policy-neutral, never policy-prescriptive" (www.ipcc.ch/organization/organization.htm).

average global forcing from a limited set of human climate forcings. Further, it devised a mitigation strategy based on global model predictions.

Besides GHGs, they single out several other factors:

In addition to greenhouse gas emissions, other first-order human climate forcings are important to understanding the future behavior of Earth's climate. These forcings are spatially heterogeneous and include the effect of aerosols on clouds and associated precipitation ..., the influence of aerosol deposition (e.g., black carbon (soot) ... and reactive nitrogen ...), and the role of changes in land use/land cover.

All of these would be relevant for political action, and maybe even more amenable to political intervention compared to the massive reductions envisaged for CO_2 emissions. There would be the additional advantage of reducing local and regional vulnerability, no matter whether it arises from extreme weather events, natural climate variation, or anthropogenic climate variation.

The role of scenarios

Let us return to one of the important policy-brokers in the field of knowledge and global governance who has written on this topic. Robert Watson was involved in both the ozone and the climate change debates, and was IPCC chair from 1997 until 2002. In a piece written for the Royal Society, he tells us that in order to

influence decision-making we have to understand the underlying causes of environmental change and the process of decision-making. Although sound science is necessary for informed public policy and decision-making, it is not sufficient. We have to identify the problem, identify what the policy choices are, implement those policy choices and then monitor and evaluate the effects of those policy choices. Furthermore, we must recognize that decision-making processes are highly value-laden, combining political and technocratic elements, that they operate at a range of spatial scales from the village to the global level, and that, to have any chance of being effective, they must be transparent and participatory, involving all relevant stakeholders. (Watson 2005: 473)

After this very useful exposition of the role of knowledge and the need for a broad social participation in the decision-making process, he then narrows his focus to science:

There is solid evidence that key decision-makers, including governments, the private sector and the general public, are influenced in their decisions by sound, solid scientific knowledge. Developing sound scientific knowledge requires national and internationally coordinated public and private sector research programmes, combining local indigenous knowledge with institutional knowledge

where appropriate, and the free and open exchange of information. This knowledge then needs to be placed in an appropriate format for decision-making.
(Watson 2005: 473)

In this book we differentiate between "knowledge for practice" and
"practical knowledge." This distinction is important, since the pragmatic relevance of knowledge is by no means certain a priori. For knowledge to be turned to knowledge for action, several conditions must
be met. According to Mannheim ([1929] 1965: 143), the successful
"deployment" of findings in concrete situations for action demands that
for such contexts the possibilities for action, as well as an understanding of the actors' latitude for action and their chances of shaping events,
must be linked together, in order that knowledge may become practical
knowledge. In other words, scientific knowledge is not sufficient – other
knowledge forms may well be required – and knowledge needs to get
access to levers that exist in reality and that can be moved.

When Watson says that "knowledge then needs to be placed in an
appropriate format for decision-making," he touches upon this very
problem. In his view, scenarios play a special role in this process. He
claims that they are "one of the most important tools for helping to foster policy changes." Scenarios are "plausible futures, not predictions or
projections of the future." He praises the virtues of scenarios beyond
the field of environmental politics, such as "playing war games, projecting the prices of agricultural commodities and projecting energy
demand." Many multinational companies also use them, such as
Dutch Royal Shell and Morgan Stanley. As Watson puts it, "[t]he goal
for decision-makers is to explore plausible futures and understand the
underlying factors that determine those futures so that interventions
can be crafted to realize the positive outcomes and avoid the negative
outcomes" (2005: 475).[13]

However, if one looks more closely at the experience with scenarios,
some caution might be in order. Shell is often credited with its shrewd
use of scenarios to anticipate future trends and be prepared. Shell
confronted the very example of climate change in the late 1980s and
early 1990s, and it is widely regarded as a pioneer and expert in the use

[13] According to the terminology used by the IPCC, *climate predictions* are to be distinguished from *climate projections*, which are in turn to be distinguished from *scenarios*.
"A climate prediction or *climate forecast* is the result of an attempt to produce an estimate of the actual evolution of the climate in the future, for example, at seasonal,
interannual or long-term time scales." Climate *projections* "depend upon the emis-
sion/concentration/radiative forcing scenario used." And *scenarios*, in turn, "are based
on assumptions concerning, for example, future socioeconomic and technological
developments that may or may not be realised and are therefore subject to substantial
uncertainty" (www.ipcc.ch/pdf/glossary/ar4-wg1.pdf).

of scenario planning (Grant 2003; Shell 2004; Wright 2004).[14] Since 1971, Shell has explicitly addressed issues of uncertainty in its strategy formulation through scenario planning. Shell's own literature claims that the extensive use of scenario planning is based on the belief that "the only competitive advantage the company of the future will have is its managers' ability to learn faster than their competitors" (De Geus 1988).

Stubbs (2009) has carried out a detailed analysis of Shell's scenarios in the late 1980s and early 1990s. He shows that the use of these has been limited and somewhat countervails the official message:

The 1992 scenarios discuss increasing demand for finite resources, in particular fossil fuels, and the need for global agreements. This wasn't particularly innovative, given that the Brundtland report was discussing this in 1987 and that international agreements were being proposed in the run up to the United Nations summit in Rio in 1992. It is also striking that at this time senior mangers at Shell were not particularly vocal about the need for action on climate change, or proactive in discussing the management of its own environmental impacts.

The 1995 scenarios have curiously little specific discussion of environmental issues and especially climate change, especially considering that the IPCC was active and the process of negotiating a treaty to control greenhouse emissions was already well advanced. There was in fact less discussion of environmental issues than in the 1992 scenarios. It was however at about this time that senior managers at Shell started to make the public statements about supporting controls on greenhouse gas emissions. The 1998 scenarios considered the way the Kyoto protocol might be implemented and how environmental policies may be driven by emerging crises and more extreme environmental activism rather than by planned proactive action by government and business.

However, it is noteworthy that Shell defines scenarios as event-driven, and that one has to make assumptions about crucial future developments, as its website states: "scenarios provide alternative views of the future. They identify some significant events, main actors and their motivations, and they convey how the world functions" (Shell 2010).

This aspect is not appropriately emphasized by Watson or by the IPCC. They seem to use the prestige of scenario planning as a management

[14] "The scenario approach enables a continual assessment of trends and developments that may affect its business in the future" (Skjærseth and Skodvin 2001: 53). Wright claims that the use of scenario planning resulted in Shell "having considered and rehearsed its responses to the 1973 oil crisis and price collapse of 1981 before these events happened" (Wright 2004: 6); and Grant explains that "although all the [major oil] companies used scenario analysis to some extent, only Shell utilises scenarios as the foundation and centrepiece of its strategic planning process. Other companies tend to use scenarios as a complement and balance to their forecasting exercises, or to explore particular issues" (Grant 2003: 17).

tool, as is evident with some high-profile corporations. However, all scenarios are driven by specific assumptions (called "storylines" in the IPCC jargon) about population size, economic growth, and the prevailing energy mix, which means that they will vary accordingly. As the IPCC explicitly acknowledges, these storylines are subject to "substantial uncertainty." In 2000, the IPCC published a Special Report on Emissions Scenarios (SRES, see Nakicenovic and Swart 2000), which shows "four scenario families (A1, A2, B1, and B2) that explore alternative development pathways, covering a wide range of demographic, economic and technological driving forces and resulting GHG emissions." One scenario (A2) assumes that the world population in 2100 will be 15.1 billion, more than 50 percent higher than other scenarios. Such details are buried in the technical details of the report, and are rarely mentioned when communicating the findings to the public.[15] We have summarized some of the underlying assumptions ("storylines") and implications in Table 5. (Note that only the socio-demographic assumptions are contained in SRES, whereas the implications are not reported. They have been collected from TAR.)

On the basis of these four storylines (A1/2, B1/2), forty scenarios were developed, with six being presented as illustrative. In Table 5, this can be seen through the variety of scenarios based on the A1 storyline, where three additional runs have been reported, A1T, A1B, and A1FI, relating to temperature and sea-level rise. Looking at IPCC scenarios published in 1990, 1992, and 2000, Girod et al. observe an increase in the number of scenarios and authors, but a decrease in specific information; for example, the omission of descriptive titles. The 1990 scenario did contain such descriptive titles, i.e. "2030 High Emissions" and "2060 Low Emissions." Compared to previous scenarios, the SRES of 2000 shows a dramatic increase in available information. More information is an ambiguous virtue for policymakers: on the one hand, it can convey important aspects to be taken into account; on the other hand, it can lead to confusion. The coverage of uncertainties in population and income projections is beneficial because the impact of climate change strongly depends on these variables, as Nicholls and Tol (2006: 1073) point out: "The most vulnerable future worlds to sea-level rise appear to be the A2 and B2 scenarios, which primarily reflects [sic] differences in the socio-economic situation ... rather than the magnitude of sea-level rise."

---

[15] By the way, the Stern Review (2007) made liberal use of the A2 scenario for its assessment of the damages and costs of climate change.

Table 5. *IPCC storylines in SRES*
*(Note that socio-demographic assumptions are based on forecasts by 2050,
implications by 2100.)*

		A1	A2	B1	B2
Socio-demographic Assumptions	Population	9 bn	15 bn	9 bn	10 bn
	Income/capita ($)	21,000	7,200	13,000	12,000
	Educational levels	High	Uneven	High	High
	Technology innovation and transfer	High	Uneven	High	Uneven
	International cooperation	High	Low	High	Low
Implications	Average temperature rise by 2100 (C)	A1T: 2.4 A1B: 2.8 A1FI: 4.0	3.4	1.8	2.4
	Average sea-level rise by 2100 (M)	A1T: 0.20–0.45 A1B: 0.21–0.48 A1FI: 0.26–0.59	0.23–0.51	0.18–0.38	0.20–0.43

While the 1990 and 1992 scenarios included these implications (such as temperature change and sea-level rise), these were removed from the final version of SRES. The 1990 scenario used a 2030 High Emissions scenario to predict future climate change. After that, equal treatment was given to all scenarios. From 1992 onwards, the scenarios are presented without any probabilities attached to them. This can easily lead to confusion in public debate, and it is not surprising that some climate scientists want to introduce appropriate qualifications based on probability estimates, however subjective they might be. Stephen Schneider writes:

[w]e are facing the even more worrying prospect of dozens of users selecting arbitrary scenarios and climate sensitivities to construct frequency charts that … are built on implicit assumptions … I would definitely put more trust in the probability estimates of the SRES team – however subjective – than those of the myriad special interests that have been encouraged to make their own selection. Meanwhile, as we wait for the IPCC to decide whether to reassemble the team for this controversial labour, climate policy-makers will have to be vigilant, asking all advisers to justify the threshold they choose for predicting "dangerous" climate change, as well as to provide a "traceable account" of how

they selected their emissions scenarios and model sensitivities, as these jointly determine the probability of future risks.

Girod et al. (2009: 116) do not concur in the call for inclusion of probabilities. Instead, they wish to see a better identification of salient scenarios, more transparency, and an assessment of policy options based on intervention scenarios:

The challenges for the development of new IPCC's emission scenarios remain: (i) to agree on a salient number of emissions scenarios; (ii) to transparently describe and classify the scenarios (intervention/non-intervention); (iii) to assess which policies are needed to reach the low RCPs/emissions scenarios; and (iv) to transparently and fairly mediate among the scientific and intergovernmental review contributions.

When Shell communicates its scenarios, it is making clear what the assumptions are. For example, in 1992 Shell presented two scenarios called *New Frontiers* and *Barricades*. *New Frontiers* envisaged more global cooperation and an acknowledgment of the interdependence of global financial and political institutions. There would be growth in the use of all energy sources: oil, coal, gas, and unconventional oils, and significant new renewable energy sources, particularly photovoltaics. *Barricades*, in contrast, saw an increase in protectionism and insular thinking. Fears over energy security and environmental damage lead to draconian local regulation. There is a weakening of international institutions, and therefore of an ability to tackle problems globally (Stubbs 2009: 79). The IPCC makes reference to these Shell scenarios (which are used, among other sources, to construct the storyline for A1 and A2) but does not communicate its own message in a similarly clear way to the public.

Both Shell and the IPCC make one crucial, yet perhaps unconvincing, assumption in the general design of their scenarios. This is the principle that the scenarios should be constructed independently of the intervention of the organization in question. In Stubbs's (2009) words,

The language Shell uses in its literature tends to imply a distance between the planner and the scenario; it gives a sense of objectivity and legitimacy ... It is very much portrayed as a positivistic methodology that assumes a world is out there to be discovered, rather than alternative realities that are created ... It is interesting that the organisation itself is not included in the scenario. This may imply that it feels it is simply reacting to events and has no part in shaping them. The planning methodology states that the "scenarios should never contain the organisation as an actor" (Wright 2004: 10). When the organisation is a major and influential player in the field this would seem to be denying a fundamental reality.

Likewise, the IPCC has only briefly used intervention scenarios (1990). An intervention scenario is defined as "an emission scenario that makes assumptions about climate policies to reduce greenhouse gases. Policies must be directed towards mitigation." By contrast, a non-intervention scenario is "an emission scenario that does not make any assumption about climate policy to reduce greenhouse gases" (Alcamo et al. 1995: 258). In both cases it is highly implausible to assume that the organization constructing the scenarios would be irrelevant for the further development of the external world. In the case of Shell, for instance, we know that its signaling (together with BP and the insurance industry) of acceptance of the Kyoto treaty was significant for the change in attitudes of important corporate actors, and thus for the very acceptance of Kyoto (Leggett 2001). However, the IPCC makes the assumption that the world would carry on without climate policies. One might see this as a useful reminder of dangerous developments. But it gets more complicated. The SRES document thus states:

> the scenarios in this report do not include additional climate initiatives, which means that no scenarios are included that explicitly assume implementation of the United Nations Framework Convention for Climate Change (UNFCCC) or the emissions targets of the Kyoto Protocol. However, GHG emissions are directly affected by non-climate change policies designed for a wide range of other purposes. Furthermore government policies can, to varying degrees, influence the GHG emission drivers such as demographic change, social and economic development, technological change, resource use, and pollution management. This influence is broadly reflected in the storylines and resultant scenarios. (Nakicenovic and Swart 2000: 3)

What gets communicated to the public are the implications. These are plain numbers about average temperature rise and average sea-level rise. Perhaps most crucially, there is a sharp contrast between the IPCC and Shell scenarios with regard to the social science dimension. While Shell stresses the need to understand actors and their motivations, the IPCC looks only at some aggregate statistics – it tries to quantify everything in a positivistic manner. This does not mean that the IPCC is oblivious to the importance of actors and their motivations. As we will argue below, the communication of the IPCC scenarios has indeed played an important role in the policy process, and it has led to some alarming rhetoric and bandwagon effects. Still, the desired political result has not ensued.

The framing of the issue

It seems problematic to think of the policy process simply in terms of experts influencing political decision-makers (this section draws on Grundmann 2007). Nor is it very helpful to draw a sharp demarcation line between experts and non-experts. As many controversies have shown, the important opposition is between two alliances that advocate different policies, based on divergent basic values and knowledge claims (Hajer 1995). Representatives of science, politics, and the lay public are on both sides of such disputes. Scientific results and their symbolic representation in the public domain are valuable resources. Public trust and credibility are at stake, with claims from both sides being tested in public disputes (Grundmann 2001). It may well be that scientific experts are leading in the framing of issues and the invention of symbols and metaphors. But it is the engaged lay people and the wider interested public, including the mass media, that will ultimately decide on the credibility of various propositions. Such shifts in public credibility are unlikely to follow consensus models. It is more realistic to expect that one side will eventually gain hegemony over the other (Grundmann 2001; Hajer 1995). It is unlikely, however, that scientific evidence will play the most important role in this process. Witness the ozone case above, where the international treaty was agreed upon without robust scientific theory.

The media hold an important position in influencing public opinion on these matters; the framing of issues is particularly important (Spector and Kitsuse 1977; Ungar 1992; Mazur and Lee 1993). It has been suggested that there is an issue attention cycle (Downs 1972; Trumbo, 1996), but that the media's influence in the climate case is secondary, "reinforcing the perceptions of primary definers in the politics of global warming: scientists, states and corporations" (Newell 2000: 95).

Looking at the basic values that underlie climate change policies, one could identify – in an ideal-typical way – two radically opposing frames, which are related to different climatic and economic models. According to the first, the world economy would be fatally damaged if we tried to reduce GHG emissions drastically; according to the second, similar catastrophic results would follow by adopting the opposite course, and not taking action. These frames are based on fundamental values such as "preventing harm" (to the global environment, or to the economy). They also rest on some knowledge of causal chains of future climate states, their causes and effects, and on economic knowledge about costs of carbon emissions reduction. In a simplified way, one could describe the policy of the United States government as following the first frame (avoid damage to the economy as a result of GHG emissions cuts), while the European Union is following the second (avoid global environmental catastrophe).[16]

---

[16] It would be an exaggeration to claim that Europe has tried to reduce emissions drastically; it has tried to take modest first steps. But in fact, emissions in many countries of the European Union have been increasing (EEA 2005).

How influential is the IPCC on politics?

Because the IPCC is an intergovernmental body and is based on scientific consensus, it is hardly surprising that many observers (and participants) assume that the relationship between science and politics is linear, i.e. they believe that knowledge is directly influencing politics. We will discuss this most influential position first, and then turn to a less prominent view.

In its Second Assessment Report (SAR), published in 1996, the IPCC famously stated that "the balance of evidence suggests that there is a discernible human influence on global climate" (Houghton et al. 1996). Scholars have attributed the change in US climate policy to the release of this report. As Edwards and Schneider (2001) observed, after a long period in which the United States did not support binding targets in international environmental policymaking, things started to change after the release of the SAR. "On July 17, 1996, then-US Under-Secretary of State for Global Affairs Tim Wirth formally announced to COP-2 that the United States would now support 'the adoption of a realistic but binding target' for emissions. The exact degree to which the IPCC SAR influenced this policy change cannot be known. But Wirth certainly gave the impression that the report was its proximate cause." Wirth also noted that "the United States takes very seriously the IPCC's recently issued Second Assessment Report." He cited the SAR at length, stating that "the science is convincing; concern about global warming is real" (Wirth 1996, quoted in Edwards and Schneider 2001). However, such a reading is prone to overlook the fact that years before the publication of SAR, Vice-President Al Gore had written *Earth in Balance* (1992). This indicates that SAR was used by the Clinton administration to embark upon a political trajectory that had taken shape beforehand.

A second decisive episode shows that there is no direct link between scientific expert knowledge and political orientation: while the scientific assessment has not been reversed since 1996, the official US policy has. Bush called the Kyoto Protocol "fatally flawed" because it would be economically damaging, and unfair in that there would be insufficient involvement by the developing countries. Interestingly, he made explicit reference to "the incomplete state of scientific knowledge of the causes of, and solutions to, global climate change" when he withdrew the US commitment to the Kyoto Protocol and its binding targets (*New York Times*, March 17, 2001). On May 11, 2003, the White House requested a fast-track review of the state of climate science from the National Academy of Sciences. In its report, eleven leading atmospheric scientists reaffirmed the mainstream scientific view that the earth's atmosphere was getting warmer and that human activity was largely responsible. However, despite the fact that the government could not derive support from NAS, it was nevertheless able to hold firmly to the view that Kyoto was fatally flawed, and that "we cannot do something that damages the American economy" (*New York Times*, June 7, 2001). There are two issues here; one is uncertainty with respect to human influences on climate, and the other is uncertainty with respect to the impacts of Kyoto on the US economy. Clearly the Bush administration values the latter over the former, where "science" seems simply a legitimizing cover for decisions reached based on other factors. If the NAS had obliged the government in concocting a favorable review, Bush would undoubtedly have made a bigger case for scientific aspects as a reason for rejection. As it turned out, they were not needed; the economic argument was deemed to be convincing on its own.

Let us now examine the second, less prominent, position on the relation between science and policy. This position does not assume that scientific consensus is a prerequisite for regulatory action. Comparing the cases of ozone depletion and climate change, Betsill and Pielke (1997) argue that in the ozone case, scientific *uncertainty* – rather than scientific certainty – fostered the regulatory activities. They demonstrate how a specific set of (precautionary) decision rules was institutionalized in the United States in the mid 1970s and carried over to the mid 1980s. Against interpretations relying too heavily on epistemic communities and the role of scientific consensus (e.g. Haas 1992, 1993), they argue that "in some instances, scientific uncertainty, rather than consensus, may actually move policy along" (Betsill and Pielke 1997: 165). Likewise, Edwards (1999: 465–66) points out that "in politics scientific uncertainty becomes a rhetorical resource which can and will be employed by different actors in different ways." Opponents of precautionary action will usually demand more research and "proof" before regulations are deemed legitimate. But advocates of regulations also argue that *because* of scientific uncertainty, we should act now in order to avoid worst-case scenarios coming true. "Far from inhibiting decisions... uncertainty can actually provide proponents of international and national-level policymaking with one of their best arguments for near-term action" (Edwards 1996: 155).

It has also been argued that the IPCC used simple messages in order to construct a consensus, and not to confuse policymakers. An example is climate sensitivity, which was estimated for some time at a range of 1.5–4.5° C as a result of doubling CO_2 concentrations in the atmosphere. Some have argued that this "anchoring device" was not altered, despite the fact that scientists themselves were not too confident about this range; they maintained it in order not to give the impression that their findings were uncertain (van der Sluijs et al. 1998; see also Weart 2003: 173).[17]

The first assessment carried out by the US National Academy of Sciences in 1979 estimated the climate sensitivity as a result of a doubling of global CO_2 concentrations. It reached the conclusion that "the most probable" warming would be "near 3° C with a probable error of ± 1.5° C" (US NAS, 1979, as quoted in van der Sluijs et al. 1998: 298). This leads to a range of 1.5–4.5° C global warming. It is remarkable how stable this range has remained over time: the same range appears in all major modeling efforts: by the US National Academy of Sciences in 1979 and 1983; in Villach 1985; by the IPCC in 1990, 1992, and 1994; by Bolin in 1995; and by the IPCC in 1995 (see van der Sluijs et al. 1998).[18] In minute detail, van der Sluijs et al. (1998) show how the community of scientists and policymakers[19] has held on to this range of climate sensitivity for a long time. It seems plausible to assume that scientists and policymakers involved in the process have chosen this strategy in order to gain and maintain credibility. However, this consensus comes at a price. The "anchoring property" of the 1.5–4.5 range has screened out policy attention for other relevant questions, such as the possibility of regional differentiations and variations outside the range; more abrupt changes in climate; and the role of human poverty, inequity, and global consumption and land-use patterns (van der Sluijs et al. 1998: 318). All of these would be apt vehicles for promoting a preventive climate change strategy. The anchoring device has arguably helped screen out such other valid concerns. Only in later years has one of these possibilities gained in prominence: abrupt changes in climate. The new metaphor of "tipping points" lent itself to a storyline of unfolding drama.

The Third Assessment Report, published in 2001, revised the top-range limit of predictions of global warming from the previous value of 1.5–4.5° C to 1.4–5.8° C between now and 2100. Stephen Schneider

---

[17] Over time, a remarkable shift occurred with regard to the epistemological status of climate sensitivity. Early efforts used the CO_2 doubling as a heuristic tool for model inter-comparison, but during the 1980s climate sensitivity became an objective indicator of the climate system, which could be measured (van der Sluijs et al. 1998: 307).

[18] Only later, in the Third Assessment Report, was the range extended to 1.4–5.8° C (see www.ipcc.ch/pub/spm22–01.pdf).

[19] Very much an "epistemic community," which is defined by Haas (1992: 187–8) as "a knowledge-based network of specialists who share beliefs in cause-and-effect relations, validity tests, and underlying principled values and pursue common policy goals." As we shall see below, however, Haas (surprisingly?) does not see the IPCC as an epistemic community.

(2001: 17) called this revision dramatic and "sweeping." He says that it depends on "two factors that were not the handiwork of the modellers: smaller projected emissions of climate-cooling aerosols; and a few predictions containing particularly large CO_2 emissions."

Not only has the rise in the range of global mean temperature been revised, but there have also been more and more alarmist statements in recent years about the potential impacts of climate change.

What is dangerous climate change?

In 2004 the United Kingdom's chief science advisor, Sir David King, outlined the challenge posed by climate change: "In my view, climate change is the most severe problem that we are facing today – more serious even than the threat of terrorism" (King 2004: 176). A few years down the line, and the Department for Environment, Food and Rural Affairs says on its website (as of September 2009):

Climate change is the greatest challenge facing the world today. It is a global issue that demands a global response. All countries must be part of the solution. The UK plays a leading role at the international level. We are working through the European Union, the G8 and UN Framework Convention on Climate Change (UNFCCC) processes to find ways to reach global agreement on action to avert dangerous climate change. The UK Government's goal is to stabilise atmospheric greenhouse gas levels so that we avoid dangerous climate change, and to adapt to the climate change that is unavoidable. The UK Government and the EU consider that global warming must be limited to no more than 2°C temperature rise above pre-industrial times to avoid dangerous impacts.[20]

Mike Hulme (2009: 66–67) comments on these rhetorical strategies as follows:

The language and metaphorical constructions of fear and catastrophe regarding climate change have been embellished substantially in the period following 9/11. The "war on terror" provided a new benchmark against which the dangers of future climate change could be referenced, while new linguistic and metaphorical repertoires have been developed.

There are other examples of conveying a more dramatic message to the world public. Addressing the issue of dangerous anthropogenic climate change (DAI), several IPCC authors identified five "reasons for concern" (Smith et al. 2009). Their paper, published in the prestigious

[20] www.defra.gov.uk/sustainable/government/publications/uk-strategy/documents/Chap4.pdf.

Proceedings of the National Academy of Sciences and quoted extensively by the media, lists them as follows:

Risk to Unique and Threatened Systems, such as coral reefs, tropical glaciers, endangered species, unique ecosystems, biodiversity hotspots, small island states, and indigenous communities.

Risk of Extreme Weather Events, e.g. increase in the frequency, intensity, or consequences of heat waves, floods, droughts, wildfires, or tropical cyclones.

Distribution of Impacts: Some regions, countries, and populations face greater harm from climate change, whereas other regions, countries, or populations would be much less harmed – and some may benefit; the magnitude of harm can also vary within regions and across sectors and populations.

Aggregate Damages: Impacts distributed across the globe can be aggregated into a single metric, such as monetary damages, lives affected, or lives lost.

Risks of Large-Scale Discontinuities, sometimes called singularities or tipping points. Phenomena include the deglaciation (partial or complete) of the West Antarctic or Greenland ice sheets and major changes in some components of the Earth's climate system, such as a substantial reduction or collapse of the North Atlantic Meridional Overturning Circulation. (Smith et al. 2009: 2–3)

Compared to previous IPCC publications, especially the Third Assessment Report of 2001, the authors revise the sensitivities of these five concerns to increases in global mean temperature (GMT). They conclude that a lower amount of increase in GMT would contribute to increased risks. The basis for their claim is, *inter alia*, the "growing evidence that even modest increases in GMT above levels circa 1990 could commit the climate system to the risk of very large impacts on multiple-century time scales." This is a different message from the one presented above, which was to do with sensitivity ranges. Now "tipping points" have been identified, which need to be avoided before the impacts of climate change become irreversible.[21] These are either given in CO_2 concentrations (350ppm), average temperature rise (2 degrees or lower), or timeframe for action (less than ten years).[22]

Thus Lenton et al. (2008) state:

Human activities may have the potential to push components of the Earth system past critical states into qualitatively different modes of operation,

---

[21] Popularized by Malcolm Gladwell in his book of the same title, the term has also been taken up by political leaders in 2006. Tony Blair and Dutch Prime Minister Jan Peter Balkenende state in a letter to EU leaders that "we have a window of only ten to fifteen years to avoid crossing catastrophic tipping points" (quoted in Hulme 2009: 333).

[22] "Tipping points" appear for the first time in 2003, when *The Chronicle of Higher Education* published an article "Hot Air and Cold Fear: Scientists Debate Whether Global Warming Can Cause a Big Chill" before any academic papers were documented in the scientific literature on climate change. The first article dates from November 2005. Russill and Nyssa (2009) examine the diffusion of this popular concept into climate science.

implying large-scale impacts on human and ecological systems. Examples that have received recent attention include the potential collapse of the Atlantic thermohaline circulation, dieback of the Amazon rainforest, and decay of the Greenland ice sheet. Such phenomena have been described as "tipping points" following the popular notion that, at a particular moment in time, a small change can have large, long-term consequences for a system, i.e., "little things can make a big difference."

Lenton et al. (2008) examine several such possibilities of non-linear processes leading to catastrophic results, and conclude that "[s]ociety may be lulled into a false sense of security by smooth projections of global change." They identify as the greatest threats the melting of Arctic sea ice and the Greenland ice sheet. This knowledge should influence climate policy, which, however, will be "extremely challenging given the nonconvexities in the human environment system that will be enhanced by tipping elements, as well as the need to handle intergenerational justice and interpersonal equity over long periods and under conditions of uncertainty."

The conclusion highlights the typical approach from a modeling perspective based on the physical sciences: "Given the large uncertainty that remains about tipping elements, there is an urgent need to improve our understanding of the underlying physical mechanisms determining their behavior, so that policy-makers are able 'to avoid the unmanageable, and to manage the unavoidable'" (Lenton et al. 2008: 1792). In other words, we do not know enough about tipping points in various aspects of climate change. But what would a better knowledge provide? Would it change the quality of policy decisions in any way? These are difficult questions. In such a situation it appeals to some scientists to demand more money for research in order to strengthen the science; others also alarm the public and politicians, effectively suggesting that we are only a few inches away from the tipping points. Two examples may illustrate this.

False alarm

Just before the much-awaited Copenhagen climate summit (COP 15) in December 2009, twenty-six scientists (some of them working within the IPCC framework) issued a declaration, "The Copenhagen Diagnosis,"[23] which comprised statements such as these:

Accounting for ice-sheet mass loss, sea-level rise until 2100 is likely to be at least twice as large as that presented by IPCC AR4, with an upper limit of ~2m based on new ice-sheet understanding.

[23] www.copenhagendiagnosis.org/.

The argument was made that because of the early deadlines for IPCC reports and the fast-developing science, there were new insights into the rapidly rising sea levels that had not been predicted in the 2007 report. The high estimates were developed by German oceanographer Stefan Rahmstorf in a controversial paper published in 2007. The message has been taken over by the Copenhagen Diagnosis and covered by mainstream media. Only after the failed Copenhagen summit could critical voices be heard in the papers. *The Sunday Times* (January 10, 2010) quoted Jason Lowe, a leading Met Office climate researcher, saying: "These predictions of a rise in sea level potentially exceeding 6ft have got a huge amount of attention, but we think such a big rise by 2100 is actually incredibly unlikely. The mathematical approach used to calculate the rise is simplistic and unsatisfactory." Pfeffer et al. (2008) published a much-quoted study on sea level rise, in which they wrote:

We consider glaciological conditions required for large sea-level rise to occur by 2100 and conclude that increases in excess of 2 meters are physically untenable. We find that a total sea-level rise of about 2 meters by 2100 could occur under physically possible glaciological conditions but only if all variables are quickly accelerated to extremely high limits. More plausible but still accelerated conditions lead to total sea-level rise by 2100 of about 0.8 meter. These roughly constrained scenarios provide a "most likely" starting point for refinements in sea-level forecasts that include ice flow dynamics.

Note that Pfeffer et al. say that the upper bounds of 2 meters and above are physically untenable, and that "more plausible but still accelerated conditions lead to total sea-level rise by 2100 of about 0.8 meter." It is thus surprising to see studies published that give the upper bound, basing their findings on Pfeffer. For example, Overpeck and Weiss (2009) state that "the range of sea-level rise by 2100 projected by Vermeer and Rahmstorf coincides remarkably well with a completely independent assessment of glaciological constraints published last year (0.8–2.0 m; ref. 3)." This "ref. 3" is the paper by Pfeffer et al.

Simon Holgate criticized Rahmstorf's paper in *Science*, and said of his public interventions: "Rahmstorf is very good at publishing extreme papers just before big conferences like Copenhagen when they are guaranteed attention ...The problem is that his methods are biased to generate large numbers for sea-level rise which cannot be justified but which attract headlines" (quoted in the *Sunday Times*, January 10, 2010).

The second example comes right from the IPCC AR4. In Chapter 10, it says:

Glaciers in the Himalaya are receding faster than in any other part of the world (see Table 10.9) and, if the present rate continues, the likelihood of them disappearing by the year 2035 and perhaps sooner is very high if the Earth keeps warming at the current rate. Its total area will likely shrink from the present 500,000 to 100,000 km2 by the year 2035 (WWF, 2005).

As it turned out, this claim was not based on the peer-reviewed literature, but rather on a news story in the *New Scientist* published eight years before the IPCC report. When the story was made public, a comprehensive report was released by the Indian minister of environment and forestry in New Delhi, India, denying the claim. Its author, Vijay Kumar Raina, a senior glaciologist, had analyzed some twenty glaciers and concluded that it is premature to make a statement that the Himalayan glaciers are retreating abnormally because of global warming. This was endorsed by the Indian minister of environment, Jairam Ramesh. The IPCC chairman Pachauri vehemently defended the IPCC 2007 report, accusing the Indian minister of "arrogance." He told the *Guardian* (November 9, 2009): "We have a very clear idea of what is happening. I don't know why the minister is supporting this unsubstantiated research. It is an extremely arrogant statement." Who is right? Madhav Khandekar, a former research scientist from Environment Canada and expert reviewer for the IPCC 2007, has collated some of the current research, making reference to the research of Graham Cogley (Trent University, Ontario). Khandekar concludes:

In summary, the glaciers in the Himalayas are retreating, but NOT any faster than other glaciers in the Arctic and elsewhere. The two large and most important glaciers of the Himalayas show very little retreat at this point in time. The primary reason for retreat of some of the other glaciers seems to be lack of adequate winter snow accumulation. This depletion of winter snow could be due to many factors like inter-annual variability of winter precipitation or possible southward displacement of the sub-tropical jet stream which straddles the Himalayan Mountains over a long 1500 km path.

In the meantime, Pachauri has admitted his error. He has come under attack for various reasons, including alleged conflicts of interest. He also has lost credibility in the eyes of one of the main countries promoting aggressive climate change policies. UK Secretary for the Environment and Climate Change Ed Miliband wrote in a letter to Pachauri in February: "Mistakes such as the IPCC statements on Himalayan glaciers are inevitably damaging. This is a matter of concern because the reliability and good name of the IPCC is vital to ensuring all countries recognise the dangers of climate change."[24] He also states that the IPCC

[24] www.decc.gov.uk/en/content/cms/what_we_do/change_energy/tackling_clima/intl_strat/ipcc/ipcc.aspx.

needs to thoroughly review its procedures and the way it responds to public and media criticism. It should also find a way to correct errors and to minimize future problems, particularly with reports drawn from grey literature. "Clearly this is only the outline of a strategy," the letter says. "There is a great deal of work to do in turning it into a detailed plan for change. The British government is happy to assist you in that process." This does not sound like a letter of support.

While these lines are being written, there are almost daily new stories about alleged errors in the IPCC report. Interestingly, many comments either try doggedly to defend the IPCC, or condemn it in a wholesale manner. Both positions reflect the highly politicized situation, where both sides act according to the principle that it is about good and evil, and no path is possible between them. Calls for a reform of the IPCC have been issued, and an independent inquiry by the InterAcademy Council published its results.[25] Former IPCC chairman Robert Watson has clearly recognized the challenge: "The mistakes all appear to have gone in the direction of making it seem like climate change is more serious by overstating the impact. That is worrying. The IPCC needs to look at this trend in the errors and ask why it happened" (Watson 2010).

Unsubstantiated alarm will backfire and undermine the credibility of those who sound the alarm. We may not want to believe those who "cry wolf" too often. This is a lesson that a scientist activist drew in ozone politics:

As scientists we are divided – we have to warn but you cannot shout "catastrophe" all the time. If you do that too often, in the end no one listens any more. But on the other hand: we alarm the public, well knowing that we do not know everything with certainty. You can overrate the problems, but you also can underrate them. The sudden appearance of the ozone hole is an example for the latter. A difficult situation for science. (Paul Crutzen in *Die Welt*, October 23, 1989, cited in Grundmann 2001: 182)

Threshold effects and bandwagons

Granovetter's (1978) threshold model can be used to analyze social situations in which many actors make their decisions dependent on the decisions of others, and when there are few, if any, institutional guidelines for orientation and much uncertainty. As a result, bandwagon effects can emerge. A small group with a low threshold takes the lead, trying to get support from colleagues whose threshold is higher. Before they join in, they want to see better data, or other relevant and trustworthy

[25] www.interacademycouncil.net/?id=12852.

individuals or institutions who take a public stance. A scientist who was interviewed by Grundmann in his ozone study put it this way:

A lot of people were waiting to see how it comes out. For most scientists in most areas, they don't want to speak up unless they have really made an in-depth study of the area, so that they can speak on it authoritatively. The number of chemists/meteorologists who would know the chlorine chemistry and the meteorology was very, very small at that time. So, you would not expect very many people to speak up. They might say: that sounds interesting, even plausible, but if you believe it is a different question. (Grundmann 2001: 58)

As we know, this situation changed with the onset of a hot crisis, the discovery of the ozone hole. Arguably, in climate politics we do not have a hot crisis – despite the attempts to create such crises, if only symbolically (as the examples above show). No matter whether real or imagined, if situations are defined as real they are real in their consequences (as the famous "Thomas theorem" states). We therefore examine different social bandwagon effects that have convinced others that climate change is real and dangerous.

Bandwagon effect: the media

As Figure 4 shows, there is a continuous rise in levels of newspaper reporting on climate change in four selected countries. After 2005 the level of media attention rises exponentially and peaks in spring 2007 and December 2009. In 2010 it falls rapidly, but shows still relatively high levels, as seen in 2004–05 (see Grundmann and Krishnamurthy 2010 ; Grundmann and Scott 2011).

This sharp increase in attention can be attributed to various factors that have reinforced each other, such as the Group of Eight (G8) Summit in Gleneagles, Scotland in July 2005; the release of Al Gore's film *An Inconvenient Truth* in November 2006; the publication of the UK "Stern Review" on the economics of climate change at the end of October 2006; and the Twelfth Conference of the Parties to the United Nations Framework Convention on Climate Change (COP12) in Nairobi, which began approximately a week later (Boykoff 2007). In February 2007 the Fourth Assessment report of the IPCC was published, and in October 2007 the award of the Nobel Peace Prize to Al Gore and the IPCC was announced. A great deal of media interest does not mean that the tenor of the coverage is uniform. The media interest can go hand in hand with a dramatization or the opposite, with political events related to climate change or with scandals. Qualitative studies have shown that different political cultures and different newspapers portray climate change in different ways.

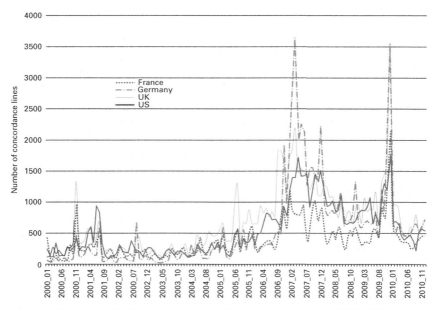

Figure 4: Media reporting on climate change in the UK, US, France and Germany. Concordance lines for the following search terms: climate change, global warming, greenhouse effect; Klimawandel, globale Erwärmung, Treibhauseffekt, Klimakatastrophe; changement climatique, effet de serre, réchauffement de la planète; réchauffement climatique. Retrieved from LexisNexis. (Source: Grundmann and Scott 2011.)

Carvalho and Burgess (2005) have analyzed British newspapers over a twenty-year period. One might think that the authority of the IPCC, and the fact that we are dealing with scientific issues, would pretty much dictate what journalists can do in terms of "spinning" a story. However, there is considerable variance between such alleged "facts" and their presentation to a mass audience. The authors conclude that

coverage of climate change has been strongly linked to the political agenda on this issue, and particularly to public pronouncements and discursive strategies of prime ministers and other top governmental figures. Furthermore, as noted above, our analysis indicates that the media build particular images of scientific knowledge and uncertainty on climate change, and emphasize or de-emphasize forecasts of impacts, in order to sustain their political preferences regarding the regulatory role of the state, individual freedom, and the general economic and social status quo. Dangerous climate change is thus both politically defined and ideologically constrained. (Carvalho and Burgess 2005: 1467)

The results of this analysis reveal a dramatic increase in the quantity of newspaper coverage of anthropogenic climate change in both the UK and the USA over the study period, but also an evolutionary shift in US newspaper coverage in 2005, from explicitly "balanced" accounts to reporting that more closely reflected the scientific consensus on attribution for climate change (Boykoff 2007: 6).

Bandwagon effect: science

In many statements from scientists, politicians, and NGOs, the point was made that "the science is settled," that we know that humans are causing climate change and that GHGs are the cause; hence the urgent need for action. One systematic study (Oreskes 2004) of research publications in the field of climate science investigated 928 abstracts in scientific journals, retrieved with the search term "global climate change." Oreskes claimed that "the scientific consensus is clearly expressed in the reports of the Intergovernmental Panel on Climate Change (IPCC)," and this "states unequivocally that the consensus of scientific opinion is that Earth's climate is being affected by human activities." Of the 928 papers she analyzed, "[r]emarkably, none of the papers disagreed with the consensus position."

At the same time as Oreskes was conducting her research, Dennis Bray was collecting data for his own survey of climate scientists (results available at http: //coast.gkss.de/staff/bray/surveyintro.html). Bray obtained different results, based on a survey of 558 climate scientists conducted in 2003.[26] One question on the survey asked, "To what extent do you agree or disagree that climate change is mostly the result of anthropogenic causes?" A value of 1 indicates "strongly agree" and a value of 7 indicates "strongly disagree." The results were:

1 strongly agree	50 (9.4% of valid responses)
2	134 (25.3% of valid responses)
3	112 (21.1% of valid responses)
4	75 (14.2% of valid responses)
5	45 (8.5% of valid responses)
6	60 (10.8% valid responses)
7 strongly disagree	54 (9.7% of valid responses)

[26] In the above-mentioned study by Grundmann, we find a similar statement from an atmospheric modeler about the confidence of the modeling community in their own ozone models: "I do remember a meeting in '78, a number of the modeler groups got together ...We went around the table and asked what people thought the change in ozone would be in reality, not from what our models were saying, because we knew

Science did not publish Bray's comment.[27]

What is interesting is that Bray based his sample on Oreskes's list for the survey and asked them directly the same question that focused Oreskes's work. Incidentally, some replied to Bray that they did not feel qualified to respond, as they were not climate scientists.[28]

From this we can conclude that there are some methodological problems with the paper by Oreskes, and that a proportion of the 928 papers referred to the climate change consensus as a fact without setting out to probe into the notion of consensus, or to what extent a consensus exists. If authors of some of the examined papers say they are not climate scientists in the strict sense, it seems plausible that they joined a bandwagon.

Bandwagon effect: scientific organizations

Richard Ordway, "the public face of NCAR," compiled the following list of scientific professional associations and posted it on Realclimate. org.[29] He says:

The following world-wide established scientifically-oriented bodies have all issued verifyable [*sic*] written statements that human caused-global warming/ human-caused climate change is now happening:

1) European Academy of Sciences and Arts – 2007
2) InterAcademy Council – 2007
3) International Council of Academies of Engineering and Technological Sciences – 2007
4) 32 national science academies (Australia, Belgium, Brazil, Cameroon, Canada, the Caribbean, China, France, Ghana, Germany, Indonesia, Ireland, Italy, India, Japan, Kenya, Madagascar, Malaysia, Mexico, Nigeria, New Zealand, Russia, Senegal, South Africa, Sudan, Sweden, Tanzania, Uganda, United Kingdom, United States, Zambia, and Zimbabwe) – 2001
5) The national science academies of the G8+5 nations, joint statement – 2009

our models had their own problems. There were a few people who thought that there would be no real net change, even an increase. But most of us were saying the change would be big, 30 to 40 years looking into the future. And there have been much larger changes than we expected, because we did not have the understanding of chemistry and physics we needed to have" (Grundmann 2001: 59).

[27] The full letter to *Science*, titled "The Not So Clear Consensus on Climate Change," can be found here: www.sepp.org/Archive/NewSEPP/Bray.htm.

[28] http://klimazwiebel.blogspot.com/2010/01/tale-of-two-consensus.html#more (comment 19).

[29] www.realclimate.org/index.php/archives/2009/11/the-cru-hack/comment-page-13/.

6) Network of African Science Academies (Cameroon, Ghana, Kenya, Madagascar, Nigeria, Senegal, South Africa, Sudan, Tanzania, Uganda, Zambia, Zimbabwe, as well as the African Academy of Sciences) – 2007
7) Royal Society of New Zealand – 2008
8) Polish Academy of Sciences – 2007
9) US National Research Council – 2001
10) American Association for the Advancement of Science – 2006
11) European Science Foundation – 2007
12) Federation of Australian Scientific and Technological Societies – 2008
13) American Geophysical Union – 2007
14) European Federation of Geologists – 2008
15) European Geosciences Union – 2005
16) Geological Society of America – 2006
17) Geological Society of Australia – 2009
18) International Union of Geodesy and Geophysics – 2007
19) National Association of Geoscience Teachers – 2009
20) American Meteorological Society – 2003
21) Australian Meteorological and Oceanographic Society – (As of 2009)
22) Canadian Foundation for Climate and Atmospheric Sciences – 2005
23) Canadian Meteorological and Oceanographic Society – 2007
24) English Royal Meteorological Society – 2007
25) World Meteorological Organization – 2006
26) American Quaternary Association – (from at least 2009)
27) American Association of Wildlife Veterinarians – (from at least 2009)
28) American Society for Microbiology – 2003
29) Australian Coral Reef Society – 2006
30) UK's Institute of Biology – (from at least 2009)
31) Society of American Foresters – 2008
32) American Academy of Pediatrics – 2007
33) American College of Preventive Medicine – 2006
34) American Medical Association – 2008
35) American Public Health Association – 2007
36) Australian Medical Association – 2004
37) World Federation of Public Health Associations – 2001
38) World Health Organization – 2008
39) American Astronomical Society – (from at least 2009)
40) American Chemical Society – (from at least 2009)
41) American Institute of Physics – (from at least 2009)
42) American Physical Society – 2007
43) American Statistical Association – 2007
44) Intergovernmental Panel on Climate Change (IPCC).

… not one *currently as of 2009* rejects anymore the IPCC findings (to the best of my knowledge) that we humans are warming the Earth. However, it was a different story several years ago before the world-wide mainstream climate science's evidence advanced enough to become indisputably solid in mainstream science (with the help of intense contrarian arguments and became so strong) …

While some of these statements go back to 2001 (and in a few individual cases, even earlier), most were published in 2007 (14) and 2009 (10).

According to Boykoff (2007: 3) and partly supported by our research (see Figure 4), the two largest increases in press coverage of climate change in the UK took place during June–July 2005 and September–November 2006, while in the USA the largest increase was in November 2006. Both peaks are well before the large increase in declarations from professional organizations. Of course, there were declarations from thirty-two National Academies of Science, which published statements in 2001,[30] and nearly every year from 2005 to 2009. The 2005 declaration stresses that the scientific case for climate change is sufficiently clear that states can take action. It expressly refers to the IPCC consensus.[31] In preparation for the thirty-third G8 Summit in 2007, the National Academies of Science of the G8 + 5 countries[32] made a statement in which they referred to the previous declaration of 2005, and also added that "it is unequivocal that the climate is changing, and it is very likely that this is predominantly caused by the increasing human interference with the atmosphere. These changes will transform the environmental conditions on Earth unless counter-measures are taken."[33]

Shortly before the thirty-fourth G8 Summit in 2008, the same National Academies of Science of the G8 + 5 countries made a statement in which the position of the 2005 statement is repeated, and it is noted "that climate change is happening and that anthropogenic warming is influencing many physical and biological systems." Among other actions, the declaration urges other states to "[t]ake appropriate economic and political measures to accelerate the transition to a low carbon society to encourage and bring about changes in the behavior of individuals and States."[34]

In May 2009, a few months before the climate summit in Copenhagen, the same academies stated, "Climate change and sustainable energy

[30] The National Academies of Science of the following countries signed: Australia, Belgium, Brazil, Cameroon, Canada, the Caribbean Islands, China, France, Ghana, Germany, Indonesia, Ireland, Italy, India, Japan, Kenya, Madagascar, Malaysia, Mexico, Nigeria, New Zealand, Russia, Senegal, South Africa, Sudan, Sweden, Tanzania, Uganda, United Kingdom, United States of America, Zambia, and Zimbabwe.
[31] The 2005 declaration was signed by eleven countries (Brazil, Canada, China, France, Germany, India, Italy, Japan, Russia, the United Kingdom, and the United States of America).
[32] The thirteen signatories were Brazil, Canada, China, France, Germany, India, Italy, Japan, Mexico, Russia, South Africa, the United Kingdom, and the United States of America.
[33] Joint Scientific Academies statement, 2007, quoted in: http: //en.wikipedia.org/wiki/Scientific_opinion_on_climate_change.
[34] Joint Scientific Academies statement, 2008.

supply are crucial challenges for the future of humanity. It is essential that world leaders agree on the emission reductions needed to combat negative consequences of anthropogenic climate change." The statement references the IPCC's AR4 of 2007, and asserts that "climate change is happening even faster than previously estimated; global CO_2 emissions since 2000 have been higher than even the highest predictions, Arctic sea ice has been melting at rates much faster than predicted, and the rise in the sea level has become more rapid."[35]

There is a clearly visible push from some science associations and National Academies to influence the political process. Some of the declarations are alarming in tone. As can be demonstrated with the media analysis, 2007 and 2009 are the years with the highest level of media activity. It is an open question whether this momentum is maintained in the coming years, or whether the media's attention dies down. One of the reasons why the issue attention cycle *à la* Downs is not observed in the case of climate change (see Grundmann and Krishnamurthy 2010) lies in the institutional structure of the sources of expertise. With the IPCC, an organization was created to disseminate regularly scientific news messages that are picked up by other scientific organizations and political and other interest groups. Thus, a certain level of coverage is guaranteed. However, it is conceivable that in the coming years we will see a relative decline, as an ever-increasing rise of media attention is impossible. What is more, public opinion is not in lockstep with media coverage. With regard to US poll data, there was more concern developing from 1998 to 2002 than from 2006 to 2008. There is even a slight decline after 2008, just at a time when media coverage goes through the roof. We reproduce a graph from Gallup below (see Figure 5).

Gallup also shows how the US public perceives the media coverage of global warming as exaggerated, just at a time when the big rise in media attention occurs (Figure 6).

This inverse relation between media coverage and public perception requires explanation. It may be that we see a healthy skepticism on the part of lay people who feel that something is being "sold" to them. Thus, Nordhaus and Shellenberger (2009) offer the following account:

They may not know climate science very well, but they are not going to be muscled into accepting apocalyptic visions about our planetary future – or embracing calls to radically transform "our way of life" – just because environmentalists or climate scientists tell them they must. They typically give less credit to expert opinion than do educated elites, and those of us who tend to pay more attention to these questions would do well to remember that expert

---

[35] Joint Scientific Academies statement, 2009.

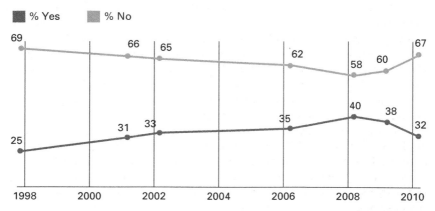

Figure 5: US poll data on global warming.

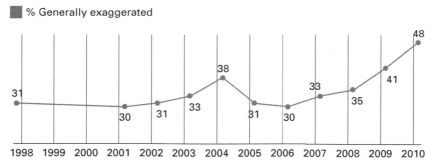

Figure 6: US public perception of credibility of media reports on
global warming.

opinion and indeed, expert consensus, has tended to have a less sterling track
record than most of us might like to admit.

These same efforts to increase salience through offering increasingly dire
prognosis [*sic*] about the fate of the planet (and humanity) have also probably
undermined public confidence in climate science. Rather than galvanizing public demand for difficult and far-reaching action, apocalyptic visions of global

warming disaster have led many Americans to question the science. Having been told that climate science demands that we fundamentally change our way of life, many Americans have, not surprisingly, concluded that the problem is not with their lifestyles but with what they've been told about the science. And in this they are not entirely wrong, insofar as some prominent climate advocates, in their zeal to promote action, have made representations about the state of climate science that go well beyond any established scientific consensus on the subject, hyping the most dire scenarios and most extreme recent studies, which are often at odds with the consensus of the Intergovernmental Panel on Climate Change.

We think that this captures an important insight into the relation between public opinion, expert opinion, and mass media. If anyone was operating under the assumption that the public could be convinced by the "best science," they have been wrong. If anyone drew the conclusion that the message about the "best science" got lost because the skeptics had started a media war, and one needed to ratchet up the rhetoric in this public relations exercise (in order to win the media war), then they have been proven wrong again. Society, it seems, is a strange beast – not easily seduced, not easily bullied. This is not to say that the public "knows best." It certainly has reasons to believe some voices more than others. There are strong mechanisms to align one's own life and values with external demands. As Nordhaus and Shellenberger (2009) explain:

Combine these two psychological phenomena – a low sense of imminent threat (what psychologists call low-threat salience) and system justification – and what you get is public opinion that is highly resistant to education or persuasion. Most Americans aren't alarmed enough to pay much attention, and efforts to raise the volume simply trigger system-justifying responses. The lesson of recent years would appear to be that apocalyptic threats – when their impacts are relatively far off in the future, difficult to imagine or visualize, and emanate from everyday activities, not an external and hostile source – are not easily acknowledged and are unlikely to become priority concerns for most people. In fact, the louder and more alarmed climate advocates become in these efforts, the more they polarize the issue, driving away a conservative or moderate for every liberal they recruit to the cause.

These are interesting, even plausible, explanations, which at the same time raise questions that need further investigation, both by psychologists and by social scientists more broadly.

Climate policy: where next?

Anthony Giddens (2009) has dedicated a book-length study to the problem of climate change, addressing several of the current policy debates in the UK and internationally. He starts by saying, "[M]any have said that to cope with [climate change] we will need to mobilize on a level comparable to fighting a war; but in this case there are no enemies to identify and confront" (p. 2). And he coins a paradox – somewhat immodestly using his own name – to describe the difficulty of acting:

The politics of climate change has to cope with what I call "Giddens's paradox." It states that, since the dangers posed by global warming aren't tangible, immediate or visible in the course of day-to-day life, however awesome they appear, many will sit on their hands and do nothing of a concrete nature about them. Yet waiting until they become visible and acute before being stirred to serious action will, by definition, be too late. (Giddens 2009: 2)

After mentioning some of the recently introduced, arguably ambitious, climate change policies in the UK, Giddens asserts that "we have no politics of climate change ... we do not have a developed analysis of the political innovations that have to be made if our aspirations to limit global warming are to become real" (p. 4).

There are several arguments in his account which seem problematic to us,[36] but elucidating them would detract from the central focus of the argument. In short, he is right to identify one of the weaknesses of much political rhetoric regarding climate change. This is the assumption that ringing the alarm bells will get decision-makers to take the proper decisions and implement climate change policies accordingly, and in a timely fashion. He says that fear is not the best motivator to get people to respond.

We furthermore agree with his skepticism about focusing too much on target-setting (which can be an excuse for inaction rather than the reverse), and his emphasis on the need to adapt to climate change in a proactive way.

Giddens makes a useful comment about the relation between public opinion and government action. He refers to Kingdon's notions of policy streams, windows of opportunities, and policy entrepreneurs. The latter are people who are offering solutions to problems that come up, or for which they have been waiting. Especially in situations of crisis, policy windows (opportunities) may open up in which it is vital to be able to present convincing solutions quickly. However, Giddens sees political entrepreneurs in too narrow a manner, focusing on traditional roles, such as politicians and decision-makers. It is interesting that in both Kingdon's and Giddens's accounts, scientific experts are largely absent from the list of actors who could act as

---

[36] Especially his repudiation of the "precautionary principle" and "sustainable development."

policy entrepreneurs. This aspect is especially important in the context of our argument and the focus of this book. Giddens mentions the importance of framing and "focusing events," and therefore the role of the media. The national mood is a central element and "has major impact upon when, where and how the problem, policy and political streams converge" (Giddens 2009: 112). While this is certainly true, and while we agree with Giddens that too much reliance should not be put on the science of climate change, we nevertheless think that the potential role of scientists as policy entrepreneurs deserves our attention. This does not mean that their role is always positive.

Undoubtedly, the IPCC has played a crucial role in setting the political agenda. Without its efforts, climate change would not be the important global political issue that it is today. However, the IPCC also exemplifies the weakness of traditional conceptions of the science-policy relation. There is an assumption that governments will follow scientific recommendations because they produce the best available knowledge through a consensus-building process. Setting aside the question of whether a consensus is necessary for political action, the IPCC has neglected the important aspect of controllability of social parameters of action. To take up a distinction made in this book, the IPCC has produced *knowledge for practice*, but not *practical knowledge*. In calling for a worldwide reduction of GHG emissions, it does not seem to take enough into account that emissions are determined by forces that are largely beyond the political control of governments. Levels of GHG emissions are linked to levels of economic activity, and it is hardly in the interest of governments to reduce the latter. A paradox follows for politics, which has to prioritize one over the other. As experience shows, economic growth has been a top political priority, whereas concerns about potential future climate crises have taken a back seat. Of course, there is no simple solution to the problem outlined here. But it seems highly problematic to leave this paradox unsolved by merely appealing to decision-makers that they should somehow show more courage and rank concern for the economy lower. There seems to be no immediately actionable path that leads to latitude in decision-making here. The only realistic orientation is a long-term restructuring of the economy into a low-carbon economy that is much more resistant to vulnerability.

One alternative to the straitjacket of emissions reductions is to look at crucial sectors of the economy (steel, cement, energy) and analyze them on the basis of the so-called Kaya Identity (after the Japanese energy economist Yoichi Kaya). This shows that total (anthropogenic) emission levels depend on the product of four variables: population, Gross Domestic Product (GDP) per capita, energy use per unit of GDP (energy intensity), and emissions per unit of energy consumed (carbon intensity of energy). We leave aside population policies, as they are politically suspect. Population growth is largely determined by socioeconomic factors, such as wealth and (female) educational levels. There is much evidence to suggest that emissions growth is primarily due to increases in economic activity. It follows that climate policies need to focus on reducing the energy intensity of wealth production, or the carbon intensity of energy production, or both. If the energy intensity of wealth production cannot be radically changed, then the remaining possibility is the reduction of carbon intensity of energy. Based on the Kaya Identity, Pielke (2009: 6) argues that

[i]f global emissions are to be reduced by 80% by midcentury, or anywhere close to this level, then the world will have to achieve rates of decarbonization that have never been achieved in large economies in recent decades ... Policy should focus less on targets and timetables for emissions reductions, and more on the process for achieving those goals, and the various steps along the way. Setting targets and timetables for sectoral efficiency gains and expansion of carbon-free energy supply would be a step in the right direction. Such a policy focused on incremental improvements in decarbonization ... offers the only feasible approach to the challenge of mitigation.

Science or technology to the rescue?

Sarewitz and Pielke (2000) claim that "scientific uncertainty about the causes and consequences of global warming emerged as the *apparent* central obstacle to action" (our emphasis). They identify this illusion as a fateful determinant for the stalling of climate policy. This illusion is much in line with the received view of the science–policy relation identified above. However, the logic of the constellation has led to a paralysis, and to deepening divisions in society. As the battle for one interpretation of climate research dominated the political scene, there was an incentive to play science as the trump card. The merits of this view for an anti-environmentalist strategy are obvious. As long as there are scientific uncertainties, the onus of proof is on those who want to take preventive action. It so happened that the American Bush [Sr.] administration "justified its huge climate-research initiative explicitly in terms of the need to reduce uncertainty before taking action." Weart (2003: 168) reports that a "White House memorandum, inadvertently released in 1990, proposed that the best way to deal with concern about global warming would be to 'raise the many uncertainties.'" But Al Gore, by then a senator, also agreed, as we have seen, explaining that "more research and better research and better targeted research is absolutely essential if we are going to eliminate the remaining areas of uncertainty and build the broader and stronger political consensus necessary for the unprecedented actions required to address this problem" (quoted in Sarewitz and Pielke 2000). In the end, a Republican administration and a Democratic Congress agreed on the need for more research, if for completely different reasons: one side looking for reasons to do nothing, the other seeking justification for action.

This analysis holds also true for the younger Bush, who in 2001 declared unilateral withdrawal from the Kyoto Protocol, yet subscribed to the need for "more research." The commitment to carry out more research is the least common denominator that everyone can agree upon. However, opponents of an ambitious climate change policy benefit more than supporters of such a policy, as the institutional decision rule (the "default condition") amounts to doing nothing. The IPCC agrees to this least common denominator for two fundamental reasons: first, the prospects of research funding; and second, the belief that eventually, a compelling case for strict controls can be made (Pielke and Sarewitz 2003). However, the readiness to fund research into climate science contrasts with a lack of investment in research and development for alternative energy and transportation. It would require huge regulatory efforts and a massive boost to R&D in order to increase energy efficiency. Such measures are not very popular in the United States, but have not been adequately developed elsewhere either.

After the Kyoto Protocol in 1997, the main policy option narrowed down to the deployment of market mechanisms. The idea of carbon markets, which would deal with emission certificates for CO_2, was launched by the USA and initially rejected by the EU (Damro and Luaces-Méndez 2003; Gilbertson and Reyes 2009). In the meantime, however, carbon trading has caught on in most developed countries. This is not the place to discuss these policies and their prospects in detail (see Lohmann 2009; Storm, 2009); but it seems obvious that flourishing carbon markets can go hand in hand with *increasing* carbon emissions. No matter what the problems with this approach, the world leaders in Copenhagen could not agree how to implement this instrument.

On balance, the strategy of investing in scientific research in order to achieve a political solution with regard to climate change has failed. This strategy was based on the assumption that true knowledge would inform policies, and that this needed to be done on an international level. Climate change is a truly global problem, but it is not clear how a global solution could work in the absence of functioning global governance structures. The UNFCCC process has tried to reduce the complexity of the climate problem (scientific, economic, sociodemographic, technological) simultaneously with the attempt to tackle the political complexity within the international community, which now counts about 200 members, of which all have to agree to a global treaty. At present it is wishful thinking that world society could build effective global governance structures and solve one of the most complex global problems at the same time.

We have argued that knowledge, in order to be practical, needs not only to have relevance for practical decisions, but also to identify levers for action. The main emphasis in the climate discourse so far has been on the level of geophysical research. A consensus view on the basics of the changing atmosphere was desired, with the view that this would enable policymakers to act. What was forgotten in all of this was the "rest" of the problem. We mention only three elements: first, what types of alternative energy production could be developed that are competitive in the market place, and in what time period? Second, what is the public support for climate policies? What level of acceptance of new technologies and willingness to change lifestyles is to be expected? Third, how can the interests of nation-states in a changing, globalizing world be aligned? How do we balance the "right to development" with climate policy targets? These are questions for research that reach far beyond the study of the geophysics of the planet. They require the involvement of engineers, civil society, political decision-makers, and social scientists. The view that a consensus on the part of climate science could provide the solution to climate policy has failed spectacularly.

5   Conclusion

The reader will recall that we introduced several models, questions, and theses in previous chapters, to which we will now return. Let us start with the model of instrumentality, which states that true knowledge is reliable and useful in practical contexts. This model, which may still be widely shared among observers and policymakers, has not come up with a convincing answer to the question of how it is possible that science ("true knowledge") is effective only in some cases, but not always. To answer this question, we developed the thesis that in order to become practically relevant, knowledge must include the policy options that need to be manipulated, so that the intended change can be effected. To this end we have introduced the distinction between "knowledge for practice" and "practical knowledge." The former provides knowledge that could be relevant in practical contexts (which highlights the fact that not all knowledge has this property), while the latter provides knowledge that identifies the "levers for action." We also suggested that in order to be effective, knowledge need not reflect all aspects or variables of reality. Taken together, these points amount to a critical reevaluation of traditional models of the knowledge/power relation, no matter whether they rely on a specific epistemology; on a "linear" conception of the relation between knowledge and power; or on a concept that postulates that in order to be effective, a theory needs first of all to reflect the complexity of reality.

How do the case studies compare to these considerations? What are the practical aims in each of these cases? In economic science and policy, the goal was to use financial instruments available to government in order to compensate for market failure and to overcome a deep economic crisis. Specifically, these policies aimed at the reduction of unemployment and the stimulation of economic activity. In race science and policy, the aim was to bring about a "healthy" population and to weed out "unworthy" life through population policies, ranging from forced sterilization to extermination. In climate science and policy, it is the prevention of dangerous climate change through appropriate mitigation strategies and adaptation to inevitable climate change.

In what follows, we will address several of the issues raised by our thesis. The three cases under examination are different in various aspects. They take place in different historical, geographical, political, and cultural settings. The knowledge basis is located in different scientific disciplines, and the experts advising policymakers vary from Keynes's one-man show (economic discourse) to a scientific establishment that has close links to the power elite (race and climate discourse), and to one that has close links to governments all over the world (IPCC). While the cases of race and climate are similar, in that there is a mainstream view that has become dominant and is taken up by the media, institutions, and decision-makers, the discrepancy in their effectiveness is striking. Racist policies became practical in a relatively short time span in Nazi Germany, while climate policies are not achieving what they are supposed to achieve, according to the main players in the climate science and climate policy fields. In what follows we will examine the three cases and ask where, when, and why knowledge became influential politically. We will start with an account of Keynesianism.

Success and failure

As we have shown in Chapter 2, Hall's (1989a) analysis provides a valuable account for the explanation of the rise of Keynesianism. He identifies three interrelated factors: theoretical and academic credibility, administrative viability, and political viability. He also examines the importance of the political orientation of the party in power. If the governing party had strong trade union links and if unemployment was a big concern, Keynesian policies were more likely to be implemented. He also refers to exogenous shocks and crises, such as the economic crisis of the 1930s and World War II. In what follows we will apply these aspects to the two other case studies examined in this book.

The theoretical appeal of racist theories was strong in the 1930s, with very little opposition to them. The German state administration was in the control of a dictatorial regime, and there was no resistance from civil servants, no real attempt to undermine the organization of mass extermination. Politically, the racist discourse was broadly supported by the public. One could say that there was a "spontaneous consent" (Gramsci 1971: 12), or at least "permissive consensus" (Key 1961).

With regard to climate change the theoretical appeal is evident. Citizens in many countries see climate change as a reality and "already know" that more extreme weather events are harbingers of a grim future. They tend to believe scientists who assert that such events will become more frequent because climate change is a fact, not a theory. In a way, the public no longer needs the science to prove the point. Administratively, in all countries there are tensions within government, especially between the departments of the environment and finance/energy. As Levy and Egan (2003: 818) point out, "The Clinton administration was almost paralysed by internal dissent over the economic impact of emission reductions, with the Department of Energy generally supportive of industry's position, the Environmental Protection Agency opposed, and Commerce split." Similar observations hold for other countries.

Let us turn to political viability. As we know from other cases, when political elites have consensus, the public tends to follow (Brulle, Carmichael, and Jenkins 2012). In Europe, both left-wing and right-wing governments enact climate change policies. Germany started this trend under Chancellor Helmut Kohl, and it has been continued by a red-green coalition government. The British Labour Party enacted the Climate Change Act, but Margaret Thatcher had joined the chorus of concerned voices about climate change in the late 1980s. However, in the United States party politics has seized upon the climate issue, with Democrat governments of Clinton/Gore and now Obama being more proactive compared to the Republican Bush governments. As a result, in the United States the science is contested and has become the battleground for politics.

It only takes a few important players in global climate policy to veto international treaties. The failure of globally binding climate policies should thus come as no surprise. The other two cases examined in this book did not rely on international agreements. Let us therefore proceed further by trying to understand why racist policies in Nazi Germany and Keynesian policies in postwar Europe and America were effective.

We offer two explanations. One is the dictatorial nature of the German political regime at the time of the implementation of the racist policies (and of Keynesian policies, too). These were pushed through by terrorist means that intimidated opponents of the regime, yet met with the tacit or open approval of large parts of society. There were, after all, beneficiaries of racist policies; for example, as a result of the expulsion of non-Aryan persons from their workplaces and property.

With Keynesianism, the explanation of its relative success concerns another aspect of government authority, which is related to the setting of interest rates and money supply. These were under the control of governments from the 1930s and enabled them to change macroeconomic parameters at the stroke of a pen. This applies to the authoritarian regimes in Germany as well as Japan. Dictatorships tend to increase the number of parameters for control. It is much more difficult to explain how Keynesian ideas moved into the accepted toolbox of economic policy in Western societies.

There was a gradual ascendency of Keynesian ideas replacing traditional economic views, especially in the aftermath of World War II. It is perhaps no coincidence that Keynesian macroeconomic policies were adopted widely at a time when major countries had experienced government interventions into society on a large scale as a result of the war effort. It was only after World War II that such a shift took place in major economies.

Climate change: complex issues, complex negotiations

The lure of authoritarian solutions has been evident in both racist and economic policies. However, there are those who think that we need to reform our democratic institutions in order to deal with global climate emergency. Very much as in wartime, we should suspend democratic rights and push through with the aggressive changes needed to tackle "dangerous climate change." Even before the climate change debate, there were "green" voices advocating drastic government measures (for some early advocacy of such policies, see Hardin 1974; Harich 1975). More recently, Australian scientists Shearman and Smith (2007) have argued that we need an authoritarian form of government in order to implement the scientific consensus on greenhouse gas emissions. The well-known climate researcher James Hansen laments that "the democratic process does not work" in the case of climate change. And in *The Vanishing Face of Gaia*, James Lovelock emphasizes that we need to abandon democracy in order to meet the challenges of climate change head on. We are in a state of war. There is talk of a new war effort, in order to pull the world out of its state of lethargy (see Stehr and von Storch 2009 for a critical assessment).

This thinking assumes that we need only to ascertain the political will in order to change policies. But it is not that simple. Opinion polls show that two-thirds of the population in all major countries worry about climate change and would, to some extent, support policies targeting it. The problems are how much could be changed on the basis of existing lifestyles and technologies, and how much people would be prepared to pay. It is here that politicians hesitate when prompted to make radical changes. As Nordhaus and Shellenberger (2009) point out, "Having been told that climate science demands that we fundamentally change our way of life, many Americans have, not surprisingly, concluded that the problem is not with their lifestyles but with what they've been told about the science."[1]

As opinion polls also show, economic concerns trump concerns over the environment. The Pew Research Center published data for 2010 under the headline, "Public's Priorities for 2010: Economy, Jobs, Terrorism." The article finds that "global warming ranks at the bottom of the public's list of priorities; just 28% consider this a top priority, the lowest measure for any issue tested in the survey."[2] This means that successful climate policies will have to combine both concerns: the environment and the economy. A strategy of frontal attack on carbon emissions is bound to fail. If emissions vary with economic activity, what scope for action is there?

Governments worldwide realize that economic downturns are to be avoided, if necessary at the cost of environmental goals. GHG emission reductions are tightly coupled to economic activity, and it is unlikely that governments will decide to sacrifice economic growth to "save the planet" (Pielke Jr. 2010). The Stern Review (2007) is telling in that it tries to address the economics of climate change in order to make an argument for self-interest in the language of cost–benefit analysis. Of course, the recommended instruments stop short of advocating regulatory steps that could be a burden for the economy. Carbon markets form the major political instrument that has been proposed and adopted in the UK and the EU. Why? One interpretation looks at the role that public pressure has played in these countries. This interpretation suggests that governments have given in to environmental NGOs and Green parties in the search for "green votes." But the acknowledgement of climate change as a policy issue has not been intended to adopt the radical green proposals (such as

---

[1] They also draw attention to the fact that "when asked in open-ended formats to name the most serious problems facing the country, virtually no Americans volunteer global warming. Even other environmental problems, such as air and water pollution, are often rated higher priorities by US voters than global warming, which is less visible and is experienced less personally than many other problems. What is arguably most remarkable about US public opinion on global warming has been both its stability and its inelasticity in response to new developments, greater scientific understanding of the problem, and greater attention from both the media and politicians. Public opinion about global warming has remained largely unchanged through periods of intensive media attention and periods of neglect, good economic times and bad, the relatively activist Clinton years and the skeptical Bush years."

[2] http://people-press.org/report/584/policy-priorities-2010.

opposing globalization, renewable energy without the nuclear option, de-industrialization, etc.). The coalition-building effort includes the green voters, sustainable businesses, the renewable sector and, not least, "carbon trading" specialists who are central to the UK as a key financial marketplace. What is more, a coalition between the UK and EU could be established despite otherwise fraught discussions about EU–UK relations. Carbon trading does not address the energy intensity and carbon intensity of energy in an actionable manner. There is no policy lever that would provide such a tool within a market-based approach. Nevertheless, market instruments provided a broad enough platform for a political alliance to support (nominally) radical carbon reductions. We say "nominally," because it must not be forgotten that the most ambitious target (the UK's 80 percent CO_2 reductions by 2050) is a long-term target, and there is the distinct possibility of shifting the burden of painful action to future governments. All that we see is cheap talk, or so the argument goes.

So what prospects are there for a successful climate change policy? Drawing on Lindblom's distinction (summarized in Chapter 1), we juxtapose a (in our view unrealistic) "synoptic view" with an incremental approach. The IPCC's global managerial approach (Eastin et al. 2011) can be interpreted as exemplifying such a synoptic approach, which attempts to get the full picture of all relevant elements for a decision, but ultimately singles out massive CO_2 reductions as the main goal and lever for action. But what would an incremental approach look like? Hulme (2010) suggests that apart from CO_2 there are other, potentially more effective, levers of action that have so far been left untried. He differentiates between "interventions for short-lived and long-lived climate forcing agents" and identifies several strategic policy initiatives that would make a difference, among them the eradication of black carbon, the protection of tropical forests, and the full use of the Montreal Protocol.[3]

This pragmatic approach of exploiting low-hanging fruit, improving energy efficiencies in key industries, reducing soot ("black carbon"), or managing tropical forests seems to make sense, as there is a range

---

[3] Black carbon is a public health hazard, and contributes massively to warming of polar ice regions. Tropical forests are a key asset for humanity's future, not merely because of their carbon store, but also because of their husbandry of biodiversity, their timber and non-timber products, and their wider livelihood functions for indigenous peoples. Some long-lived gases, such as sulphur hexafluoride and halocarbons, are climate-warming but non-ozone-depleting gases. They could be controlled through a modification of the Montreal Protocol; there is no need to tie this initiative to the much more challenging task of reducing fossil carbon emissions (see Hulme 2010).

of so-called "no regrets" policies, which have an impact on climate forcings but would make sense for other reasons as well. In addition, such proposals have the major advantage that they can be tackled without first reaching a global agreement (see also Prins et al. 2010). Such targets can be tackled on the regional level (or, as in the case of the Montreal Protocol, an international umbrella already exists).

Until now, the governments of more than 190 different nations have been locked into inaction on a global level because of their pursuit of self-interest. They tried to agree on many complex issues that were "stitched together into one single impossible package" (Hulme 2010). Even if they acknowledged the severity of the looming climate crisis, no nation had wanted to bear more of the burden of the costs compared to others.

There is another, ironic aspect in the calls for less democracy and more government power. Such proposals forget all too easily that such a "solution" might be worse than the problem. The very attempt to install dictatorial regimes in the West would in all likelihood be followed by civil unrest and disruption of social organization – which is one of the main detrimental consequences of climate change, according to those who make such proposals.

Knowledge, society, and experts

Between the 1920s and 1930s and the late 1980s, there have been important developments and changes in the relation between science and politics and, perhaps most importantly in our context, in the social science reflection of these changes. Gone are the days of scientific innocence and promise. After the deployment of nuclear bombs at the end of World War II and numerous disasters of large-scale technology, the faith of Western civilization in the blessings of science and technology has diminished. Society is now much more aware of a discrepancy between scientific and social progress. Society is also more aware of the political use of knowledge claims, and especially scientific knowledge claims, for the legitimation of specific decisions. Science has become suspicious. We all know that expertise is partial, and that it can be mustered by opposing positions in a political battle. The end of certainty has been decried by some, and celebrated by others (such as the postmodern strand in the social sciences and humanities). Still, the old view has not vanished completely. It still seems to make sense to appeal to science as an arbiter in contested issues. We still look for rigorous and impartial research to cut through the ideological and political battles, even in the knowledge that science cannot live up to these expectations.

It is under these changed circumstances that the issue of climate change has unfolded.

This change seems to be lost on previous generations of scientists; Jim Lovelock, for example, laments the fact that more people have access to higher education and, as a result, science is no longer performed by elites. He is critical of the current system of research: "science, not so very long ago, pre-1960s, was largely vocational. Back when I was young, I didn't want to do anything else other than be a scientist. They're not like that nowadays. They don't give a damn. They go to these massive, mass-produced universities and churn them out. They say: 'science is a good career. You can get a job for life doing government work.' That's no way to do science." There may be some truth to this criticism, but Lovelock overlooks the fact that there is an overall increase in knowledge in contemporary society, with many more people being informed about science and politics.

Does science help to de-politicize issues, and therefore make solutions easier? This idea has been expressed by Peter Haas, who coined the term "epistemic communities." The idea that cognitive consensus makes political action easier has become a truism for many, and has been embraced by several observers and practitioners. It would appear that the IPCC is the paradigmatic case for such an epistemic community; but not according to Haas. He has the following to say about the IPCC:

The IPCC is of interest because it highlights the way in which states may choose to shape the science advisory process. A closer look at the interplay of science and power in the IPCC reveals empirically how this dynamic interaction operates in this key contemporary issue, as well as analytically establishing the political limits to autonomous science and social learning. The scientific consensus is not yet strong, and thus the available scientific knowledge is not fully usable. Yet, in the case of climate change, the fact that usable knowledge is not yet available for climate change has much to do with the political choices associated with the design of the IPCC, and thus suggests the political limits to states' willingness to confer some degree of autonomy to scientific institutions and to defer to their guidance. (Haas 2004: 580)

Haas is right to point out that governments wanted to regain control over a potentially volatile situation that existed in the mid 1980s, when the governments of the industrialized countries got tired "of being lambasted by UNEP in multilateral environmental negotiations, and were concerned that uncontrolled scientific panels may give rise to policies that they did not deem warranted." Various scientific meetings from 1985 to 1988 had forcefully put the issue of global warming on the international agenda, culminating in the 1988 Toronto conference, which most memorably called for 20 percent reductions in greenhouse gas emissions. In short, governments "wished to rein in any independent political pressure that would be generated from an organized scientific involvement in collective discussions on climate change" (Haas 2004: 584). However, at the same time there were strong tendencies within the scientific community that saw advantages in coordinating assessment reports from different countries into one enterprise. Scientists with concerns about global warming very much cherished the prospect of speaking with one voice. Speaking truth to power was perceived to be much easier if there were not several voices to be heard (see Grundmann 2007 for an assessment). In the end, the politicians' thrust to control the science coincided with the scientists' interest in getting the message across in the most efficient way without "confusing the public."

Haas makes reference to principal-agent theory when claiming that governments ("the principal") carefully designed the IPCC in such a way as to avoid any surprises that might come out of its reports. However, there is clear evidence that the reports have become more dramatic over time. And the "principal" is not one actor, but many. For some, the increasing dramatization has been used as a political tool for advocating specific policies (especially by the EU); for others, it may have appeared more of a problem. However, what Haas misses is the lack of "useful knowledge" contained in the IPCC reports or, to use our terminology, the lack of "practical knowledge." Contra Haas, we think that the problem with the IPCC is not so much a lack of scientific consensus about key issues of anthropogenic warming and its causes; the problem is rather that it lacks actionable knowledge that could inform governments in a practical way.

When Haas evaluates the lack of impact the IPCC has made on climate policy, he cites a lack of scientific understanding as a reason for its failure to deliver. He says that "[t]he state of scientific understanding of the key global systems that affect global warming remains relatively immature … The accuracy of the IPCC science remains limited. The estimates of global warming and their effects are crude, and global carbon models are unable to account fully for the global carbon cycle." He also states that its scenarios are "sufficiently crude that they do not engage any significant political interests in any of the member countries" (Haas (2004: 581–82). This is partly true, but misses the point. Haas implies that a better scientific understanding would lead to a political agreement on climate policies. This puts him in a politically unique position, indistinguishable from skeptics who demand more robust scientific knowledge before climate change policies are justified. One cannot avoid the impression that the failure of the IPCC is unexpected for him, because it should represent the "epistemic community" par excellence. Haas retreats to a position that regards the IPCC as an "extreme case," and contrasts it with "most other transboundary and global environmental issues" where a scientific consensus preceded political discussions. As we have demonstrated with the example of the ozone layer, this was not the case. Here, knowledge development took place in parallel to the political process, and some crucial elements of scientific understanding came only after the important decisions had been taken. Keynes developed his theory while advising government. Only eugenics had been established scientifically in the form of Darwinist evolutionary theory. But Haas's conclusion – that climate science needs to be shielded from politics – is well taken, especially in the light of the recent credibility crisis after Climategate. However, Haas seems to expect too much from a scientific consensus that could sway politics.

Crisis

Hall (1989a) mentions a further possibility that a new, radical policy will be adopted – because everything else has failed. Likewise, Oliver and Pemberton (2004: 416) maintain "that the power of existing institutions to channel forces of change requires the presence of a powerful exogenous shock (or shocks) sufficient to undermine a well-entrenched policy paradigm." The importance of crises for the restructuring of discourses has also been captured by Jessop and Oosterlynck (2008: 1158–59), who note that

there is constant variation, witting or unwitting, in apparently routine social practices. This poses questions about the regularization of practices in normal conditions and about possible sources of radical transformation, especially in periods of crisis. The latter typically lead to profound cognitive and strategic disorientation of social forces and a corresponding proliferation in discursive interpretations and proposed material solutions. Nonetheless the same basic mechanisms serve to select and consolidate radically new practices and to stabilize routine practices.

In a comparison of the industrial policies in 1930s France, the UK, and the USA, Dobbin (1993: 1) argues that "governments ... tried to reverse the economic downturn by reversing their traditional strategies" – that is to say, they tried and tested everything from their conventional toolboxes; only to find that nothing worked, while the crisis got more serious. He states:

[W]hereas new macro-economic policies took roughly the same form in different nations, new industrial policies took very different forms. New macro-economic policies were similar because these countries rejected similar macro-economic traditions; but new industrial policies were different from one another because these countries rejected very different industrial traditions. The United States abandoned market regulation in favour of state-led cartelization; Britain supplanted policies designed to sustain small firms with policies designed to create huge monopolies; and France replaced *étatisme* with liberalism. (Dobbin 1993: 1)

The crux of his argument is "that the Great Depression falsified the tenets of extant industrial cultures and caused nations to try to counteract the effects of pre-existing policy paradigms, which they believed had contributed to the economic decline. Political-conflict arguments are contradicted by the fact that in each country the political party that gained power pursued new industrial policies that were inconsistent with its long-held ideological goals – but that promised to reverse the traditional industrial strategy, which appeared to have precipitated the decline" (p. 8). This argument points to the possibility that governments are prepared to try out something completely different from what their normal repertoire offers (only) in times of severe crisis.

Some say that only a deep ecological crisis would bring about more radical instruments for the decarbonization of our current techno-structure. Sir John Houghton told the *Sunday Telegraph* in 1995: "If we want a good environmental policy in the future we'll have to have a disaster." And Jim Lovelock said in an interview with the *Guardian* in 2010 that "[t]here has been a lot of speculation that a very large glacier [Pine Island glacier] in Antarctica is unstable. If there's much more melting, it may break off and slip into the ocean. It would be enough to produce an immediate sea-level rise of two metres, something huge, and tsunamis … That would be the sort of event that would change public opinion … Another IPCC report won't be enough. We'll just argue over it like now."

Provided that this disaster will happen and effect a shift in public support in favor of drastic action, it will in all likelihood be too late to prevent the worst.

Haas, too, highlights the role of crises, saying that "[u]sable knowledge is … heeded to the extent that it is, after widely publicized shocks or crises" (2004: 576). While this may be generally true, much depends on how the crisis is socially constructed. If we rehearse the three case studies, we note that there was a clearly perceived economic crisis in the 1920s and 1930s, in Great Britain and elsewhere. No disagreement about the definition of the situation could be seen. The debates were about causes and remedies.

In a slightly different way, the definition of a crisis related to racial hygiene was accomplished by the political leaders of Germany, who combined the racial discourse with a discourse of imperial expansion. Here we witness a very close alliance between the key scientific experts and political power-holders. Both were adherents of the pan-German political and military project, and both had strong beliefs about the hierarchy of races and the aim to exterminate "unworthy lives." All the measures of population control that were taken were largely shared among political and scientific elites (with very few exceptions, such as the German Association of Socialist Physicians, see Proctor 1988a). A sense of urgency was constructed in a historical juncture which led into World War II. The Holocaust and World War II were thus inextricably linked from the viewpoint of the fascist regime in Germany. No such imminent crisis was perceived in other countries where race science had been institutionally established as a legitimate scientific endeavor and eugenics laws had been passed (but no mass extermination of "unworthy life" had taken place, see Sewell 2010).

In the case of climate change, much of the scientific and political debate revolves around the very question of whether we face an imminent crisis or not. Using ozone politics as an analogue, many actors and observers have suggested that the situation with regard to climate change, while perhaps not showing signs of a "hot crisis" (Ungar 1992), could turn out to be much worse. And some have tried to construct such a sense of crisis with various rhetorical tools, such as the "hockey stick," which advertised "unprecedented temperatures" on planet Earth, or "tipping points" which would set the climate system onto a path of no return, ultimately triggering a downward spiral of collapse. Others have resisted such a dystopian construal, and insist that scare mongering is counterproductive.

Indeed, the case of ozone politics has shown how the scientists closely involved with the study of the ozone layer were taken completely by surprise when the ozone hole was discovered. They simply did not have such a huge phenomenon on their list of possible scenarios. The shock was genuine, and quickly reverberated through the expert and policy communities and the mass media. At the time, it was not clear whether, or how quickly, the local and temporal phenomenon (massive springtime Antarctic ozone losses) could spread globally. Experts involved in this experience were primed for the next global environmental emergency, dangerous climate change. They started to go beyond the relatively unexciting model projections of average temperature rise by slipping in the message that we could see surprises (like in the case of the ozone hole). As a result, the public has been put into a state of constant alarm.

However, unlike in the case of Keynesianism or racism, loud voices could be heard in the climate discourse that did not accept this alarmism.

For a long time, these voices were limited to relatively a small "sceptical" community, which was marginal (and mainly based in the United States, where it received more media attention than elsewhere). From 2005 to 2009 it seemed nearly extinct, when the mass media (also in the United States) joined the bandwagon to "prevent dangerous climate change." With the failure of the political project in Copenhagen and the loss of scientific integrity in the wake of the CRU email scandal, many actors and observers have begun to reposition and redefine central claims and frames of the climate discourse.

Let us ponder the idea of what the appeal to scientific authority ("economic viability" in Hall's language) explains. In the case of race science, most of the science had been established before the Nazis took power and started their racial policies. In fact, racism (based on Darwin's theory) was seen as the established scientific authority, which "demanded" that "inferior" or "unworthy" lives be exterminated. As we have argued, the program of racial hygiene combined a philosophy of biological determinism with a firm conviction that science can provide the legitimation for solving social problems in a specific way. The Nazis were intent to root out all forms of racial, social, or spiritual "disease."

This example should serve as a cautionary tale when considering climate science and policy. Here, too, specific courses of action have been justified with reference to scientific authority, disregarding the fact that it is largely a political choice to identify and implement sound and just policies. In the case of race science, we said that even if findings from race science were "true," it would not automatically follow that persons should be labeled as "unworthy," or that they should be exterminated. And if such a position, based on human rights and solidarity, had been firmly established, race extermination policies would have been much more difficult to justify through science. Conversely, in the absence of a human rights discourse, the availability of race science and its authority made it much easier for the Nazi government to initiate and carry through its policies.

What follows for climate policy? Let us tackle this question indirectly, starting with the conclusion just reached, and asking: Can policymakers appeal to a body of scientific knowledge and authority? And what non-scientific principles could be used to reach sensible policies? While there is a robust consensus among scientific authorities regarding detection (and perhaps also attribution) of anthropogenic global warming, this does not tell us what to do. To be sure, some scientific authorities demand cutting CO_2 emissions radically within the next decades. But this may be an "impractical" strategy, so to speak. In the short term, levers for action in this regard have to be seen with pessimism, as argued above. What is more, if society were prepared to take preventative and/ or adaptive measures with regard to climate change, it would not need to wait for scientific studies to deliver the foundations for this belief. And if climate change were seen as a risk we want to avoid, we should try to reduce our vulnerability and take adaptive measures (coastline protection, increasing agricultural and infrastructure resilience). As in other policy fields, we face the prospect of acting on the basis of limited information, where Lindblom's principle of incrementalism should be followed. Social and economic policies are prime examples of areas where we do this all the time, mostly without waiting for yet another improved report on the state of knowledge (bearing in mind that such reports, if available, will in all likelihood be used as "trump cards" if they fit the proposed policy option – otherwise they will be ignored).

One would have thought that in the early twenty-first century, our economic models were so much better compared to the 1930s that today we could manage economic downturns much better. It turns out that such a belief is illusory. It does not follow that the economics profession has made no progress in the last seven decades; the contrary is the case. But it follows that political decisions and policies can and do develop without authoritative knowledge, sometimes even in opposition to it. Likewise, our knowledge of the geophysics of the climate system has increased and will increase further. Yet at the same time, our capacity to act has not increased accordingly. Whether it ever will depends very much on technological innovation and social practices, which need to be developed.

There is another striking similarity between the discourses of race and climate. Both exemplify a technocratic approach to policymaking; neither presents us with a political choice, but rather tell us what "the science demands." Political decisions thus get transformed into scientific and technical issues. The Nazis "took major problems of the day – problems of race, gender, crime, and poverty – and transformed them into medical or biological problems ... [they] argued that Germany was teetering on the brink of racial collapse, and that racial hygiene was needed to save Germany from 'racial suicide'" (Proctor 1988a: 286). And climate scientists have told us that the science demands 80 percent reductions in GHG emissions by 2050 in order to save the planet.

Speaking a few months before the Copenhagen summit, Ban Ki-moon, the UN secretary-general, said: "The climate negotiations are proceeding at glacial speed. The world's glaciers are now melting faster than human progress to protect them and us. Failure to reach broad agreement in Copenhagen would be morally inexcusable, economically short-sighted and politically unwise ... The science demands it. The world economy needs it" (The Associated Press, September 22, 2009).

There is also an important difference between the case of eugenics and climate change. In the former case, science became practical knowledge as it identified levers for policy action; in the latter it failed to do so. However, climate science has put the issue on the political agenda, framing it and shaping public opinion in certain ways. Politicians in both cases used the science as legitimation for decisions.

Finally, let us return to the hope which was expressed by Otto Neurath and others. The hope is to unite society through science, to solve political conflicts or stalemate through rational scientific argumentation. Recall Neurath's dictum: "Metaphysical terms divide; scientific terms unite." If we interpret the "metaphysical" to comprise ideological and political aspects, we arrive at a truly astonishing conclusion. In the example of Keynes, the practical policies and agreements that were implemented were first and foremost based on politics. Keynes himself may have subscribed to a technocratic (and elitist) worldview, but he practiced differently. His economic policy proposals were based on the recognition of the "stickiness of wages" and a respect of trade union power. He developed his policy in opposition to neoclassical market equilibrium models. With regard to racism, we realize that the Nazis used an ideology to unite a majority of the German people and enrolled race science to bolster additional support for the extermination programs. So what happened in the climate discourse? Again, we see a widespread political agreement about the serious implications of climate change. But when it comes to action, ironically, science has been used to divide, not to unite. Because of a misunderstanding of the relation between authoritative knowledge and political power, a battle has been waged for the "correct" understanding of the climate system as a precondition for action. This has alienated many citizens who would be prepared to discuss preventative policies (as expressed in opinion polls). Many perceive that they are expected to subscribe to a platform that is either beyond their grasp or suspicious. It is perhaps the ultimate irony that the science war about climate change has all the overtones of a religious war.

As we indicated in the introductory chapter, we do not claim to provide a general theory of how knowledge becomes practical and effective in policymaking. We also indicated that even if knowledge has the hallmarks of being practical, this does not mean that it will be implemented and thus automatically become effective in practice. Too many factors influence policymaking, and the unpredictable nature of historical processes inevitably thwarts any kind of determinism. The many different possible combinations of policy streams, windows of opportunity, and active policy entrepreneurs lead to different policy outcomes, over time and in different jurisdictions.

But even where practical knowledge is developed, this does not create the conditions for its own practical success. Political and cultural forces are usually far more important for decision-making. So does our study on the power of scientific knowledge end with the conclusion that it does not yield any? It certainly does not in the literal sense of the term. However, scientists can act as agenda setters, influencing the belief systems of decision-makers and providing legitimation for decisions taken. A science push model, as mentioned in the introductory chapter, is highly improbable. As the cases of eugenics and Keynesianism show, even the most practical knowledge does not create the conditions for its own implementation. And the case of climate change provides another lesson, the futility of trying to influence policymaking without practical knowledge.

Bibliography

Abelshauser, Werner. 1999. "War Industry and 'Wirtschaftswunder': Germany's Economic Mobilization for World War II and Economic Success in the Postwar Period." *Vierteljahrshefte für Zeitgeschichte* 47(4): 503–38.

Adler, Emanuel, and Peter M. Haas. 1992. "Conclusion: Epistemic Communities, World Order, and the Creation of a Reflective Research Program." *International Organization* 46: 367–90.

Alcamo, Joseph, et al. 1995. "An Evaluation of the IPCC IS92 Emission Scenarios." In IPCC (eds.), *Climate Change 1994*. Cambridge University Press.

Aly, Götz and Susanne Heim. [1991] 2004. *Vordenker der Vernichtung: Auschwitz und die deutschen Pläne fur eine neue europäische Ordnung*. Frankfurt am Main: Fischer.

Andresen, Steinar, and Shardul Agrawala. 2002. "Leaders, Pushers and Laggards in the Making of the Climate Regime." *Global Environmental Change* 12(1): 41–51.

Arrhenius, Svante. 1896. "On the Influence of Carbonic Acid in the Air upon the Temperature of the Ground." *The London, Edinburgh and Dublin Philosophical Magazine and Journal of Science* 5: 237–76.

Ash, Mitchell, G. 1999. "Kurt Gottschaldt and Psychological Research in Nazi and Socialist Germany." In Kristie Macrakis and Dieter Hoffmann (eds.), *Science under Socialism: East Germany in Comparative Perspective*. Cambridge, MA: Harvard University Press, 286–301.

Ashley, David, and David Michael Orenstein. 1995. *Sociological Theory: Classical Statements*. Boston: Allyn & Bacon.

Bacon, Francis. [1620] 1858. *Novum Organum*, ed. James Spedding, Robert Leslie Ellis, and Douglas Denon Heath. London: Longmans.

Balz, Dan. 1997. "Sweden Sterilized Thousands of 'Useless' Citizens for Decades." *The Washington Post* 120 (August 29): A1.

Banton, Michael. 1998. *Racial Theories*. Second edition. Cambridge University Press.

Barkan, Elezar. 1992. *The Retreat of Scientific Racism. Changing Concepts of Race in Britain and the United States between the World Wars*. Cambridge University Press.

Barnes, Barry. 1988. *The Nature of Power*. Urbana and Chicago: University of Illinois Press.

Baur, Erwin, Eugen Fischer, and Fritz Lenz. [1921] 1931. *Human Heredity*. London: George Allen & Unwin.
Bell, Daniel. 1987. "The World and the United States in 2013." *Daedalus* 116: 1–31.
Benedick, Richard E. 1991. *Ozone Diplomacy: New Directions in Safeguarding the Planet*. Cambridge, MA: Harvard University Press.
Berenbaum, Michael. 1993. *The World Must Know: The History of the Holocaust as Told in the United States Holocaust Memorial Museum*. Boston: Little, Brown and Company.
Beyer, Janice M., and Harrison M. Trice. 1982. "The Utilization Process: A Conceptual Framework and Synthesis of Empirical Findings." *Administrative Science Quarterly* 27: 591–622.
Biddis, Michael Denis. 1970. *Father of Racist Ideology. The Social and Political Thought of Count Gobineau*. New York: Weybright and Talley.
Bleaney, Michael. 1985. *The Rise and Fall of Keynesian Economics: An Investigation of Its Contribution to Capitalist Development*. New York: St. Martin's Press.
Block, Fred. 1990. "The Market." In Fred Block, *Postindustrial Possibilities: A Critique of Economic Discourse*. Berkeley, CA: University of California Press, 46–74.
Block, Fred, and Larry Hirschhorn. 1979. "New Productive Forces and the Contradictions of Contemporary Capitalism." *Theory and Society* 7: 363–95.
Boas, Franz. 1935. "Race. " In Edwin R. A. Seligman (ed.), *Encyclopedia of the Social Sciences*, Vol. XIII. New York: Macmillan, 25–34.
Boehmer-Christiansen, Sonja. 1994a. "Global Climate Protection Policy: The Limits of Scientific Advice." Part 1. *Global Environmental Change* 4: 140–59. 1994b. "Global Climate Protection Policy: The Limits of Scientific Advice." Part 2. *Global Environmental Change* 4: 185–200.
Bombach, Gottfried et al. (eds.). 1963. *Der Keynesianismus IV: Die beschäftigungspolitische Diskussion in der Wachstumsepoche der Bundesrepublik Deutschland. Dokumente und Analysen*. Berlin: Springer-Verlag.
Bormann, F. von. 1937. "Ist die Gründung einer europäischen Familie in den Tropen zulässig?" *Archiv für Rassen- und Gesellschafts-Biologie* 31: 89–114.
Boykoff, Maxwell T. 2007. "Logging a Dead Norm? Newspaper Coverage of Anthropogenic Climate Change in the United States and United Kingdom from 2003 to 2006." *Area* 39(2): 470–81.
Broberg, Gunnar, and Nils Roll-Hansen. 1996. *Eugenics and the Welfare State: Sterilization Policy in Denmark, Sweden, Norway and Finland*. East Lansing, MI: Michigan State University Press.
Brooks, Harvey. 1982. "Stratospheric Ozone, the Scientific Community and Public Policy." In Frank A. Bower and Richard B. Ward (eds.), *Stratospheric Ozone and Man*. Boca Raton: CRC Press, 201–16.
Brossard, Dominique, James Shanahan, and Katherine McComas. 2004. "Are Issue-Cycles Culturally Constructed? A Comparison of French and American Coverage of Global Climate Change." *Mass Communication & Society* 7(3): 359–77.
Brothwell, John. 1988. "The General Theory after Fifty Years: Why Are We Not All Keynesians?" In John Hillard (ed.), *J. M. Keynes in Retrospect. The Legacy of the Keynesian Revolution*. Aldershot: Edward Elgar, 45–63.

Browning, Christopher R. 1992. *Ordinary Men: Reserve Police Battalion 101 and the Final Solution in Poland.* New York: HarperCollins.

Brulle, Robert J., Jason Carmichael, and J. Craig Jenkins. 2012. "Shifting Public Opinion on Climate Change: An Empirical Assessment of Factors Influencing Concern over Climate Change in the U.S., 2002–2010." *Climatic Change.* DOI 10.1007/s10584-012-0403-y

Brüning, Heinrich. 1970. *Memoiren 1918–1934.* Stuttgart: Deutsche Verlags-Anstalt.

Brunner, Karl, and Allan Meltzer. 1977. "The Explanation of Inflation: Some International Evidence." *American Economic Review* 67(5): 148–54.

Burleigh, Michael, and Wolfgang Wippermann. 1991. *The Racial State: Germany 1933–1945.* Cambridge and New York: Cambridge University Press.

Bush, Vannevar. 1945. *Science: The Endless Frontier – A Report to the President by Vannevar Bush, Director of the Office of Scientific Research and Development, July 1945.* Washington, DC: United States Government Printing Office.

Caplan, Nathan. 1979. "The Two-Communities Theory and Knowledge Utilization." *American Behavioral Scientist* 22(3): 459–70.

Cartwright, Nancy, J. Cat, L. Fleck, and T. E. Uebel. 1996. "Introduction." In N. Cartwright, J. Cat, L. Fleck, and T. E. Uebel (eds.), *Otto Neurath: Philosophy between Science and Politics.* Cambridge University Press.

Carvalho, Anabela, and Jacquelin Burgess. 2005. "Cultural Circuits of Climate Change in UK Broadsheet Newspapers, 1985–2003." *Risk Analysis* 25(6): 1457–69.

Chamberlain, Houston Stewart. [1900] 1968. *Foundations of the Nineteenth Century,* New York: Howard Fertig.

Chick, Victora. 1987. "Money Matters." *Times Higher Educational Supplement.* January 2, 1987.

Christie, Maureen. 2001. *Ozone Layer: A Philosophy of Science Perspective.* Cambridge University Press.

Coddington, Alan. 1974. "What Did Keynes Really Mean?" *Challenge* (November–December): 13–19.

Cohen, Michael D., James G. March, and Johan P. Olsen. 1972. "A Garbage Can Model of Organizational Choice." *Administrative Science Quarterly* 17(1): 1–25.

Collingridge, David, and Colin Reeve. 1986. *Science Speaks to Power: The Role of Experts in Policymaking.* London: Frances Pinter.

Collins, H. M. 1985. *Changing Order.* London: Sage.

Crane, Diana. 1972. *Invisible Colleges: Diffusion of Knowledge in Scientific Communities.* University of Chicago Press.

Crew, David F. (ed.). 1994. *Nazism and German Society.* London and New York: Routledge.

Dahl, Robert A. 1994. "A Democratic Dilemma: System Effectiveness versus Citizen Participation." *Political Science Quarterly* 109: 23–34.

Damro, Chad, and Pilar Luaces-Méndez. 2003. "The Kyoto Protocol's Emissions Trading System: An EU-US Environmental Flip-Flop." *Earth:* 1–19.

Daston, Lorraine, and Peter Galison. 2007. *Objectivity.* Boston: Zone Books.

Davidson, Paul. 1978. *Money and the Real World.* New York: Wiley.

2009. *The Keynes Solution: The Path to Global Economic Prosperity.* New York: Palgrave Macmillan.

De Geus, A. (1988). "Planning as Learning." *Harvard Business Review* (Mar./Apr.): 74.

Diesing, Paul. 1982. *Science and Ideology in the Policy Sciences.* New York: Aldine.

Dobbin, Frank R. 1993. "The Social Construction of the Great Depression: Industrial Policy during the 1930s in the United States, Britain, and France." *Theory and Society* 22(1): 1–56.

Downs, Anthony. 1972. "Up and Down with Ecology: The 'Issue-Attention Cycle.'" *The Public Interest* 28: 38–50.

Drucker, Peter F. 1971. "The New Markets and the New Capitalism." In Daniel Bell and Irving Kristol (eds.), *Capitalism Today.* New York: Basic Books, 44–79.

[1980] 1981a. "Toward the Next Economics." In Peter F. Drucker, *Toward the Next Economics and Other Essays.* New York: Harper and Row, 1–21.

1981b. "Toward the Next Economics." In Daniel Bell and Irving Kristol (eds.), *The Crisis of Economic Theory.* New York: Basic Books, 4–18.

[1981] 1984. "Auf dem Wege zur nächsten Wirtschaftstheorie." In Daniel Bell and Irving Kristol (eds.), *Die Krise in der Wirtschaftstheorie.* Berlin: Springer, 1–19.

1986. "The Changed World Economy." *Foreign Affairs:* 768–91.

Dryberg, Torben Bech. 1997. *The Circular Structure of Power, Politics and Identity.* London: Verso.

Durkheim, Emile. [1897] 1952. *Suicide: A Study in Sociology.* London: Routledge and Kegan Paul.

[1912] 1965. *The Elementary Forms of Religious Life.* New York: Free Press.

[1909] 1978. "Sociology and the Social Sciences." In Emile Durkheim, *On Institutional Analysis.* University of Chicago Press, 71–87.

[1955] 1983. *Pragmatism and Sociology.* Cambridge University Press.

East, Edward M. 1929. *Heredity and Human Affairs.* New York and London: Charles Scribner's Sons.

Eastin, Joshua, Reiner Grundmann, and Aseem Prakash. 2011. "The Two 'Limits' Debates: 'Limits to Growth' and *Climate Change.*" *Futures* 43: 16–26.

Edwards, Paul N. 1996. "Global Comprehensive Models in Politics and Policymaking." *Climatic Change* 32: 149–61.

1999. "Global Climate Science, Uncertainty and Politics: Data-laden Models, Model-Filtered Data." *Science as Culture* 8: 437–72.

Edwards, Paul N., and Stephen H. Schneider. 2001. "Self-Governance and Peer-Review in Science-for-Policy: The Case of the IPCC Second Assessment Report." In C. A. Miller and P. Edwards (eds.), 219–46.

EEA (European Environment Agency). 2005. *Annual Report 2004.* Luxembourg: Office for Official Publications of the European Communities.

Efron, John M. 1994. *Defenders of the Race: Jewish Doctors and Race Science in Fin-de-siècle Europe.* New Haven, CT: Yale University Press.

Elster, Jon. 1979. "Risk, Uncertainty and Nuclear Power." *Social Science Information* 18: 371–400.

Elzinga, Aant. 1995. "Shaping Worldwide Consensus: The Orchestration of Global Climate Change Research." In Aant Elzinga and Catharina Landström (eds.), *Internationalism in Science*. London: Taylor and Graham, 223–55.

Entman, Robert M. 1993. "Framing: Toward Clarification of a Fractured Paradigm." *Journal of Communication* 43(4): 51–58.

Farman, J. C., B. G. Gardiner, and J. D. Shanklin. 1985. "Large Losses of Total Ozone in Antarctica Reveal Seasonal ClOx/NOx Interaction." *Nature* 315: 207–10.

Feuer, Lewis S. 1954. "Causality in the Social Sciences." *The Journal of Philosophy* 51: 681–95.

Finkelstein, Norman. 1997. "Daniel Jonah Goldhagen's 'Crazy' Thesis: A Critique of Hitler's Willing Executioners." *New Left Review* 224: 39–87.

Fischer, Eugen. 1913. *Die Rehobother Bastards und das Bastardisierungsproblem beim Menschen. Anthropologische und ethnographische Studien am Rehobother Bastardvolk in Deutsch-Südwestafrika*, Jena: G. Fischer.

Fischer, Frank. 1990. *Technocracy and the Politics of Expertise*. London: Sage.

Foucault, Michel. 1980. *Power/Knowledge: Selected Interviews and other Writings, 1972–1977*. New York: Vintage.

Fourier, J. B. J. 1824. "Remarques générales sur les températures du globe terrestre et des espaces planétaires." *Annales de Chimie et de Physique* 27: 136–67.

Freeman, Christopher. 1977. "Economics of research and development." In Ina Spiegel-Rösing and Derek de Solla Price (eds.), *Science, Technology and Society: A Cross-Disciplinary Perspective*. Beverly Hills, CA: Sage, 223–75.

Freiburg, Jeanne. 1993. "Counting Bodies: The Politics of Reproduction in the Swedish Welfare State." *Scandinavian Studies* 65: 226–36.

Funtowicz, Silvio O. and Jerome R. Ravetz. 1993. "Science for the Post-Normal Age." *Futures* 25(7): 735–55.

Galton, F. 1962 [1892], *Hereditary Genius: An Inquiry into Its Laws and Consequences*. London : Collins.

Garver, Kenneth L., and Bettylee Garver. 1991. "Historical Perspectives: Eugenics – Past, Present, and the Future." *American Journal of Human Genetics* 49: 1109–18.

Giddens, Anthony. 2009. *The Politics of Climate Change*. Cambridge: Polity Press.

Gieryn, Thomas F. 1995. "Boundaries of Science." In Sheila Jasanoff et al. (eds.), *Handbook of Science and Technology Studies*. Thousand Oaks, CA: Sage, 393–443.

Gilbertson, Tamra, and Oscar Reyes. 2009. "Carbon Trading: How It Works and Why It Fails." Critical Currents No.7. Uppsala: Dag Hammarskjöld Foundation.

Gilman, Sander L. 1991. *The Jew's Body*. New York: Routledge.

  1993. "Mark Twain and the Diseases of the Jew." *American Literature* 65: 95–116.

  1996. *Smart Jews: The Construction of the Image of Jewish Superior Intelligence*. Lincoln: University of Nebraska Press.

Girod, Bastien, Arnim Wiek, Harald Mieg, and Mike Hulme. 2009. "The Evolution of the IPCC's Emissions Scenarios." *Environmental Science & Policy* 12: 103–18.

de Gobineau, Arthur. 1915. *The Inequality of Human Races*. New York: G. P. Putnam's Sons.

Godin, Benoit 2006. "The Linear Model of Innovation." *Science, Technology & Human Values* 31(6): 639–67.

Goffman, Irving. 1974. *Frame Analysis*. Cambridge, MA: Harvard University Press.

Goldhagen, Daniel Jonah. 1996. *Hitler's Willing Executioners: Ordinary Germans and the Holocaust*, New York: Alfred A. Knopf.

Goldstein, Judith. 1994. *Ideas, Interests, and American Trade Policy*. Ithaca: Cornell University Press.

Goldstein, Judith, and Robert O. Keohane (eds.). 1993. *Ideas and Foreign Policy: Beliefs, Institutions and Political Change*. Ithaca: Cornell University Press.

Gormley, W. T. 2007. "Public Policy Analysis: Ideas and Impacts." *Annual Review of Political Science* 10: 297–313.

Gorz, André. [1980] 1982. *Farewell to the Working Class: An Essay on Post-Industrial Socialism*. London: Pluto Press.

Gottweis, Herbert 1998. *Governing Molecules: The Discursive Politics of Genetic Engineering in Europe and the United States*. Cambridge, MA: MIT Press.

Gourevitch, Peter Alexsis. 1984. "Breaking with Orthodoxy: The Politics of Economic Responses to the Depression of the 1930s." *International Organization* 38: 95–130.

1989. "Keynesian Politics: The Political Sources of Economic Policy." In P. A. Hall (ed.), *The Political Power of Economic Ideas*, 87–106.

Graham, Loren R. 1977. "Science and Values: The Eugenics Movement in Germany and Russia in the 1920s." *American Historical Review* 82: 1133–64.

Gramsci, Antonio. 1971. *Selections from the Prison Notebooks of Antonio Gramsci*, ed. and trans. Q. Hoare and G. Smith. London: Lawrence & Wishart.

Granovetter, Mark. 1978. "Threshold Models of Collective Behavior." *American Journal of Sociology* 83: 1420–43.

Grant, Madison. 1918. *The Passing of the Great Race or the Racial Basis of European History*. New York: Charles Scribner's Sons.

Grant, Robert M. 2003. "Strategic Planning in a Turbulent Environment." *Strategic Management Journal* 24(6): 491.

Greene, Wade. 1974. "Economists in recession." *New York Times Magazine*, May 12: 64.

Grundmann, Reiner. 2001. *Transnational Environmental Policy: Reconstructing Ozone*. London: Routledge.

2007. "Climate change and knowledge politics.' *Environmental Politics* 16: 414–32.

2009. "The Role of Expertise in Governance Processes." *Forest Policy and Economics* 11: 398–403.

2012. "'Climategate' and the Scientific Ethos." *Science, Technology & Human Values*. DOI 10.1177/0162243911432318.

Grundmann, Reiner, and Ramesh Krishnamurthy. 2010. "The Discourse of Climate Change: A Corpus-Based Approach." *Critical Approaches to Discourse Analysis across Disciplines* 4(2): 125–46.

Grundmann, Reiner, and Mike Scott 2011 "Disputed Climate Science in the Media: Do Countries Matter?" Ms.

Günther, Hans F. K. 1919. *Rassenkunde des deutschen Volkes*. Munich: Lehmann.

[1925] 1927. *The Racial Element of European History*. London: Methuen.

Haas, Peter M. 1992. "Introduction: Epistemic Communities and International Policy Coordination." *International Organization* 46: 1–35.

1993. "Stratospheric Ozone: Regime Formation in Stages." In Oran R. Young and Gail Osherenko (eds.), *Polar Politic: Creating International Environmental Regimes*. Ithaca: Cornell University Press, 152–85.

2004. "When Does Power Listen to Truth? A Constructivist Approach to the Policy Process." *Journal of European Public Policy* 11(4): 569–92.

Habermas, Jürgen. 1964. "Dogmatismus, Vernunft und Entscheidung – Zur Theorie und Praxis in der wissenschaftlichen Zivilisation." In Jürgen Habermas, *Theorie und Praxis*. Neuwied: Luchterhand, 231–57.

1970. *Technology and Science as "Ideology"* trans. Jeremy J. Shapiro. Boston: Beacon Press.

1973. *Theory and Practice*. Boston: Beacon Press.

Hacking, Ian. 2005. "Why Race Still Matters." *Daedalus* 134(1): 102–16.

Hagstrom, Warren O. 1965. *The Scientific Community*. New York: Basic Books.

Hajer, Maarten A. 1995. *The Politics of Environmental Discourse: Ecological Modernisation and the Policy Process*. Oxford University Press.

Hall, Peter A. (ed.). 1989a. *The Political Power of Economic Ideas: Keynesianism across Nations*. Princeton University Press.

1989b. "Introduction." In Peter A. Hall (ed.), *The Political Power of Economic Ideas*, 3–26.

1989c. "Conclusion: The Politics of Keynesian Ideas." In Peter A. Hall, (ed.), *The Political Power of Economic Ideas*, 361–91.

1993. "Policy Paradigms, Social Learning, and the State: The Case of Economic Policymaking in Britain." *Comparative Politics* 25: 275–96.

Hankins, Frank Hamilton. 1926. *The Racial Basis of Civilization. A Critique of the Nordic Doctrine*. New York: Alfred A. Knopf.

Hansen, Alvin H. 1952. *A Guide to Keynes*. New York: McGraw-Hill.

Hardin, Garrett. 1974. "Living on a Lifeboat." *Bioscience* 24(10): 561–68.

Harich, Wolfgang. 1975. *Kommunismus ohne Wachstum? Babeuf und der 'Club of Rome.' Sechs Interviews mit Freimut Duve und Briefe an ihn*. Reinbek bei Hamburg: Rowohlt.

Harrod, Roy F. 1951. *The Life of John Maynard Keynes*. New York: Harcourt, Brace.

Hart, David M., and David G. Victor. 1993. "Scientific Elites and the Making of US Policy for Climate Change Research, 1957–74." *Social Studies of Science* 23(4): 643–80.

Haupt, Joachim. 1933. "Freie Forschung im Dritten Reich?" *Volk im Werden* 1(2): 1–2.

Hayek, Friedrich A. 1952. *The Counter-Revolution of Science: Studies on the Abuse of Reason*. Glencoe, IL: Free Press.

[1945] 1969. "The Use of Knowledge in Society." In Friedrich A. Hayek, *Individualism and Economic Order*. University of Chicago Press, 77–91.

Heclo, Hugh. 1978. "Issue Networks and the Executive Establishments." In Anthony D. King (ed.), *The New American Political System*. Washington: American Enterprise Institute, 87–124.

Hellpach, Willy H. 1938. "Kultur und Klima." In Heinz Wolterek (ed.), *Klima-Wetter-Mensch*. Leipzig: Quelle & Meyer, 417–38.

Hernes, Gudmund. 2008. "The Interface between Social Research and Policy Making." *European Sociological Review* 24: 257–65.

Herrnstein, Richard J., and Charles Murray. 1994. *The Bell Curve: Intelligence and Class Structure in American Life*, New York: Free Press.

Hicks, John R. 1937. "Mr. Keynes and the Classics: A Suggested Interpretation." *Econometrica* 5: 147–59.

1974. *The Crisis of Keynesian Economics*. Oxford: Basil Blackwell.

1985. "Keynes and the World Economy." In Fausto Vicarelli (ed.), *Keynes's Relevance Today*. London: Macmillan, 21–27.

Hirschman, Albert O. 1989. "How Keynes Was Spread from America." *States and Social Structures Newsletter* No. 10, 1–5.

Hirst, Paul, and Grahame Thompson. 1992. "The Problem of 'Globalization': International Economic Relations, National Economic Management and the Formation of Trading Blocs." *Economy and Society* 21: 357–96.

Horkheimer, Max. [1932] 1972. "Notes on Science and the Crisis." In Max Horkheimer, *Critical Theory: Selected Essays*. New York: Continuum, 3–9.

Horowitz, Irving L. 1970. "Social Science Mandarins: Policymaking as a Political Formula." *Policy Sciences* 1: 339–60.

1980. *Taking Lives: Genocide and State Power*, New Brunswick, NJ: Transaction Publishers.

1995. "Searching for Enemies." *Society* 33: 42–50.

Hotz-Hart, Beat. 1983. "Regierbarkeit im wirtschaftlichen Strukturwandel. Der weltwirtschaftliche Umbruch als Herausforderung wirtschaftspolitischer Institutionen", *Schweizerisches Jahrbuch für politische Wissenschaft* 23(5): 293–314.

Houghton, J. T. et al., eds. 1996. *Climate Change 1995: The Science of Climate Change*. Cambridge University Press.

Houghton, J. T. et al., eds. 2001, *Climate Change 2001: The Scientific Basis*. Cambridge University Press.

Howitt, Peter. 1996. "On Some Problems in Measuring Knowledge-Based Growth." In P. Howitt (ed.), *The Implications of Knowledge-Based Growth for Micro-Economic Policies*. University of Calgary Press.

Hulme, Mike. 2009. *Why We Disagree About Climate Change*. Cambridge University Press.

2010. "Moving beyond Climate Change." *Environment* 52(3):15–19.

Huntington, Ellsworth. 1907. *The Pulse of Asia*. Boston: Houghton Mifflin.

[1915] 1924. *Civilization and Climate*. New Haven: Yale University Press.

1927. *The Human Habitat*. New York: D. Van Nostrand.

1935. *Tomorrow's Children: The Goal of Eugenics*. New York: J. Wiley.

1945. *Mainsprings of Civilization*. New York: J. Wiley.

Inter Academy Council. 2010. *Review of the IPCC: Review of the Processes and Procedures of the Intergovernmental Panel on Climate Change.* http:// reviewipcc.interacademycouncil.net/report.html.

Jacobsen, John Kurt. 1995. "Much Ado about Ideas: The Cognitive Factor in Economic Policy." *World Politics* 47: 283–310.

Jaensch, Ehrich. 1927. *Der nordische Gedanke unter den Deutschen.* Munich: J. F. Lehmann.

1930. *Rassenkunde des Jüdischen Volkes.* Munich: J. F. Lehmann.

James, Harold. 1989. "What Is Keynesian about Deficit Financing? The Case of Interwar Germany." In Peter A. Hall (ed.), *The Political Power of Economic Ideas,* 231–61.

Jasanoff, Sheila. 1990. *The Fifth Branch: Science Advisers as Policymakers.* Cambridge, MA: Harvard University Press.

1987. "Contested Boundaries in Policy-Relevant Science." *Social Studies of Science* 17: 195–230.

Jaspers, Karl. [1947] 1965. "Die Wissenschaft im Hitlerstaat." In Karl Jaspers, *Hoffnung und Sorge: Schriften zur deutschen Politik 1945–1965.* Munich: Piper, 41–46.

Jencks, Christopher. 1985. "Methodological Problems in Studying 'Military Keynesianism.'" *The American Journal of Sociology* 91(2): 373–79.

Jessop, Bob, and Stijn Oosterlynck. 2008. "Cultural Political Economy: On Making the Cultural Turn without Falling into Soft Economic Sociology." *Geoforum* 39(3): 1155–69.

Johnson, Chalmers. 2007. *Nemesis: The Last Days of the American Republic* (American Empire Project). New York: Metropolitan Books.

Johnson, Elizabeth S., and Harry G. Johnson. 1978. *The Shadow of Keynes: Understanding Keynes, Cambridge and Keynesian Economics.* Oxford: Blackwell.

Kaldor, Nicholas. 1983. *Grenzen der "General Theory."* Berlin: Springer.

Katz, Jacob. 1980. *Exclusiveness and Tolerance: Studies in Jewish-Gentile Relations in Medieval and Modern Times.* Westport, CT: Greenwood Press.

Katz, Steven T. 1994. *The Holocaust in Historical Perspective.* Vol. II: *The Holocaust and Mass Death before the Modern Age.* New York. London 1994.

Keane, John, 1988. *Democracy and Civil Society.* London: Verso.

Keane, John, and John Owens. 1986. *After Full Employment.* London: Routledge.

Key, V.O., Jr. 1961. *Public Opinion and American Democracy.* New York: Alfred A. Knopf.

Keynes, John M. [1930] 1971. *Treatise on Money.* Vol. I: *The Pure Theory of Money. Collected Writings.* Vol. V. Cambridge University Press.

1932a: "The World's Economic Outlook." *The Atlantic Monthly,* May 1932.

1932b. "Die wirtschaftlichen Aussichten für 1932." *Wirtschaftsdienst* Heft 5 (January): 15.

1936. *The General Theory of Employment, Interest and Money.* London: Macmillan.

1938. "Letter to Roy Harrod (July 4, 1938)." In John M. Keynes, *Collected Writings.* Vol. XIV.

[1931] 1963a. *Essays in Persuasion*. New York: Norton.

1963b. *Collected Writings*. Vol. X: *Essays in Biography*. London: Macmillan.

[1933] 1972a. *The Means to Prosperity*. In John M. Keynes, *Collected Writings*. Vol. IX: *Essays in Persuasion*. London: Macmillan.

[1949]1972b. *Collected Writings*. Vol. X: *Essays in Biography*. London: Macmillan.

1978. *Collected Writings*. Vol. XVIII: *Activities 1922–1932*, ed. Elizabeth Johnson. London: Macmillan.

1980. *Collected Writings*. Vol. XXVII: *Activities 1940–1946*, ed. Donald Moggridge. London: Macmillan.

1981. *Collected Writings*. Vol. XX: *Activities 1929–1931*. London: Macmillan.

1982. *Collected Writings*. Vol. XXI: *Activities 1931–1939: World Crises and Policies in Britain and America*, ed. Donald Moggridge. London: Macmillan.

[1932] 1982a. "The Economic Prospects 1932." In John M. Keynes, *Collected Writings*. Vol. XXI, 39–48.

[1932] 1982b. "The World's Economic Crisis and the Way of Escape" (Halley-Stewart Lecture). In John M. Keynes, *Collected Writings*. Vol. XXI, 50–62.

[1930] 1984a. "Economic Possibilities for Our Grandchildren." In John M. Keynes, *Collected Writings*. Vol. IX: *Essays in Persuasion*. Cambridge University Press, 321–32.

[1929] 1984b "Can Lloyd George Do It?" In John M. Keynes, *Collected Writings*. Vol. IX: *Essays in Persuasion*. Cambridge University Press, 86–125.

[1926] 1984c. "The End of Laissez-Faire." In John M. Keynes, *Collected Writings*. Vol. IX: *Essays in Persuasion*. Cambridge University Press, 253–71.

[1930] 1984d. "The Great Slum of 1930." In John M. Keynes, *Collected Writings*. Vol. IX: *Essays in Persuasion*. Cambridge University Press, 126–34.

[1931] 1984e. "Economy." In John M. Keynes, *Collected Writings*. Vol. IX: *Essays in Persuasion*. Cambridge University Press, 135–49.

[1931] 1984f. "Proposals for a Revenue Tariff." In John M. Keynes, *Collected Writings*. Vol. IX: *Essays in Persuasion*. Cambridge University Press, 231–44.

[1973] 1987. *Collected Writings*. Vol. XIII: *The General Theory and After: Part I: Preparation*, ed. Donald Moggridge. London : Macmillan.

Khandekar, Madhav. 2009. "Global Warming and Glacier Melt-Down Debate: A Tempest In A Teapot?' Guest blog on http://pielkeclimatesci.wordpress. com/2009/12/01/global-warming-and-glacier-melt-down-debate-a-tempest-in-a-teapot/, 1 December.

King, David A. 2004. "Climate Change Science: Adapt, Mitigate, or Ignore?" *Science* 303 (January): 176–77.

Kingdon, John W. 1984. *Agendas, Alternatives, and Public Policies*. Boston: Little Brown.

Kirshner, Jonathan. 2009. "Keynes, Legacies, and Inquiry." *Theory and Society* 38: 527–41.

Klemperer, Victor. 1995. *Ich will Zeugnis ablegen bis zum Letzten: Tagebücher 1933–1941*. Berlin: Aufbau-Verlag.

Kolnai, Aurel. 1977. *Ethics, Values, and Reality: Selected Papers*. London: Athlone Press.

Krasner, Stephen D. 1993. "Westphalia and All That." In Judith Goldstein and Robert O. Keohane (eds.), *Ideas and Foreign Policy: Beliefs, Institutions and Political Change*. Ithaca: Cornell University Press, 235–64.

Krohn, Claus-Dieter. 1981. *Wirtschaftstheorien als politische Interessen: Die akademische Nationalökonomie in Deutschland 1918–1933*. Frankfurt am Main: Campus.

1987. *Wissenschaft im Exil: Deutsche Wirtschafts- und Sozialwissenschaftler in den USA und die New School of Social Research*. Frankfurt am Main: Campus.

Kroll, Gerhard. 1958. *Von der Weltwirtschaftskrise zur Staatskonjunktur*. Berlin: Duncker & Humblot.

Kroto, Harold. (no date). http: //thesciencenetwork.org/docs/BB3/Kroto_ Theories.pdf.

Kühl, Stefan. 1994. *The Nazi Connection: Eugenics, American Racism, and German National Socialism*. New York: Oxford University Press.

1997. *Die Internationale der Rassisten: Aufstieg und Niedergang der internationalen Bewegung für Eugenik und Rassenhygiene im 20. Jahrhundert*. Frankfurt am Main: Campus.

Kuhn, Thomas S. [1962] 1970. *The Structure of Scientific Revolutions*. Second edition. Chicago University Press.

Kuznets, Simon. 1971. *Qualitative Economic Research: Trends and Problems*. New York: Columbia University Press.

Landfried, Christine. 1976. "Wissenschaft und Politik in der Krise um 1930 in Deutschland." In Bernard Badura (ed.), Seminar: Angewandte Sozialforschung. *Studien über die Voraussetzungen und Bedingungen der Produktion, Diffusion und Verwertung sozialwissenschaftlichen Wissens*. Frankfurt am Main: Suhrkamp 151–83.

Landmann, Oliver. 1981. "Theoretische Grundlagen für eine aktive Krisenbekämpfung in Deutschland 1930–1933. " In Gottfried Bombach et al. (eds.), *Der Keynesianismus III: Die geld- und beschäftigungstheoretische Diskussion in Deutschland zur Zeit Keynes: Dokumente und Analysen*. Berlin: Springer-Verlag, 215–420.

Landsberg, Paul Ludwig. 1993. "Rassenideologie und Rassenwissenschaft: Zur neuesten Literatur über das Rassenproblem." *Zeitschrift für Sozialforschung* 2: 388–406.

Lasswell, Harold D., and Abraham Kaplan. 1950. *Power and Society: A Framework for Political Inquiry*. New Haven: Yale University Press.

Latour, Bruno. 1993. *We Have Never Been Modern*. Cambridge, MA: Harvard University Press.

1987. *Science in Action: How to Follow Scientists and Engineers through Society*. Cambridge, MA: Harvard University Press.

Lekachman, Robert. 1968. *The Age of Keynes*. New York: Random House.

Leggett, Jeremy K. 2001. *The Carbon War*. London: Routledge.

Lenger, Friedrich, 1994. *Werner Sombart 1863–1941: Eine Biographie*. Munich: C. H. Beck.

Lenton, Timothy M. et al. 2008. "Tipping Elements in the Earth's Climate System." *Proceedings of the National Academy of Sciences* 105(6): 1786.

Lenz, Fritz. 1924. "Eugenics in Germany." *Journal of Heredity* 15: 223–31.

1925. "Oswald Spenglers 'Untergang des Abendlandes' im Lichte der Rassenbiologie." *Archiv für Rassen- und Gesellschafts-Biologie* 17: 289–309.

1931. "Die Stellung des Nationalsozialismus zur Rassenhygiene." *Archiv für Rassen- und Gesellschafts-Biologie* 25: 300–08.

1933. *Die Rasse als Wertprinzip: Zur Erneuerung der Ethik.* Munich: Lehmann.

Leontief, Wassily. 1985. "Introduction to the Transaction Edition: Academic Economics." In Wassily Leontief, *Essays in Economics.* New Brunswick: Transaction Books, ix–xii.

Lerner, Daniel. 1959. "Social Science: Whence and Whither?" In Daniel Lerner (ed.), *The Human Meaning of the Social Sciences: Original Essays on the History and the Application of the Social Sciences.* Cleveland, OH: The World Publishing Company, 13–39.

Lerner, Richard M. 1992. *Final Solutions. Biology, Prejudice, and Genocides.* University Park, PA: University of Pennsylvania Press.

Levy, David L., and Daniel Egan. 2003. "A Neo-Gramscian Approach to Corporate Political Strategy: Conflict and Accommodation in the Climate Change Negotiations." *Journal of Management Studies* 40(4): 803–29.

Lieberman, Leonard, and Larry T. Reynolds. 1995. "The Future Status of the Race Concept." *Michigan Sociological Review* 9 (Fall 1995): 1–18.

Liesner, Thelma. 1985. *Economic Statistics 1900–1983: United Kingdom, United States of America, France, Germany, Italy, Japan.* New York: Facts on File Publications.

Lindblom, Charles E. 1959. "The Science of Muddling Through." *Public Administration Review* 19: 79–88.

1972. "Integration of Economics and Other Social Sciences through Policy Analysis." In James C. Charlesworth (ed.), *Integration of the Social Sciences through Policy Analysis.* Philadelphia: AAPSS, 1–14.

1979. "Still Muddling, Not Yet Through." *Public Administration Review* 39: 517–26.

Lipset, Seymour M. 1979. "Predicting the Future of Post-Industrial Society." In Seymour M. Lipset (ed.), *The Third Century: America as a Post-Industrial Society.* University of Chicago Press, 1–35.

[1979] 1985. "Predicting the Future: The Limits of Social Science." In Seymour M. Lipset, *Consensus and Conflict: Essays in Political Sociology.* New Brunswick: Transaction Books, 329–60.

1994. "The State of American Sociology." *Sociological Forum* 9: 199–220.

Lipsey, Richard G. 1991, "Global Change and Economic Policy." In Nico Stehr and Richard V. Ericson (eds.), *The Culture and Power of Knowledge: Inquiries into Contemporary Society,* 279–300.

Lohmann, L. 2009. "Climate as Investment." *Development and Change* 40(6): 1063–83.

Lomborg, Bjørn. 2001. *The Skeptical Environmentalist.* Cambridge University Press.

Lösch, Niels C. 1997. *Rasse als Konstrukt: Leben und Werk Eugen Fischers.* Frankfurt am Main: Peter Lang.

Lovelock, James. 2010. "Humans Are too Stupid to Prevent Climate Change." www.guardian.co.uk/environment/blog/2010/mar/29/james-lovelock.

Lowe, Adolph. 1965. *On Economic Knowledge: Toward a Science of Political Economics*. New York: Harper & Rowe.

    1977. *On Economic Knowledge: Toward a Science of Political Economics*. Enlarged edition. White Plains, NY: M. E. Sharpe.

Loyal, Steven, and Barry Barnes. 2001. "'Agency' as a Red Herring in Social Theory." *Philosophy of the Social Sciences* 31: 507–24.

Luhmann, Niklas. 1984. *Soziale Systeme: Grundriß einer allgemeinen Theorie*. Frankfurt am Main: Suhrkamp.

    1992. *Beobachtungen der Moderne*. Opladen: Westdeutscher Verlag.

Lyons, Andrew P. 1974. "The Question of Race in Anthropology from the Time of J. F. Blumenbach to that of Franz Boas, with Particular Reference to the Period 1830 to 1890 (approx.)." PhD dissertation, University of Oxford.

Lyotard, Jean-François [1979] 1984. *The Postmodern Condition: A Report on Knowledge*. Minneapolis: University of Minnesota Press.

Lysgaard, Sverre, and Louis Schneider. 1953. "The Deferred Gratification Pattern." *American Sociological Review* 18 (April): 142–59.

Mann, Michael E., Raymond S. Bradley, and Malcolm K. Hughes. 1998. "Global-Scale Temperature Patterns and Climate Forcing over the Past Six Centuries." *Nature* 392: 779–87.

    1999. "Northern Hemisphere Temperatures during the Past Millennium: Inferences, Uncertainties, and Limitations." *Geophysical Research Letters* 26(6): 759–62.

Mannheim, Karl. 1929. *Ideologie und Utopia*. Bonn: Cohen.

    [1929] 1936. *Ideology and Utopia: An Introduction to the Sociology of Knowledge*. London: Routledge and Kegan Paul.

    1932. *Die Gegenwartsaufgaben der Soziologie: Ihre Lehrgestalt*. Tübingen: J. C. B. Mohr (Paul Siebeck).

    1940. *Man and Society in an Age of Reconstruction*. London: Routledge and Kegan Paul.

    [1928] 1952. "Competition as a Cultural Phenomenon." In Karl Mannheim, *Essays on the Sociology of Knowledge*. London: Routledge and Kegan Paul, 191–229.

March, James G., and Herbert A. Simon. 1958. *Organizations*. New York: Wiley.

Marks, Jonathan. 1995. *Human Biodiversity: Genes, Race and History*. New Jersey: Aldine Transaction.

Marsh, David, and R. A. W. Rhodes. 1992. *Policy Networks in British Government*. Oxford: Clarendon Press.

Marshall, Alfred. [1890] 1948. *Principles of Economics*. New York: Macmillan.

Mason, Tim. 1993. *Social Policy and the Third Reich: The Working Class and the "National Community."* Oxford and Providence: Berg Publishers.

Massin, Benoit. 1996. "From Virchow to Fischer: Physical Anthropology and 'Modern Race Theories' in Wilhelmine Germany." In George W. Stocking Jr. (ed.), *Volksgeist as Method and Ethic: Essays on Boasian Ethnography and the German Anthropological Tradition*. History of Anthropology, Vol. 8. Madison: University of Wisconsin Press, 79–154.

Mazur, Allan, and Jinling Lee. 1993. "Sounding the Global Alarm: Environmental Issues in the US National News." *Social Studies of Science* 23: 681–720.

McIntyre, Stephen, and Ross McKitrick. 2003. "Corrections to the Mann et al. (1998) Proxy Data Base and Northern Hemispheric Average Temperature Series." *Energy & Environment* 14(6): 751–71.

McKee, James. 1994. *Sociology and the Race Problem: The Failure of a Perspective*, Urbana: University of Illinois Press.

Meja, Volker, and Nico Stehr. 1985. "Sozialwissenschaftlicher und erkenntnistheoretischer Diskurs." *Soziale Welt* 36: 361–80.

1988. "Social Science, Epistemology, and the Problem of Relativism." *Social Epistemology* 2: 263–71.

Melman, Seymour. 1970. *Pentagon Capitalism: The Political Economy of War*. New York: McGraw-Hill Publishing Company.

Merton, Robert K. 1937. "The Unanticipated Consequences of Purposive Social Action." *American Journal of Sociology* 1: 894.

1949. "The Role of Applied Social Science in the Formation of Policy: A Research Memorandum." *Philosophy of Science* 16: 161–81.

[1949] 1957. *Social Theory and Social Structure*. Revised and enlarged edition. New York: Free Press.

1963. "Basic Research and the Potentials of Relevance." *The American Behavioral Scientists* 6: 86–90.

1975. "Social Knowledge and Public Policy: Sociological Perspectives on Four Presidential Commissions." In Mirra Komarovsky (ed.), *Sociology and Public Policy: The Case of Presidential Commissions*. New York: Elsevier, 153–77.

1995. "The Thomas Theorem and the Matthew Effect." *Social Forces* 74: 379–424.

Mill, John Stuart. 1950. *Philosophy of Scientific Method*. New York: Hafner.

Miller, Clark A. 2001. "Hybrid Management: Boundary Organizations, Science Policy, and Environmental Governance in the Climate Regime." *Science, Technology & Human Values* 26(4): 478–500.

Miller, Clark A., and Paul N. Edwards (eds.). 2001. *Changing the Atmosphere: Expert Knowledge and Environmental Governance*. Cambridge University Press.

Mintz, Alex, and Alexander Hicks. 1984. "Military Keynesianism in the United States, 1949–1976: Disaggregating Military Expenditures and their Determination." *The American Journal of Sociology* 90(2): 411–17.

Montford, A. W. 2010. *The Hockey Stick Illusion: Climategate and the Corruption of Science*. London: Stacey International.

Mosse, George L. 1978. *Towards the Final Solution: The Failure of a Perspective*. Urbana, IL: University of Illinois Press.

Muir Russell, Alastair. 2010. *The Independent Climate Change E-mails Review*. http://www.cce-review.org/.

Nakicenovic, N., and R. Swart (eds.). 2000. *IPCC Special Report on Emissions Scenarios*. Cambridge University Press.

National Academy of Science. 1969. *The Behavioral Sciences: Outlook and Needs*. Englewood Cliff, NJ: Prenctice-Hall.

Neurath, Otto. 1913. "Probleme der Kriegswirtschaftslehre. " *Zeitschrift fuer die Gesamte Staatswissenschaft* 69: 438–531.

Newell, Peter. 2000. *Climate for Change: Non-State Actors and the Global Politics of the Greenhouse.* Cambridge University Press.

Nicholls, Robert J., and Richard S. J. Tol. 2006. "Impacts and Responses to Sea-Level Rise: A Global Analysis of the SRES Scenarios over the Twenty-First Century." *Philosophical Transactions: Series A, Mathematical, Physical, and Engineering Sciences* 364: 1073–95.

Nordhaus, Ted, and Michael Shellenberger. 2009. "Apocalypse Fatigue: Losing the Public on Climate Change. " *Yale Environment* 360. http: // e360.yale.edu/content/feature.msp?id=2210.

O'Connor, James. 1984. *Accumulation Crisis.* Oxford: Blackwell.

O'Donnell, Timothy. 2000. "Of Loaded Dice and Heated Arguments: Putting the Hansen-Michaels Global Warming Debate in Context." *Social Epistemology* 14: 109–27.

Oliver, Michael J., and Hugh Pemberton. 2004. "Learning and Change in 20th-Century British Economic Policy." *Governance* 17(3): 415–41.

Oppenheimer, Michael, Brian C. O'Neill, Mort Webster, and Shardul Agrawala. 2007. "Climate Change: The Limits of Consensus." *Science* 317(5844): 1505–06.

Oreskes, Naomi. 2003. "The Role of Quantitative Models in Science." In Charles D. Canham, Jonathan J. Cole, and William K. Lauenroth (eds.), *Models in Ecosystem Science.* Princeton University Press, 13–31.

　　2004. "Beyond the Ivory Tower: The Scientific Consensus on Climate Change." *Science* 306(5702): 1686.

Oreskes, Naomi, Kristin Shrader-Frechette, and Kenneth Belitz 1994. "Verification, Validation, and Confirmation of Numerical Models in the Earth Sciences." *Science* 263(5147): 641–46.

Overpeck, Jonathan T., and Jeremy L. Weiss. 2009. "Projections of Future Sea Level Becoming More Dire." *Proceedings of the National Academy of Sciences of the United States of America* 106(51): 21461–2.

Oxburgh, Ron. 2010. *Report by Lord Oxburgh's Science Assessment Panel.* www.uea.ac.uk/mac/comm/media/press/CRUstatements/SAP.

Parker, Richard. 2005. *John Kenneth Galbraith: His Life, His Politics, His Economics.* New York: Farrar, Straus and Giroux.

Parkin, Michael, and Robin Bade. 1986. *Modern Macroeconomics.* Second edition. Scarborough, Ontario: Prentice-Hall.

Parsons, Talcott. 1938. "The Role of Ideas in Social Action." *American Sociological Review* 3(5): 652–64.

Patinkin, Don. 1982. *Anticipations of the General Theory? And other Essays on Keynes.* University of Chicago Press.

Perrow, Charles. 1984. *Normal Accidents.* New York: Basic Books.

Pfeffer, W. T., J. T. Harper, and S. O'Neel, 2008. "Kinematic Constraints on Glacier Contributions to 21st-Century Sea-Level Rise." *Science* 321: 1340–43.

Pielke, Roger A., Jr. 2007. *The Honest Broker: Making Sense of Science in Policy and Politics.* Cambridge University Press.

　　2009. "The British Climate Change Act: A Critical Evaluation and Proposed Alternative Approach." *Environmental Research Letters* 4, 024010.

2010. *The Climate Fix. What Scientists and Politicians Won't Tell You about Global Warming.* New York: Basic Books.

Pielke, Roger A., Jr., and Michele M. Betsill. 1997. "Policy for Science for Policy: A Commentary on Lambright on Ozone Depletion and Acid Rain." *Research Policy* 26(2): 157–68.

Pielke, Roger A., Jr., and Daniel Sarewitz. 2003. "Wanted: Scientific Leadership on Climate." *Issues in Science and Technology* (Winter): 27–30.

Pielke, Roger A., Jr., Daniel Sarewitz, and Radford Byerly, Jr. 2000. "Decision Making and the Future of Nature: Understanding and Using Predictions." In Daniel Sarewitz, Roger A. Pielke, Jr., and Radford Byerly, Jr., *Prediction: Science, Decision Making and the Future of Nature.* Washington, DC: Island Press, 361–87.

Pierson, Paul. 1993. "When Effect Becomes Cause: Policy Feedback and Political Change." *World Politics* 45: 595–628.

Ploetz, Alfred. 1911. "Die Begriffe Rasse und Gesellschaft und einige damit zusammenhängende Probleme." In *Verhandlungen des Ersten Deutschen Soziologentages vom 19.-22. Oktober 1910 in Frankfurt am Main.* Tübingen: J. B. C. Mohr (Paul Siebeck), 111–36.

Poliakov, Leon. 1974. *The Aryan Myth: A History of Racist and Nationalist Ideas in Europe.* New York: Basic Books.

Popper, Karl R. 1956. *Three Views Concerning Human Knowledge in Conjectures and Refutations.* London: Routledge, 130–60.

1963. *Conjectures and Refutations: The Growth of Scientific Knowledge.* London: Routledge.

1972a. "Epistemology without a Knowing Subject." In Karl R. Popper, *Objective Knowledge: An Evolutionary Approach.* Oxford: Clarendon Press, 106–52.

[1957] 1972b. *The Poverty of Historicism.* London: Routledge and Kegan Paul.

Price, Derek de Solla. 1963. *Little Science, Big Science … And Beyond.* New York: Columbia University Press.

Prins, Gwyn, Isabel Galiana, Christopher Green, Reiner Grundmann, Mike Hulme, Atte Korhola, Frank Laird, Ted Nordhaus, Roger Pielke Jr., Steve Rayner, Daniel Sarewitz, Michael Shellenberger, Nico Stehr, and Hiroyuki Tezuka. 2010. *The Hartwell Paper: A New Direction for Climate Policy after the Crash of 2009.* Institute for Science, Innovation and Society, University of Oxford.

Proctor, Robert N. 1988a. *Racial Hygiene: Medicine under the Nazis.* Cambridge, MA: Harvard University Press.

1988b. "From *Anthropologie* to *Rassenkunde* in the German Anthropological Tradition." In George W. Stocking Jr. (ed.), *Bones, Bodies, Behavior: Essays on Biological Anthropology.* History of Anthropology, Volume 5. Madison, WI: The University of Wisconsin Press, 138–79.

Rice, Thurman B. 1929. *Racial Hygiene: A Practical Discussion of Eugenics and Race Culture.* New York: Macmillan.

Rich, Georg. 1983. "Weltwirtschaftliche Verflechtung und geldpolitische Handlungsfähigkeit der Schweiz." *Schweizerisches Jahrbuch für Politische Wissenschaft* 23: 271–91.

Robinson, E. A. G. 1956. "John Maynard Keynes 1883–1946." In John
    Maynard Keynes, *Politik und Wirtschaft: Männer und Probleme: Ausgewählte
    Abhandlungen*. Tübingen: J. C. B. Mohr (Paul Siebeck),1–69.
Roll-Hansen, Nils. 1989. "Geneticists and the Eugenics Movement in
    Scandinavia." (Genetics, Eugenics and Evolution: Special Issue in
    Commemoration of Bernard Norton 1945–1984.) *The British Journal for
    the History of Science* 22(3): 335–46.
Röpke, Wilhelm. 1932. *Krise und Konjunktur*. Leipzig: Quelle & Meyer.
Rosecrance, Richard. 1987. *Der neue Handelsstaat: Herausforderungen für Politik
    und Wirtschaft*. Frankfurt am Main: Campus.
Rosenberg, Charles E. 1976. *No Other Gods: On Science and American Social
    Thought*. Baltimore: The Johns Hopkins University Press.
Rosenstrauch, Hazel. 1988. *Aus Nachbarn werden Juden: Ausgrenzung und
    Selbstbehauptung 1933–1942*. Berlin: Transit.
Rügemer, H. 1927. "Die 'Nature' eine Greuelzeitschrift." *Zeitschrift für die
    gesamte Staatswissenschaft* 3: 475–79.
Philippe J. Rushton, Philippe J. 1995. *Race, Evolution, and Behavior: A Life
    History Perspective*. New Brunswick, NJ: Transaction Publishers.
Russill, Chris, and Zoe Nyssa. 2009. "The Tipping Point Trend in
    Climate Change Communication." *Global Environmental Change* 19(3):
    336–44.
Salant, W. 1989. "The Spread of Keynesian Doctrines and Practices in the United
    States." In P. Hall (ed.), *The Political Power of Economic Ideas*, 27–51.
Salter, Liora, Edwin Levy, and William Leiss 1988. *Mandated Science: Science
    and Scientists in the Making of Standards*. Dordrecht: Springer.
Samuelson, Paul A. 1959. "What Economists Know." In Daniel Lerner (ed.),
    *The Human Meaning of the Social Sciences: Original Essays on the History
    and the Application of the Social Sciences*. Cleveland: The World Publishing
    Company, 183–213.
Sanmann, Horst. 1965. "Daten und Alternativen der deutschen Wirtschafts-
    und Finanzpolitik in der Aera Brüning." *Hamburger Jahrbuch für
    Wirtschafts- und Gesellschaftspolitik* 10: 109–40.
Sapper, Karl. 1932. "Über die Grenzen der Akklimatisationsfähigkeit des
    Menschen." *Geographische Zeitschrift* 38(7): 385–98.
Sarewitz, Daniel. 1998. "Science in Policy: An Excess of Objectivity?"
    Geological Society of America 30(7): 202.
    2004. "How Science Makes Controversies Worse." *Environmental Science &
    Policy* 7: 385–403.
Sarewitz, Daniel, and Richard Nelson. 2008. "Three Rules for Technological
    Fixes." *Nature* 456 (18 December): 871–72. www.nature.com/nature/journal/
    v456/n7224/full/456871a.html – a2.
Sarewitz, Daniel, and Roger Pielke, Jr. 2000. "Breaking the Global-Warming
    Gridlock." *Atlantic Monthly* (July): 54–64.
Schattschneider, E. E. 1960. *The Semi-Sovereign People*. Hinsdale: Dryden.
Schell, Jonathan. 1989. "Our Fragile Earth." *Discover* 10(10): 44–50.
Schelling, Thomas C. 1960. *The Strategy of Conflict*. New York: Oxford
    University Press.
Scherf, Harald. 1986. *Marx und Keynes*. Frankfurt am Main: Suhrkamp.

Schiller, Karl. 1987. "'Wir sollten jetzt ein Zeichen setzen.' Spiegel-Gespräch mit Karl Schiller. " *Der Spiegel* 45: 40–55.

Schleiff, Harmut. 2009. "Der Streit um den Begriff Rasse in der frühen Deutschen Gesellschaft für Soziologie als ein Kristallisationspunkt ihrer methodologischen Konstitution." *Leviathan* 27: 367–88.

Schmölders, Günter, et al. 1956. *John Maynard Keynes als Psychologe*. Berlin: Duncker & Humblot.

1962. *Geschichte der Volkswirtschaftslehre*. Reinbek bei Hamburg: Rowohlt.

Schneider, Stephen H. 1991. "Three Reports of the Intergovernmental Panel on Climate Change." *Environment* 33(1): 25–30.

2001. "What Is Dangerous Climate Change? " *Nature* 411 (3 May): 17–19.

Schon, Donald A. 1963. *The Displacement of Concepts*. London: Tavistock.

Schumpeter, Joseph A. 1946a. "Science and Ideology." *American Economic Review* 34: 345–59.

1946b. "John Maynard Keynes 1883–1946." *American Economic Review* 34: 495–518.

1949. "English Economists and the State-Managed Economy." *Journal of Political Economy* 57: 371–82.

[1912] 1951. *Theory of Economic Development*.

1952. *Ten Great Economists*. London: Allen and Unwin.

1954. *History of Economic Analysis*. New York: Oxford University Press.

Scott, Daryl Michael, 1997. *Contempt and Pity: Social Policy and the Image of the Damaged Black Psyche, 1880–1996*. Chapel Hill: University of North Carolina Press.

Scott, Robert A., and Arnold R. Shore. 1974. "Sociology and Policy Analysis." *American Sociologist* 9: 51–59.

1979. *Why Sociology Does Not Apply: A Study of the Use of Sociology in Public Policy*. New York: Elsevier.

Sebenius, James K. 1992. "Challenging Conventional Explanations of International Cooperation: Negotiation Analysis and the Case of Epistemic Communities." *International Organization* 46: 323–65.

Semple, Ellen Churchill. 1911. *Influences of Geographic Environment on the Basis of Ratzel's System of Anthropo-Geography*. New York: Henry Holy and Company.

Sewell, Dennis. 2010. *The Political Gene: How Darwin's Ideas Changed Politics*. London: Picador.

Shackley, Simon, and Brian Wynne. 1995. "Integrating Knowledges for Climate Change." *Global Environmental Change* 5(2): 113–26.

Shapin, Steven. [1982] 1986. "History of Science and Its Sociological Reconstructions." In Robert S. Cohen and Thomas Schnelle (eds.), *Cognition and Fact:Materials on Ludwik Fleck*. Dordrecht: D. Reidel, 325–86.

1994. *A Social History of Truth: Civility and Science in Seventeenth-Century England*. University of Chicago Press.

Shaw, Alison, and John Robinson. 2004. "Relevant but Not Prescriptive? Science Policy Models within the IPCC." *Philosophy Today* 48(5): 84–95.

Shearman, David J. C., and Joseph Wayne Smith. 2007. *The Climate Change Challenge and the Failure of Democracy*. Westport, CT: Praeger.

Shell. 2004. "The Shell Global Scenarios to 2025: The Future Business Environment – Trends, Trade-Offs and Choices." www-static.shell.com/static/aboutshell/downloads/our_strategy/shell_global_scenarios/exsum_23052005.pdf (last accessed February 1, 2012).

2010. "What Are Scenarios?" www.shell.com/home/content/aboutshell/our_strategy/shell_global_scenarios/what_are_scenarios/what_are_scenarios_30102006.html (last accessed March 19, 2010).

Shepherd, John. 2009. "Geoengineering the Climate: Science, Gvernance and Uncertainty. Workshop on the Engineering Response to Global Climate Change." RS Policy, Vol. 1. Royal Society. http://royalsociety.org/geoengineeringclimate/.

Siebenhüner, Bernd. 2003. "The Changing Role of Nation States in International Environmental Assessments: The Case of the IPCC." *Global Environmental Change* 13(2): 113–23.

Simmel, Georg. 1890. *Über sociale Differenzierung: Sociologische und psychologische Untersuchungen*. Leipzig: Duncker & Humblot.

1919. *Philosophische Kultur: Gesammelte Essais*. Second, enlarged edition. Leipzig: Alfred Kröner.

Skidelsky, Robert. 1979. "The Decline of Keynesian Politics." In Colin Crouch (ed.), *State and Economy in Contemporary Capitalism*. London: Croom Helm, 55–87.

1992. *John Maynard Keynes: The Economist as Saviour 1920–1937*. London: Macmillan.

Skjærseth, Jon Birger, and Tora Skodvin. 2001. "Climate Change and the Oil Industry: Common Problems, Different Strategies." *Global Environmental Politics* (November): 43–64.

Skodvin, Tora. 2000. *Structure and Agent in the Scientific Diplomacy of Climate Change: An Empirical Case Study of Science-Policy Interaction in the Intergovernmental Panel on Climate Change*. Dordrecht: Kluwer Academic Publishers.

Smith, Cyril S. 1987. "Networks of Influence: The Social Sciences in Britain Since the War." In Martin Bulmer (ed.), *Social Science Research and Government: Comparative Essays on Britain and the United States*. Cambridge University Press, 61–76.

Smith, David N. 1997. "Judeophobia, Myth, and Critique." In S. Daniel Breslauer (ed.), *The Seductiveness of Jewish Myth: Challenge or Response?* Albany: State University of New York Press, 119–50.

Smith, Joel B. 2009. "Assessing Dangerous Climate Change through an Update of the Intergovernmental Panel on Climate Change (IPCC) 'Reasons for Concern.'" PNAS Early edition: www.pnas.org_cgi_doi_10.1073_pnas.0812355106.

Sombart, Werner. 1911. *"Discussion."* In *Verhandlungen des Ersten Deutschen Soziologentages vom 19.-22. Oktober 1910 in Frankfurt am Main*. Tübingen: J. C. B. Mohr (Paul Siebeck), 165.

[1930] 2001. "Capitalism." In Nico Stehr and Reiner Grundmann (eds.), *Economic Life in the Modern Age*. New Brunswick, NJ: Transaction Books, 3–29.

Sorokin, Piritim A. 1928. *Contemporary Sociological Theories: Through the First Quarter of the Twentieth Century*. New York: Harper & Brothers.

Spahn, Heinz-Peter. 1976. "Keynes in der heutigen Wirtschaftspolitik." In Gottfried Bombach et al. (eds.), *Der Keynesianismus I: Theorie und Praxis keynesianischer Wirtschaftspolitik*. Berlin: Springer-Verlag, 213–92.

Spector, M. and J. Kitsuse, 1977. *Constructing Social Problems*. Menlo Park, CA: Cummings Publishing.

Spencer, Herbert. 1887. *The Factors of Organic Evolution*. London: Williams and Norgate.

   1961. *The Study of Sociology*. Ann Arbor: University of Michigan Press.

   [1862] 1873. *First Principles*. New York: Appleton.

Starr, Kevin. 1986. *Inventing the Dream: California through the Progressive Era (Americans and the California Dream)*. Oxford University Press.

Stehr, Nico. 1992. *Practical Knowledge: Applying the Social Sciences*. London: Sage.

Stehr, Nico 1994. *Knowledge Societies*. London: Sage.

   1996. "The Ubiquity of Nature: Climate and Culture." *Journal of the History of the Behavioral Sciences* 32: 151–59.

   2001. *The Fragility of Modern Societies: Knowledge and Risk in the Information Age*. London: Sage.

   2008. *Moral Markets*. Boulder, CO: Paradigm Press.

Stehr, Nico, and Wilhelm Baldamus. 1983. "Accounts and Action: The Logic(s) of Social Science and Pragmatic Knowledge." In Burkart Holzner et al. (eds.), *Realizing Social Science Knowledge*. Würzburg: Physica, 73–78.

Stehr, Nico, and Reiner Grundmann. 2011. *Experts: The Knowledge and Power of Expertise*. London: Routledge.

   (eds.) (2001) *Werner Sombart: Economic Life in the Modern Age*, New Brunswick, NJ, and Oxford: Transaction Books.

Stehr, Nico, and von Storch, Hans. 1997. "Rückkehr des Klimadeterminismus?" *Merkur* 51: 560–62.

   2009. "Wenn Forschern die Demokratie lästig wird," *Der Spiegel online*, 29 December 2009. www.spiegel.de/wissenschaft/mensch/0,1518,669398,00. html (last accessed February 2, 2012).

Steindl, Josef. 1985. "J. M. Keynes: Society and the Economist." In Fausto Vicarelli (ed.), *Keynes's Relevance Today*. London: Macmillan, 99–125.

Stern, Nicholas. 2007. *The Economics of Climate Change*. Cambridge University Press.

Stichweh, Rudolf. 1999. "Globalisierung von Wirtschaft und Wissenschaft: Produktion und Transfer wissenschaftlichen Wissens in zwei Funktionssytemen der modernen Gesellschaft. " *Soziale Systeme* 5: 27–39.

Stoddard, Lothrop. 1924. *Racial Realities in Europe*. New York: C. Scribner's Sons.

Stolarski, R. S. 1986. "Nimbus 7 Satellite Measurements of the Springtime Antarctic Ozone Decrease." *Nature* 322: 808–11.

Storm, Servaas. 2009. "Capitalism and Climate Change: Can the Invisible Hand Adjust the Natural Thermostat?" *Development and Change* 40(6): 1011–38.

Strauss, Anselm. (1978). *Negotiations: Varieties, Processes, Contexts, and Social Order*. San Francisco: Jossey-Bass.

Stubbs, Graham. 2009. "The Fossil Fuel Industry and the Challenge of Climate Change: A Study of Shell's Position." PhD thesis, Aston University, Birmingham.

Tenbruck, Friedrich H. 1986. *Geschichte und Gesellschaft*. Berlin: Duncker & Humblot.

Tobin, James. 1986. "Keynes's Policies in Theory and Practice." In Harold L. Wattel (ed.), *The Policy Consequences of John Maynard Keynes*. London: Macmillan, 13–21.

Toke, Dave. 1999. "Epistemic Communities and Environmental Groups." *Politics* 19: 97–102.

Tol, Richard. 2010. "Richard Tol on Working Group 3 of IPCC." http://klimazwiebel.blogspot.com/2010/02/richard-tol-on-wg3-of-ipcc.html.

Traweek, Sharon. 1988. *Beamtimes and Lifetimes: The World of High Energy Physicists*. Cambridge, MA: Harvard University Press.

Trumbo, Craig. 1996. "Constructing Climate Change: Claims and Frames in US News Coverage of an Environmental Issue." *Public Understanding of Science* 5(3): 269.

Truzzi, Marcello, 1996. "Pseudoscience." In Gordon Stein (ed.), *The Encyclopedia of the Paranormal*. Buffalo, NY: Prometheus Books, 560–75.

Twain, Mark. [1895] 1985. *Concerning the Jews*. Philadelphia: Running Press.

Tyaglyy, Mikhail I. 2004. "The Role of Antisemitic Doctrine in German Propaganda in the Crimea, 1941–1944." *Holocaust and Genocide Studies* 18(3): 421–59.

Tyndall, John. 1863. *Heat as a Mode of Motion*. London: Longman.

Ungar, Sheldon. 1992. "The Rise and (Relative) Decline of Global Warming as a Social Problem." *The Sociological Quarterly* 33: 483–501.

United Nations. "1992 Framework Convention on Climate Change." http://unfccc.int/resource/docs/convkp/conveng.pdf.

van Der Sluijs, Jeroen, Josée van Eijondhoven, Simon Shackley, and Brian Wynne. 1998. "Anchoring Devices in Science for Policy: The Case of Consensus around Climate Sensitivity." *Social Studies of Science* 28(2): 291–323.

Virchow, Rudolf. [1885] 1922. "Über Akklimatisation." In Karl Sudhoff, *Rudolf Virchow und die deutschen Naturforscherversammlungen*. Leipzig: Akademische Verlagsanstalt, 214–39.

von Mises, Ludwig. 1931. *Die Ursachen der Wirtschaftskrise*. Tübingen: J. C. B. Mohr (Paul Siebeck).

von Schelting, Alexander. 1934. *Max Webers Wissenschaftslehre*. Tübingen: J. C. B. Mohr (Paul Siebeck).

Wagner, Peter. 1990. *Sozialwissenschaften und Staat: Frankreich, Italien und Deutschland 1870–1980*. Frankfurt am Main: Campus.

Watson, Robert T. 2005. "Turning Science into Policy: Challenges and Experiences from the Science-Policy Interface." *Philosophical Transactions of the Royal Society of London. Series B, Biological Sciences* 360(1454): 471–77. doi: 10.1098/rstb.2004.1601.

2010. "UN Must Investigate Warming 'Bias,' Says Former Climate Chief." *Sunday Times* (February 15).

Wattel, Harold L. 1985. "Introduction." In Harold L. Wattel (ed.), *The Policy Consequences of John Maynard Keynes*. London: Macmillan, 3–12.

Weart, Spencer R. 2003. *The Discovery of Global Warming*. Cambridge, MA: Harvard University Press.

1911. *'Discussion.'* In *Verhandlungen des Ersten Deutschen Soziologentages vom 19.-22. Oktober 1910 in Frankfurt am Main*. Tübingen: J. C. B. Mohr (Paul Siebeck), 151–164.

Weber, Alfred. 1931. "Grundlagen und Grenzen der Sozialpolitik. *"Schriften des Vereins für Sozialpolitik* 182: 23–58.

1932. *Volkswirtschaftslehre: Eine Einführung*. Vol. II. Munich and Leipzig: Duncker & Humblot.

[1935] 1956. *Kurzgefasste Volkswirtschaftslehre: Siebente, neuberabeitete Auflage*. Berlin: Duncker & Humblot.

Weber, Max. [1921] 1958. *Gesammelte politische Schriften*. Zweite Auflage. Tübingen: J. C. B. Mohr (Paul Siebeck).

[1903–1906] 1975. *Roscher and Knies: The Logical Problems of Historical Economics*. New York: Free Press.

[1922] 1978a. "Ethnic Groups." In Max Weber, *Economy and Society*, 385–98.

[1922] 1978b. "Race Relations." In W. G. Runciman (ed.), *Weber: Selections in Translation*, trans. Eric Matthews. Cambridge University Press (alternative translation), 359–69.

[1922] 1978c. *Economy and Society: An Outline of Interpretive Sociology*. Berkeley, CA: University of California Press.

[1909–09] 1988a. "Zur Psychophysik der industriellen Arbeit." In Max Weber, *Gesammelte Aufsätze zur Soziologie und Sozialpolitik*. Tübingen: J. C. B. Mohr, 61–225.

[1924] 1988b. "Diskussionsreder zum Vortrag von F. Oppenheimer über, Die rassentheoretische Geschichtsphilosophie." In Max Weber, *Gesammelte Aufsätze zur Soziologie und Sozialpolitik*, 488–91.

Weingart, Peter, and Nico Stehr (eds.). 2000. *Practising Interdisciplinarity*. University of Toronto Press.

Weingart, Peter, Anita Engels, and Petra Pansegrau. 2000. "Risks of Communication: Discourses on Climate Change in Science, Politics, and the Mass Media." *Public Understanding of Science* 9(3): 261.

Weingart, Peter, Jürgen Kroll, and Kurt Bayertz, 1988. *Rasse, Blut und Gene. Geschichte der Eugenik und Rassengeschichte in Deutschland*, Frankfurt am Main: Suhrkamp.

Weinstein, Jay. 1997. *Social and Cultural Change: Social Science for a Dynamic World*. Boston: Allyn & Bacon.

Weir, Margaret. 1989. "Ideas and Politics: The Acceptance of Keynesianism in Britain and the United States." In Peter A. Hall (ed.), *The Political Power of Economic Ideas*, 53–86.

Weiss, Carol H. 1977. "Research for Policy's Sake: The Enlightenment Function of Social Research." *Policy Analysis* 3: 531–45.

1978. "Broadening the Concept of Research Utilization." *Sociological Symposium* 21: 20–31.

1983. "Three terms in search of reconceptualization: Knowledge, Utilization, and Decision-Making." In Burkart Holzner, Karin D. Knorr, and Hermann Strasser (eds.), *Realizing Social Science Knowledge*. Würzburg: Physica, 201–19.

Weiss, Carol H., with Michael J. Bucuvalas. 1980. *Social Science Research and Decision-Making*. New York: Columbia University Press.

Weiss, Janet A., and Carol H. Weiss. 1981. "Social Scientists and Decision-Makers Look at the Usefulness of Mental Health Research." *American Psychologist* 36: 837–47.

Weiss, Sheila Faith. 1987. "The Race Hygiene Movement in Germany." *Osiris* (second series) 3: 193–236.

1992. "Race and Class in Fritz Lenz's Eugenics." *Medizinhistorisches Journal* 27: 5–25.

Winch, Donald. 1972. *Economics and Policy: A Historical Study*. London: Hodder and Stoughton.

1989. "Keynes, Keynesianism, and state intervention." In Peter A. Hall (ed.), *The Political Power of Economic Ideas*, 107–28.

Wistrich, Robert, 1988. *Who's Who in Nazi Germany*. New York: Macmillan.

Wright, Alex. 2004. *A Social Constructionist's Deconstruction of Royal Dutch Shell's Scenario Planning Process*. University of Wolverhampton Working Paper (Vol. 44). www.wlv.ac.uk/uwbs.

Wynne, Brian. 2005. "Risk as Globalizing Democratic Discourse? Framing Subjects and Citizens." In Melissa Leach, Ian Scoones, and Brian Wynne (eds.), *Science and Citizens: Globalization and the Challenge of Engagement*. London: Zed Books, 66–82.

Yad Vashem. 1995. *Yad Vashem Guidebook*. Jerusalem: Yad Vashem.

Yee, Albert S. 1996. "The Causal Effects of Ideas on Policies." *International Organization* 50: 69–108.

Index